CRY HAVOC!

Nelson D. Lankford is the author of *Richmond Burning* and *The Last American Aristocrat*, and the editor of *Eye of the Storm* and *Images from the Storm*. He edits *The Virginia Magazine of History and Biography*, the quarterly journal of the Virginia Historical Society, and lives in Richmond, Virginia.

CRY! HAVOC!

THE CROOKED ROAD TO CIVIL WAR, 1861

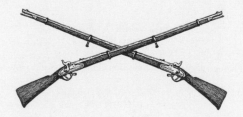

NELSON D. LANKFORD

PENGUIN BOOKS

PENGUIN BOOKS

Published by the Penguin Group

Penguin Group (USA) Inc., 375 Hudson Street, New York, New York 10014, U.S.A. • Penguin Group
(Canada), 90 Eglinton Avenue East, Suite 700, Toronto, Ontario, Canada M4P 2Y3 (a division of
Pearson Penguin Canada Inc.) • Penguin Books Ltd, 80 Strand, London WC2R 0RL, England •
Penguin Ireland, 25 St Stephen's Green, Dublin 2, Ireland (a division of Penguin Books Ltd) • Penguin
Group (Australia), 250 Camberwell Road, Camberwell, Victoria 3124, Australia (a division of Pearson
Australia Group Pty Ltd) • Penguin Books India Pvt Ltd, 11 Community Centre, Panchsheel Park,
New Delhi – 110 017, India • Penguin Group (NZ), 67 Apollo Drive, Rosedale, North Shore 0632, New
Zealand (a division of Pearson New Zealand Ltd) • Penguin Books (South Africa) (Pty) Ltd, 24 Sturdee
Avenue, Rosebank, Johannesburg 2196, South Africa

Penguin Books Ltd, Registered Offices:
80 Strand, London WC2R 0RL, England

First published in the United States of America by Viking Penguin,
a member of Penguin Group (USA) Inc. 2007
Published in Penguin Books 2008

9   10

Copyright © Nelson D. Lankford, 2007
All rights reserved

Photographs from the collection of the Library of Congress

ISBN 978-0-670-03821-3 (hc.)
ISBN 978-0-14-311279-2 (pbk.)
CIP data available

Printed in the United States of America
Set in Aldus
Designed by Amy Hill

*For the men and women of the
armed forces, who continue to defend
the nation forged by their ancestors*

CONTENTS

Maps appear on pages 14, 52, 140, and 160

CRY HAVOC!

PROLOGUE

Harpers Ferry, October 1859

Cry "Havoc!" and let slip the dogs of war . . .

—William Shakespeare,
Julius Caesar, act 3, scene 1

John Brown lay on the rough floor of the paymaster's office. Dried blood smeared his hands and clothes. A sword had gashed his scalp, and his head was now swathed in crude bandages. Lying there, he seemed much diminished, no longer the mesmeric figure he had appeared when standing erect, with his long flowing white beard and piercing eyes. In all, seventeen people had died. The first was Shepard Hayward, a station baggage porter, shot when he accosted the raiders on the rail line into Harpers Ferry. He was a free black man, the first death in Brown's war to free the slaves.[1]

The invader-liberators had entered the village in northern Virginia just across the river from Maryland on the chilly Sunday night of October 16, 1859. They quickly captured the federal arsenal at the point where the Shenandoah River floods into the Potomac. Then Brown hesitated. He cut the telegraph wire but unaccountably let an eastbound Baltimore & Ohio train continue on its journey. He allowed aroused townspeople to coop up his little band in the armory. By the next morning, church bells and frantic riders had spread the alarm: abolitionists had arrived with the thing white southerners most feared—a bloody insurrection to free the slaves. As soon as the B&O train stopped in Maryland, the crew telegraphed Washington. A company of marines under the command of an army colonel, Robert E. Lee, hurried to crush the threat before it spread. Within thirty-six hours it was all over, Brown and his men captives, fugitives, or dead. The slaves had not rallied to their standard.

As Brown lay in pain on the cold floor, a wounded prisoner, his mission an utter failure, he became the object of scornful curiosity to a parade of gloating state officials, journalists, and congressmen. They thought him ridiculous. Ridiculous to have imagined that a handful of malcontents armed with muskets and medieval pikes could have resisted the government's overwhelming military might. Ridiculous to have expected that this pitiful band could have sparked a slave revolt. When Brown had asked Frederick Douglass to join him, the fiery African American abolitionist prudently declined. Douglass called it a suicide mission, "going into a perfect steel-trap."[2] In the North as much as in the South, Americans breathed with relief at the outcome.

Then, in defeat, Brown exerted mastery over his destiny in a way more consequential than anything he had done before. He spurned efforts to rescue him or to argue in his behalf that he was deranged. Instead, he placed his hopes in the redemptive power of martyrdom. "I am ready for my fate," he quietly informed a hushed magistrate's court nine days after his capture. "I have been *whip[p]ed*," he wrote his wife, "but am sure I can recover all the lost capital occasioned by the disaster, by only hanging a few moments by the neck."[3]

Such was the grim and oddly rational calculus of a gloomy religious zealot, a man alienated from society and driven by obsession but by no means insane. For Brown intended to transform his personal misery into a purgative that would convulse the nation and free it from the incubus of slavery.[4] It would be a large role, indeed, for a sometime farmer, shepherd, tanner, and storekeeper who had failed at every one of the two dozen occupations he tried and left a spoor of bankruptcies and lawsuits across the Midwest. Even when he fixed upon the grandiose goal of eradicating human chattel slavery, so far he had accomplished little beyond the murder of innocents, first in Kansas and now in Virginia. But he was a man driven by the conviction that God had chosen him for a holy mission. Manacled in jail, without a hope left in the world, when an interrogator asked, "Do you consider yourself an instrument in the hands of Providence?" he replied plainly, "I do."[5]

The governor, Henry Alexander Wise, insisted on questioning this demon who had dared to violate the borders of the Old Dominion. An incendiary southern partisan, conceited, mercurial, and cranky, Wise impulsively defended his region against northern slights. His long hair and gaunt, angular features had always given him the look of a dangerous man. In fact, in both appearance and in temperament there was something similar about the governor and the prisoner.[6]

Wise approached their meeting angry at what Brown had attempted and perhaps embarrassed that he had so easily captured the arsenal. He was not prepared for the figure lying there on a bed of rags, a pathetic, defeated criminal who could expect no mercy from his captors. He saw there was nothing passive or defeated about the man. Brown flashed his gray eyes at Wise when the governor suggested he best be thinking of the next life. "You are not likely to be more than fifteen or twenty years behind me in the journey to eternity," Brown shot back with calm, uncanny asperity, "a very trifling distance, and I want you to be prepared . . . you Slaveholders have a heavy responsibility, and it behooves you to prepare more than it does me."[7]

Wise came away frankly expressing respect for Brown. "He is a bundle of the best nerves I ever saw," the governor conceded. Even more, the prisoner struck him as "cool, collected and indomitable . . . and he inspired me with great trust in his integrity as a man of truth. He is a fanatic, vain and garrulous, but firm, truthful and intelligent." Despite their differences, Wise recognized an affinity with Brown. Ralph Waldo Emerson called it "a bond of union between two enemies."[8]

Now, like Brown at his moment of decision at the arsenal, Wise hesitated. Perhaps the unlooked-for empathy that he discovered at their meeting gave him pause. He considered locking up Brown in a lunatic asylum but did not, believing him both sane and courageous. As governor, he could have recommended commutation of the death sentence handed down by the local court. If he had done so, he would certainly have frustrated Brown's wishes. He thereby might even have diverted the course of American history into a different channel. In the end, he gave the prisoner what he desired. He may have suspected that Brown would be proven a better prophet than revolutionary.

The prophecy came just before his jailers took him to the place of execution on the crisp morning of December 2. At that point, the prisoner handed a guard a scrap of paper bearing his final admonition: "I John Brown am now quite *certain* that the crimes of this *guilty land: will* never be purged *away;* but with Blood."[9] According to a romantic, enormously popular, but apocryphal story, repeated by those who wished it had been so, as he left the jail, Brown stopped to kiss a child held up by a black woman. He rode to the gallows in a furniture wagon, sitting on the box that contained his black walnut coffin. He was dressed oddly in white socks, red slippers, black pants, and the same shabby black frock coat he had worn when he rode out of the darkness and descended upon the sleeping town of Harpers Ferry and the conscience of a fearful nation.[10]

Once he had made up his mind on the course to follow, Henry Wise was determined to thwart any attempt to rescue Brown. Across the Potomac, Wise's counterpart, Thomas Hicks, the governor of neighboring Maryland, feared such an effort by "Northern fanatics" and put his militia on alert. Wise ordered nearly three thousand Virginia troops arrayed in a hollow square around the gallows at Charles Town, the county seat a few miles west of Harpers Ferry.[11]

They were farmers and townsmen from across the state. Prof. Thomas Jonathan Jackson, not yet called "Stonewall," was there with his students from the Virginia Military Institute. Among them stood Edmund Ruffin, editor, curmudgeon, and fire-eating secessionist, who had finagled a ludicrous temporary appointment as a cadet. Also standing in the militia ranks was a handsome actor, John Wilkes

Booth, who looked on in wonder, transfixed as the prisoner mounted the scaffold. Booth called Brown "a man inspired, the grandest character of the century," a role he later sought with twisted malice to appropriate for himself.[12]

The raid on Harpers Ferry inflamed the South. It engendered bloodcurdling paranoia about slaves rising up and slitting their masters' throats in the night. That fear might have subsided as white southerners nervously congratulated themselves on the swift collapse of Brown's enterprise and the lack of response from slaves. But Brown's eloquence during his interrogation and trial, his letters from jail, and his cool embrace of death turned his defeat into something else. A little more than a month passed between the sentence handed down by a Virginia court and the execution. In that time, in many northern eyes Brown converted himself from pathetic failure to transfigured hero. Martyrdom, of course, was essential. "I *almost fear*," fretted Henry David Thoreau, "that I may yet hear of his deliverance, doubting if a prolonged life, if *any* life, can do as much good as his death."[13] He need not have worried.

People gathered to bear witness in towns across the North on the day of execution. At the hour the trapdoor opened and ushered Brown, as he had chosen, to eternity, they marked the occasion with prayer vigils and solemn assemblies. In Cleveland, black abolitionist Charles Langston told thousands of mourners that the American people had murdered Brown because of their "union with slavery."[14] Thoreau called Brown "an angel of light." It was Emerson who made an electrifying analogy and by doing so taught sympathetic northerners how to view Brown in a different light. The martyr's death, he proclaimed grandiloquently, "will make the gallows as glorious as the cross."[15]

Such comments filled white southerners with horror and revulsion. Secessionists who despaired of their cause took heart. The North's reaction to Brown invigorated them. Here, they cried, was tangible proof that the South could no longer abide safely within the hated United States of America. Edmund Ruffin took home from Harpers Ferry some of the pikes that Brown had brought to arm rebellious slaves. He sent one of these macabre souvenirs to each southern governor as a warning: secession was now the only choice for survival.

In fact, Brown's undoubted influence in ripening the conditions for civil war was based in part on misperception. Adulation of the martyr was real enough in abolition circles, but they were a tiny minority. Sympathy for Brown in a broader swath of northern opinion was apparent when he was executed, but it was fleeting. White southerners misconstrued the meaning of Harpers Ferry. They failed to understand that the North had little appetite for interfering with slavery, and increasingly, they fell prey to the alarms spread by radicals. Thus, southern devotion to the Union eroded apace. The allure of secession beckoned—independence for the South, bright shining as the sun.

Brown's raid, whether its legacy flowed from misperception or reality, painfully bruised the sectional wound that had suppurated for decades. And it highlighted in stark relief how the actions of one man could influence the course of history. By the end of the 1850s, political parties were no longer able to appeal to a national base. In the presidential election that followed a year after Harpers Ferry, all the parties became narrowly sectional. In the fevered minds of secessionist radicals, the minority Republican victory by itself justified leaving the Union. To them, Abraham Lincoln had no legitimacy. The lower South began to act on that belief. Moderate opinion in the upper South trembled for the future.

As Lincoln's inaugural approached, therefore, so too did the prospect for conflict. After the new president took office on March 4, 1861, came the last weeks of calm, a time when the final chances for peace, however tenuous, persisted a while longer but then vanished in a matter of days. Though the Civil War was a long time in coming, when it did, it burst upon the nation with lightning speed. When the sixteenth president repeated the oath of office, however, no one could divine that horrible future. The course of the war that broke out a few weeks later was by no means decided or preordained. Would the seven lower South states that had proclaimed the Confederacy be allowed to leave the Union peacefully? If not, what would be the decision of the upper South, those eight slave states that still remained in the Union when Lincoln became president?

A month of quiet followed the inauguration, and then came the explosion at Fort Sumter. After smoke rose above the battered outpost in South Carolina, the focus instantly shifted hundreds of miles to the north. To those who lived through it, time seemed to accelerate with dizzying speed. What happened over the next few weeks in Virginia and Maryland fatefully influenced the path of the fault line that zigzagged across America. Decisions by individuals in those two states powerfully affected the course of all the border states. In consequence, a second earthquake of secession rent the nation and aligned the fragments on the threshold of civil war.

This is the story of the unfolding of those events as Americans experienced them, not knowing the outcome any more than we can know the outcome of events in our own day before they happen. Long-running discord over slavery and sectional rights prepared the way. That antipathy long predated Abraham Lincoln and Jefferson Davis and all the other actors of 1861. Perhaps by then war could not have been avoided. But the particular way that it began was in the hands of individuals, not impersonal, irresistible historical forces.

This, then, is also the story of how the prologue to war took the shape it did because of the resolve, indecision, and stubbornness of those people. For it was quirks of timing, character, and place—particularly in Virginia and Maryland—that influenced the course of events during those critical weeks, the final hiatus of uncertainty between peace and war, the vestibule leading to national tragedy. What gave precise shape to the conflict was a chain of decisions and reactions, of demands and miscalculations, of swollen vanity and wishful thinking. It was the actions of individuals in spring 1861 before uniformed armies took the field—actions even more consequential than those a year and a half before at Harpers Ferry—that finally let slip the dogs of war.

CHAPTER 1

FAITHFULLY EXECUTE

Washington, D.C., March 4, 1861

In your hands, my dissatisfied fellow countrymen, and not in mine, is the momentous issue of civil war.

—Abraham Lincoln, inaugural address, March 4[1]

In the park facing the east portico, an expectant crowd numbered in the tens of thousands. So many young men and boys clambered up the trees that they bent under the weight. It was a blustery day, sunny but raw. The unfinished new dome of the Capitol towered over the people. It echoed the condition of that other symbol of the republic at the far end of the Mall, the stump of the incomplete monument to George Washington. Protruding above the dome's base, the black arms of the crane that lifted cast-iron panels into place stood still for a day. Capitol Hill was a vast building site strewn with marble and newly sawn lumber. The plaster model of *Armed Freedom*, Thomas Crawford's statue intended eventually to stand on top of the finished dome, lurked forlornly in the weeds.[2]

It was late morning on March 4. To the accompaniment of "Hail to the Chief" and cheers from the crowd, the president and president-elect took their seats in an open carriage at the Willard Hotel. They rode down Pennsylvania Avenue, surrounded by cavalrymen led by southern officers of questionable loyalty. The most conspicuous

element in the procession was a large vehicle that was lavishly festooned, surmounted by a golden eagle, and carrying little girls in
white frocks waving a flag for each state of the Union, including,
pointedly, the seven that had seceded. General of the Army Winfield
Scott took to heart the rumors of violence that had swirled through
town and posted sharpshooters on rooftops along the parade route.
When the presidential party reached the north side of the Capitol, it
passed through an improvised wooden corridor erected to discourage
assassins. Soldiers stood ready at the windows of the building. Others camped under the temporary inaugural platform because of the
whispered threats that secessionists planned to blow it up during the
proceedings.[3]

A hundred yards to the east, New York photographer George Stacy
set up a special giant camera and prepared to take pictures of the ceremony. Down below, detectives scanned the crowd for suspicious-
looking characters. They did nothing to help spectators being fleeced
by the gangs of pickpockets drawn to such a large assembly. Just after
1:00 p.m., the dignitaries emerged from the Capitol and processed
out onto the platform. A discerning eyewitness with a good view
could have spotted most of the prominent figures of American politics. They huddled together in a sea of sober black cloaks and hats,
leavened here and there by the bright coats of women and the splendid ribbons and badges of diplomats in full court dress. And, as one
reporter snidely put it, among them "a host of minor great men"
preened upon the stage.[4]

When the notables had all found their places and the last patriotic
flourish from the marine band faded away, an old acquaintance of
Lincoln, English-born senator Edward Baker of Oregon, introduced
the president-elect. Lincoln bowed repeatedly to acknowledge the
cheers from below. He slipped his papers from his coat pocket, placed
them on a small, unsteady table, and tried to shield them from the
wind with his cane. It was not easy, and having to hold on to his tall
silk hat did not help. Sen. Stephen A. Douglas, his Illinois adversary
and one of the failed candidates in the recent presidential election,
reached out and in a gesture of grace took Lincoln's hat to relieve

him of the awkwardness. Now the president-elect was prepared to speak in the thin, high-pitched, but strong voice he was accustomed to using at public meetings, with his characteristic slow cadence that would admit no misunderstanding by his audience. What would he say?[5]

BY THE TIME Lincoln adjusted his spectacles and began to read from his text to the crowd, and by extension the nation, it had been almost seventeen months since John Brown strode into Harpers Ferry. The intervening period had not been a straight march into the abyss of disunion, however. Daily life went on for ordinary Americans. They were inured to the passions of extremists and the deeper undercurrents of sectional tension. The rhythm of the seasons still governed the lives of most people in a predominantly agricultural nation. If they thought about it, few of them could remember a time when there was no sectional controversy.

It was true that in the recent election none of the four parties fielded candidates with nationwide appeal. The result was a minority president whose plurality rested on votes in one section. And it was true that southern radicals had taken the first step toward creating an independent republic when South Carolina declared itself out of the Union in December 1860. But there was no war. Victorious Republicans told themselves that secession was just bluster meant to extort concessions for slave owners, nothing more. If politicians had been able to patch up their quarrels before, why not again? The tedious kabuki of constitutional dispute and compromise had become ingrained in the pattern of things.

The climate began to change as the new year of 1861 began, however. Observers of politics had reason to become increasingly nervous in January and February. Six more states in the Deep South followed South Carolina's example. Now it was no longer a hypothetical question about the right of a state to secede but a practical matter of whether the federal government would resist an actual attempt to undo the eternal compact of Union. Yet no one could see clearly where this ominous new situation might lead. It was a time of

fear on all sides. Conspiracy theories abounded. It seemed to many in
the North that abolitionist dread of a great "slave power" plot to
hijack the levers of government really was justified after all. To many
white southerners, the approaching inauguration meant that Lincoln
and his "Black Republican" hordes had done their own hijacking.[6]

The prospect of Americans fighting one another began to color
the predictions of some of the most alarmist commentators on the
national scene, but by no means all of them. Others, equally persua-
sive, believed different, more pacific outcomes were just as likely.

The Constitution mandated four months of interregnum between
election in November and inauguration the next March. That hiatus
induced lethargy in lame-duck Washington. At the same time, it
gave secessionists an opening they seized with the vigor of men who
believed their day had come. All the energy, it seemed, was with
the Deep South. At noon on February 4, delegates from the seceded
states—South Carolina, Georgia, Alabama, Mississippi, Florida, and
Louisiana, later joined by Texas—assembled at the capital of Alabama.

Montgomery was a somnolent port on the Alabama River, in the
center of the cotton South. It boasted a few new public buildings and
a population of only nine thousand, half black, half white. The delegates gathered there ostensibly to confer and return to their states
with recommendations for the creation of a separate republic. But
once assembled, they realized they would lose the initiative if they
only consulted. Almost by common consent, they decided on bold
action and wildly exceeded their instructions. For they presented to
the wider world the new southern republic itself, not just recommendations. In the form of a provisional government, they set the
process of building a nation into high gear. A constitution, and its
ratification by state election, could come later.[7]

They rushed into the task so that they could negotiate for peaceful separation from the United States. If that was not possible, they
would have an army in being by the time Lincoln put his administration together. Their work was done in two weeks. In partial secrecy
and without explicit authority from their states, barely three dozen

men in Montgomery had wrought a formidable fait accompli by the time Inauguration Day in Washington arrived in its slow, good time.[8]

At his own inauguration on February 18 as provisional president of the Confederate States of America, Jefferson Davis gravely proclaimed, "Our true policy is peace." He said he and his fellow secessionists had committed no wrong but claimed they suffered from "wanton aggression on the part of others." A conservative who came to secession late, not a radical, he reluctantly concluded that the North threatened basic southern rights. Like many southerners who once valued the Union, he decided that there was no place in that confederation, as Republicans conceived it, because they excluded his way of life. They had driven him out. They were the aggressors. Davis thus put a conservative face on a revolution that talked of peace but could purchase it only at the cost of killing the Union.[9]

While the delegates to Montgomery created a national government, at the local level their supporters took over one federal facility after another in the Deep South. United States customhouses, arsenals, revenue cutters, forts, the mint in New Orleans—all fell to the Confederates without bloodshed. On the day of Davis's inauguration, a faithless general surrendered U.S. Army posts in Texas. All that remained in federal hands by the end of February were scattered frontier outposts across the Mississippi and a few pitifully undermanned coastal forts in the East.

In the face of Confederate achievement, in Washington the enfeebled administration of James Buchanan denied the right of secession but then disclaimed any power to stop it. If the president confronted the southern radicals, he risked civil war. If he acknowledged their rebellion, he would fail the Union. In the latter case, he said, he would be able to travel home to Pennsylvania "by the light of my own burning effigies." So the weak, roundly vilified chief executive sought only to hang on until March, when he would gladly hand over the crisis to his successor. Congress dithered. Buchanan cried and prayed. A New Yorker listening in the visitors' gallery to congressional debate was repulsed by the lack of imagination. He left in

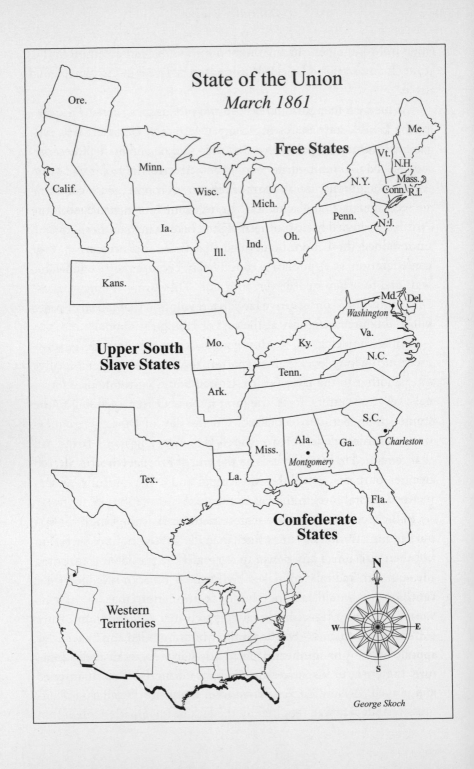

disgust for the Smithsonian Institution, finding more agreeable the "stuffed penguins and pickled lizards to the dishonest gabble of the Senate."[10]

In response to secession, each house of Congress created a committee to seek a Union-saving compromise. The auguries were not good. In the toxic atmosphere that prevailed, members had become accustomed to threatening one another with physical violence. Many came to the Capitol literally armed for mortal combat. Both committees stalemated, though the Senate one, named for Kentuckian John Crittenden, kept hope for a settlement alive as the clock ticked toward Inauguration Day. Chief among the convoluted provisions of this plan was the notion to revive the old Missouri Compromise line and extend it west, dividing slave territory from free.

Various clauses of the proposed deal, however, angered strong-willed partisans on either side. The backward-looking efforts of Crittenden, tinkering with a fistful of resolutions that parsed the legal limits of and protections for slavery, could not assuage the Deep South states. By then, they were unwilling to return to the Union of their own volition. Nor could Crittenden convince hard-line Republicans that they ought to make any concessions to the slave states. Some in the North were ready to be rid of them entirely. If compromise meant "a new drain on the negro's blood," seethed Frederick Douglass, "then . . . let the Union perish."[11]

For supporters of the Union in the upper South, surprising flowers of hope bloomed in the frost of midwinter. In retrospect, they were a frail, misleading sign, but at the time no one could tell, for with dramatic effect, a backlash in the region stopped the secessionist advance cold. Special elections either rejected a call for secession conventions or sent solid unionist majorities to those that did gather. Voters in Tennessee overwhelmingly rejected a convention. They did so narrowly in North Carolina. Maryland's governor resisted appeals of the pro-southern Democratic Party to recall the legislature. In Kentucky, a special session of the General Assembly refused to authorize a convention. Arkansas, Missouri, and Virginia each did convene one, but secessionists despaired when they saw the massive unionist majorities among the delegates elected.

Unionists in the upper South, cautious men, dreaded upheaval and doubted that Lincoln posed the threat that radicals claimed. They persuaded a majority of voters in their region to discount the alarm. The thought of leaving the Union of their fathers was inconceivable to many men of the border. The sentiment one of them expressed before the presidential election still rang true. Disunion, he said, "would be of a piece with the Madness & folly of committing suicide for fear of dying."[12]

The special state elections in winter 1861 thus gave hope that the crisis might be resolved and the Union restored. That prospect terrified the Confederates and gave urgency to their deliberations in Montgomery. At the same time, unionists in the upper South knew that to consolidate their gains they had to find a resolution to the sectional dispute quickly. Otherwise, a clash of arms might occur and sweep away their momentary ascendancy. For a time, they believed they had the energy to match that of the Confederates, purposefully fashioning a new nation. So for a time, many more white southerners hoped for peace and held back from the secessionist experiment than supported it.

At the national level, however, the flame of that hope guttered on the brink of extinction. As Congress fitfully pursued a solution, a Peace Conference, first proposed by Virginia, invited delegates to Washington. The Confederates ignored them. Newspaper baron Horace Greeley, who wielded enormous influence through caustic, witty columns in his *New York Tribune*, peered over his wire-rimmed glasses to damn the delegates as "political fossils, who would not have been again disinterred" were it not for the sectional crisis. Sen. Solomon Foot of Vermont branded the proceedings "a fraud, a trick, a deception" fomented by traitors. Seven seceded states and three free ones refused to attend.[13]

Those delegates that did gather cobbled together a package that revived much of the Crittenden proposals. The effort was doomed from the start: it fiddled with the conditions of slavery when the issue was actual disunion. On the eve of inauguration, secessionists on the one hand and rigid Republicans on the other joined forces in both houses of Congress to reject the Peace Conference's proposal. Secessionists called it "an abortion, a sham and a delusion," no more than mortician's makeup to powder the decaying corpse of the republic.[14]

Like other skeptics, Lincoln thought the southerners were bluffing. Even after they had created their government at Montgomery, he declared that *"there is no crisis,* excepting such a one as may be gotten up at any time by designing politicians." With many northerners, he underestimated the zeal of the disunionists. He made no policy pronouncements before his inauguration, but behind the scenes he urged supporters to resist compromise. In the face of his obstinacy, conciliatory Republicans despaired of reaching a solution that upper South unionists could accept and use to derail secession in their region.[15]

Shortly after arriving in Washington, Lincoln received a delegation from the Peace Conference at his suite at the Willard Hotel. The members probably did not know he privately had concluded that nothing good would come of their efforts. But by the time they left, he might as well have said as much to their faces. After polite introductions, conversation quickly degenerated into a testy exchange. James Seddon, a brilliant, dyspeptic Virginian with a salt-and-pepper goatee, emaciated features, and no sense of humor, denounced Republicans as abolitionist dupes who incited slave rebellion. The meeting broke up with everyone in a bad humor.

Four days later, Lincoln invited a small group of unionists from the upper South to call on him. Among them was another Virginian, the venerable, scholarly William Cabell Rives, a former diplomat and U.S. senator. The president-elect repeated his vow to protect slavery where it already existed. But he bristled at a request that he abandon all federal forts in the seceded states to avoid conflict. His visitors warned him that southern states still in the Union would leave if it came to fighting with the Confederacy. In reply, according to an account written later by one of the participants, Lincoln held out this hope: If Virginia would stay in the Union, he would withdraw from Fort Sumter in Charleston Harbor. In response, Rives predicted, "If you do that it will be one of the wisest things you have ever done."[16]

Despite this off-the-cuff suggestion of flexibility by the president-elect, the so-called fort-for-a-state proposal, nothing came of it. What would have happened if his interlocutors had pressed the point rather than dropping it was one of the many "might have beens" that littered the history of that spring. As it was, the encounter ended inconclusively. It was followed by the failure of the Peace Conference, which cast a pall over the upper South.[17] By the eve of the inauguration, southern unionists were increasingly apprehensive. "We will break up . . . ," grieved the young Tennessean Robert Hatton; "God will hold some men to a fearful responsibility. My heart is sick."[18] He had only thirteen months to live. He would be killed in action wearing the uniform not of his beloved Union but of a brigadier general in Confederate service. Such were the radical, wrenching changes he and the nation would make in the coming days.

As the inauguration approached, the country was at peace. The seven states of the lower South may have proclaimed they were no longer part of that country, but there was no fighting. The mails were still delivered, trains still ran, and telegraphs still operated across the divide between the states that declared their independence and the rest, which ignored that declaration.

Washington in 1861 was a town of barely seventy-five thousand. Bonds of kinship linked most residents of the District of Columbia to the two surrounding states, Maryland and Virginia. Like them, the District accepted slavery as a given of daily life. Gas lamps lit the main roads, and the need for street signs and house numbers attested to the growing population. But Washington possessed only disjointed pretensions of being a metropolis. It was "an idea set in a wilderness."[19]

A few grand public buildings were separated by vast expanses of open space, tribute to either the planners' optimism or their vanity. A giant aqueduct bringing fresh water from the falls of the Potomac powered a large public fountain near the Capitol. It did so, however, in sight of the open cesspool that was the city canal, where the runoff from sewers collected. Hogs ranged freely in the streets. A hint of intellectual and scientific life glimmered in the Smithsonian Institution's redbrick castle on the Mall and in the small Naval Observatory. A single rail line connected the town to the outside world.[20]

Rumors and threats of violence in Washington had begun to fly as soon as Lincoln's election. When told that disunionists might disrupt the official count of the electoral college in February, pompous, vain Gen. Winfield Scott, so ancient that his original commission had been signed by Thomas Jefferson, fumed in anger. "Old Fuss and Feathers" vowed to lash any malefactor to the mouth of a cannon, like defeated rebels in the recent uprising in British India, and "manure the hills of Arlington with fragments of his body!" On the day of the count, he posted two batteries of field artillery near the Capitol to make his point. A secessionist crowd spat insults at soldiers on guard. Inside, southern congressmen and their friends in the galleries vented their spleen at Scott, denouncing him as a "dotard," "coward," and "free-state pimp."[21]

The lame-duck vice president and champion of southern rights, John Breckinridge, a handsome Kentuckian who had lost to Lincoln in the four-way general election, discharged his duty by announcing the electoral majority for the Republican victor. The event came off with nothing more violent than verbal taunts. But the experience confirmed Scott in his determination to meet any threat to the inauguration with overwhelming force.

On Inauguration Day, uniforms were in evidence throughout the city. Scott himself did not attend the ceremony but stationed his carriage near an artillery battery a short distance away on Capitol Hill, the better to direct troop movements in case of trouble. The attitudes of the District of Columbia militia mirrored those of a divided nation. Some thirty new companies had formed since the election; Scott figured he could rely on only half of them. The Washington Rifles proudly accompanied Lincoln in the procession to and from the Capitol, while the National Rifles, known for secessionist proclivities, remained in their armory.

That morning, after an early breakfast, Robert Lincoln, about to enroll at Harvard, read the inaugural address aloud to his father, who made a few final revisions. The president-elect had drafted his speech before leaving Illinois for a slow, roundabout progress by train across the free states to Washington. He showed the text to others. Some made small suggestions for change, which he accepted. Former New York governor William Seward, soon to be secretary of state, agreed with the general line of argument, but he thought the speech was too provocative and urged numerous changes to soften it. The multiple hands on the draft were no secret. Unkind press reports even alleged that until the night before the ceremony, the president-elect's advisers were with him "toning down the Inaugural."[22]

With his country lawyer's faith in plain reasoning, Lincoln sought in the address to persuade his audience with words of resolve and conciliation—to assure the North of his devotion to the Union and to allay a nervous South's apprehensions. At the outset, he referred his uneasy listeners to his previous speeches, in which he had disclaimed any legal right or wish "to interfere with the institution of slavery in the States where it exists."[23]

After all the talk of compromise in the past months, one slender hope remained. A vote by the Senate that same morning favored a thirteenth amendment to the Constitution. It would prevent any future Congress from interfering with slavery in any state where it was already established. Lincoln expressly endorsed this amendment in his speech. He thus publicly announced his willingness to fasten the shackles of bondage on four million slaves forever, if that was what it took to preserve the Union. Further, he renounced any effort to use force against the seceded states. "There needs to be no bloodshed or violence; and there shall be none," he promised, "unless it be forced upon the national authority."[24]

Against these emollient overtures, however, he set an adamant assertion: the Union was forever. This claim put him in complete antipathy to the men of Montgomery, who had averred the mirror opposite, that "the separation is perfect, complete, and perpetual." Lincoln did admit candidly that revolution was a basic human right, even a moral obligation in cases of outright oppression. But, he said, by no contortion of facts could anyone claim that the orderly election of the Republican ticket abridged the constitutional rights of any minority. He reminded his audience that as chief magistrate, he was bound to administer the government and pass it along unimpaired to his successor. After giving his understanding of his obligations, he did not dodge the main issue: "Plainly, the central idea of secession, is the essence of anarchy."[25]

He also included a curiously passive statement worthy of Pontius Pilate: "In *your* hands, my dissatisfied fellow countrymen, and not in *mine*, is the momentous issue of civil war." This and other pacific phrases in his lawyerly argument may have misled some listeners. It did distract some of them from his assertion that he believed in the enduring, indissoluble Union and meant to uphold it. Toward the end, he again reminded southerners that "the government will not assail *you*. You can have no conflict, without being yourselves the aggressors."[26]

In sum, he tried to have it both ways: he disavowed the use of force against the seceded states but denied them the right to leave the Union. He was not yet sure in his own mind how to achieve his goals, only that he opposed those of the lower South Confederacy. It would therefore not be surprising if different listeners came away from the inaugural with different interpretations of the new president's intentions.

In Lincoln's original draft, he had proposed a stern closing: "With you, and not with me, is the solemn question of 'Shall it be peace, or a sword?'" In a God-fearing nation whose people read the Bible devoutly and thought nothing of committing long passages of scripture to memory, no one would have mistaken this admonitory reference or, what is more, would have missed the ominous correct answer to the question. For in the Gospel of Matthew, Jesus prophesied familial conflict: "Think not that I am come to send peace on earth: I came not to send peace, but a sword."[27]

Instead of this ending, the president took Seward's suggested alternative and honed it into a soaring paean of hope for the nation, in which "the mystic chords of memory, stretching from every battle-field, and patriot grave, to every living heart and hearthstone, all over this broad land, will yet swell the chorus of the Union, when again touched, as surely they will be, by the better angels of our nature."[28]

OBSERVERS ON INAUGURATION DAY understandably contrasted the pallid James Buchanan with his robust, forceful successor as appropriate symbols of old and new. But the shriveled, aged chief justice who now shuffled forward literally to make Lincoln president with the prescribed incantation offered an equally apt foil. When Lincoln finished speaking and the applause died away, the assembled thousands removed their hats in silent unison as eighty-three-year-old Roger Taney discharged his constitutional duty. After his *Dred Scott* decision had denied the rights of citizenship to blacks, Taney had come to embody for many in the North the corrupt and tyrannical slave power that they believed bound the federal government in service to the South's peculiar institution. In turn, to the Marylander Taney, as to many white southerners, the man about to take the oath of office incarnated the rankest despotism and danger to states' rights.

The physical contrast between the two men was marked. Frail in body, embittered by the abuse of his critics, and broken in spirit by the deaths of his wife and daughter from yellow fever, Taney was the picture of ruin, "the face of a galvanized corpse," in the acidulous words of a senator's wife. His hands visibly shook with emotion as he administered the oath. At six feet four inches tall, Lincoln, in contrast, towered over the chief justice. He projected an image of strength, though already exhausted by importunate office seekers and nonstop intrigue over the constitutional issues that confronted him. With serious, deep-set eyes and a strong jaw, newly accented since the election by a trim black beard, he looked every bit like a confident leader about to grasp the reins of power with firm hands.[29]

Placing his left hand on the cinnamon velvet binding of a Bible and raising his right hand, he repeated the words Taney feebly uttered and promised to "faithfully execute" the office of president and defend the Constitution of the United States of America. But how he would define what those words enjoined him to do remained a mystery. What he meant by them and by his speech was not immediately apparent.[30]

CHAPTER 2

WAIT AND SEE

Early March

Never did oracle, in its most evasive response, receive so many, and such various interpretations, as did the President's inaugural.

—*New York Times*, March 14

Texas senator Louis Wigfall was one of the minor dignitaries on the platform when Lincoln spoke. A southern rights advocate who had not yet decamped to Montgomery, he was a strident, raffish buffoon, yet a dangerous man who enjoyed trading on his violent past as a duelist. With a full, dark beard that highlighted the permanent scowl furrowed across his large face, Wigfall exuded a coarse appearance that fit his volatile personality. He had a fierce, flashing eye, an observer wrote, "with a well of fire burning behind and spouting through it, an eye pitiless in anger."[1] He spread the radicals' gospel in the Southwest, recklessly attacking the old unionist hero of Texas independence, Sam Houston. Responding directly to the fears ignited by John Brown at Harpers Ferry, the Texas Legislature had sent Wigfall to the U.S. Senate, where he opposed all efforts at compromise to save the Union.

Eloquent but pugnacious and devoid of tact, he used his senatorial franking privileges to inform Confederate officials of federal actions and capabilities. He planned to stay on in Washington for a while after the inauguration, an open spy feasting on the federal payroll. As a forthright enemy of all the new administration stood for, he wanted to hear with his own ears what the Republican president would say. Immediately after he listened to Lincoln take the oath of office, he telegraphed a terse prediction to South Carolina's governor: "Inaugural means war."[2]

WIGFALL COULD SEND WORD instantly thanks to a recent innovation. It had been only seventeen years earlier when the first experimental telegram had flashed from Washington to Baltimore. Since then, the burgeoning new technology had flung its strands of wire across the eastern third of the continent. The industry overcame huge technical hurdles: the problems of stringing wires on poles, sending a signal uncorrupted over great distances, and agreeing on a single code for messages. What gave the invention its power, however, was the fact that it developed at the same time as the proliferation of railroad lines, alongside which wires could be run, and even more, the explosive growth in daily newspapers, which provided a voracious appetite for telegraphed news.[3]

This networking of systems transformed communications. News gathering and news dissemination were nationalized. A rudimentary arrangement called the Associated Press allowed journalists to coordinate the sending of long-distance telegrams. With the national network centered in New York, they developed a capability to "broadcast" messages to multiple recipients simultaneously. Newspapers no longer depended on the erratic mails for information beyond their localities. They were linked instantly to every other paper that had access to the telegraph. The result was a revolution that allowed residents of every modest-size town to read about the great events of the day. Because it let them do it at the same time, not after days or weeks of delay, it radically shrank their world. The linking of telegraph and daily newspaper did not cause the sectional crisis, but it did enable the drama to unfold at the same time across the nation and therefore allowed communications to influence the course of events.

Speed did not bring enlightenment. Readers of the inaugural address the day after Lincoln spoke could not be certain what policies the president intended. To some, it seemed to be an inscrutable blend of opposing, delphic promises and threats. They also knew from newspaper reports that others besides Lincoln had had a hand in composing the speech. How much was his, and how much reflected other opinions in the cabinet and the Republican Party?

The reaction in the Confederate States echoed Wigfall's verdict. Some commentators believed their own propagandistic words when they proclaimed that the speech revealed Lincoln's malign intentions toward the South. Others hoped it was true that he meant war, while secretly fearing he did not. They believed it would take bloodshed to unify the South. Only conflict, it seemed, would bring to their senses the slave states not within the fold. Still others chose to emphasize the bright Confederate future and pay no heed to the irrelevancies of what was now, to them, a foreign country. A writer in New Orleans dismissed the pronouncements in Lincoln's address as of no consequence: "To us," in the seven seceded states, he airily concluded, "they are simply anachronisms."[4]

In South Carolina, the incubator of states' rights, the *Charleston Mercury* sneered at Lincoln for spewing insane words full of "ignorance, fanaticism, brute force." As the mouthpiece of Barnwell Rhett, the self-made, rash, and aggressive godfather of secession, the newspaper claimed vindication. It had incessantly warned against the "hood-winking verbiage" of Lincoln and his vile Republicans, who intended to impose a bloated, insolent despotism. Rhett and his fellows suffered from no shortage of offensive verbiage of their own.[5]

A positive northern reaction to the speech, at least among Republicans, was as equally predictable as secessionist contempt. The text reached New York City in time to be included in the late editions of some evening papers on Inauguration Day. By the next morning, readers there and across the country at places even more distant from Washington could form their own opinions of the new president's words. A New York Republican was pleased to see that his Democratic neighbors received the speech well and applauded it for its pacific tone. "Maybe so," he wrote approvingly, "but I think there's a clank of metal in it." A government clerk in Washington, D.C., wrote with apparent pleasure, "The 4th of March has come and gone, and we have a live *Republican* President."[6]

An Indiana paper that had supported Lincoln in the election praised the speech for standing firm: "In plain, terse, wire-woven sentences, so free from useless verbiage or pretentious rhetoric as to remind one of his own gaunt, sinewy form, all bone, and iron muscle." Full of pride in Illinois's favorite son, the *Chicago Tribune* hailed the address for "breathing kindlier feelings to all sections of the country." In case anyone mistook good wishes for weakness, however, the paper also said the speech "sweeps away the noisome vapor which treason and imbecility have cast all over the land."[7]

There was no monolithic North, though. The inaugural address did not persuade those who had opposed Lincoln's election to change their opinions. A New Jersey editor showed his partisanship when he defied any supporter of the president "to point out in it a single passage of real eloquence or pathos or beauty." A New Yorker worried that Lincoln had committed a practical error by "setting up the theory of *an unbroken Union,* against the stubborn fact of a divided and dissevered one." An Ohio paper censoriously opined that Lincoln had blundered in his speech. In consequence, the wavering border states would "certainly receive the inaugural as a virtual declaration of war upon the institution of slavery."[8]

After digesting the wildly various opinions expressed about the address, a Peoria newspaper, which had supported Douglas for president, observed that they all could not be right. The editor attributed the contrary views to the tin ears and prejudices of those passing judgment. He admitted that Lincoln was not a man of polish. He nevertheless hailed the poetic closing and concluded plainly that "as a calm, earnest, and friendly appeal to the seceding states to return to their allegiance we like it."[9] Few other non-Republican northern editors were as generous. Newspapers were partisan organs that parroted the biases of their owners, usually in more strident tones than the average citizen would use. In the aggregate, however, they reflected the range of northern popular opinion. Continuing divisions within the North meant that there was nothing like a consensus about Lincoln's speech, the secession issue, or the country's future course.

In the upper South, both extremes were well represented in the reaction to the address. A tiny Republican newspaper in the mountainous panhandle of Virginia welcomed the speech. But it reported that "the long faces of the secessionists brightened" with word of Lincoln's vow to maintain the Union because they hoped he would precipitate a clash. The editor of the *Richmond Examiner*, John Moncure Daniel, greeted the address with fulsome insults. "The 'scarlet letter' of submission to Lincoln," he cried in disgust, "has been burnt into [Virginia's] brow." Calling the president "the gigantic ape who occupies the seat of George Washington," Daniel denounced Virginia's leaders for permitting their state to bow to Lincoln's will. With a jumble of angry metaphors, a rival newspaper proclaimed that the address meant civil war: "The veil drops from the false prophet. The Demon of Coercion stands unmasked. The sword is drawn and the scabbard thrown away." John Thornton, a states' rights Virginian who would die for his principles at the head of his regiment at Antietam, warned, "It is not the first time that the Almighty has placed the words of prophecy in the mouth of a wicked man."[10]

Yet despite the noisy prominence given to extreme opinions, most sentiment in the upper South fell in between. Robert Young Conrad, a Virginia unionist, wrote his wife that Lincoln's speech threatened like a sudden earthquake to upset "all our conservative plans." The president's statements had embarrassed the effort to avoid a clash, but Conrad thought cautious men would yet prevent a war. A friend writing to Gen. Winfield Scott expressed his concern that secessionists had distorted Lincoln's message: the conservative unionist majority in Virginia "will be swept away like chaff before the wind" unless the administration made plain its benign intentions. The sole unionist broadsheet in the Virginia capital, the *Richmond Whig*, argued that it was too late to discuss whether secession was right or wrong. It was a reality in the Deep South. The editor stewed over

Lincoln's hint at coercion in the speech and implored the administration to avoid confrontation.[11]

In Raleigh, the *North Carolina Standard* was more sanguine. It argued that Lincoln spoke no more warlike words than did the cautious Buchanan, whose position the newspaper had supported. "It is not unfriendly to the South. It deprecates war, and bloodshed, and it pleads for the Union."[12] That being the case, the paper expected there would be a nonviolent resolution, either a constitutional convention to heal the rift or peaceful separation of the Deep South. That the editor considered the latter option viable in Lincoln's mind suggests the extent of misunderstanding that clouded judgment on all sides.

Maryland, astride the border between the sections, had weathered the contrary political winds that howled all winter. Delegations from the Deep South entreating Marylanders to join the Confederacy had made little headway. But the renewed hope that radicals took from Lincoln's inaugural promise to defend the Union troubled many in the border state with the most to lose in any conflict. The effect of the address had been to increase agitation and revive secessionist hopes, wrote a Marylander about the reaction in Virginia. He hoped it did not imply the same for his own state.[13]

For a few weeks after the inauguration, his wishes were granted, but partisan feelings ran strong just beneath the surface in Maryland, especially in volatile Baltimore. Gov. Thomas Hicks and other Marylanders unhappy about the prospect of having to choose between North and South tentatively endorsed common action among the slave states of the border. This would be a theme repeated over and over, especially in Maryland and Virginia, during the rest of March and into April. For many like-minded citizens of the border, the prospect that they might even form a middle confederacy between the hostile sections, and thereby prevent war, gave hope throughout the spring.

WHAT WAS CLEAR to everyone after Lincoln was inaugurated was that the eight slave states of the upper South—Arkansas, Delaware, Kentucky, Maryland, Missouri, North Carolina, Tennessee, and

Virginia—still stood apart from the secessionist experiment. The installation of a Republican president had not been enough to stampede them out of the Union. Together, they had twice the number of white residents as the new southern republic. It, indeed, contained merely a tenth of the white population of the whole United States. The call for a united and independent South had failed. The South was more divided than ever.[14]

Far from drawing the region closer together, recent economic change during the prosperous 1850s further differentiated the upper South from what had become the cotton Confederacy. The bulk of the growing southern industrial base was in the upper South. Slavery there proved remarkably resilient but very unlike the plantation version farther south. In the past decade or so, a massive increase in slave hiring called forth by the demands of industry in upper South towns enabled the institution to adapt and survive even apart from agriculture.

Even so, the same harsh system that denied some Americans the promise of individual freedom bound all of the southern states together, just as surely as leg irons often bound the unfree men and women who lived there. Despite its ability to mutate and take on different shape in different parts of the South, slavery separated all of those states where it existed from the rest of the nation. Even though ending slavery was not yet even a glimmer in the minds of northerners outside a small circle of abolitionists, the institution placed a large and undeniable division between the upper South and the free states.

The slaves themselves, by their very existence, indirectly influenced events, despite their lack of any political rights. That was so because fear of slave resistance—by acts of arson, insubordination, and flight—was never absent from the minds of troubled white southerners.[15] Alleged plots of slave insurrections were more in the imagination of slave owners than in actual fact. The fear of them, though, tainted the climate in which white southerners deliberated their relationship to the Union.

In March, however, those apprehensions were not enough to tip the scales in the upper South in favor of radical action. Unionists there, still loyal to the United States, doubted the Confederacy could become viable on its own. They believed that if no more states joined, it would collapse, and the Union would be restored.

Despite Congress's rejection of the ideas put forward by the Peace Conference, upper South unionists continued to place their hopes in a resolution on that basis. The Peace Conference had proposed a complex version of the Missouri Compromise line separating free and slave territory. It was clear to the *Richmond Whig* that those who rejected this settlement were opposed to any resolution, "their object being a thorough and permanent disruption of the Union."[16] That object was anathema to the good Union citizens of the upper South. They wanted to remain a part of the great American republic, and they hoped the disaffected states of the Confederacy could be lured back into harmony with the others.

For the moment, a confrontation was averted. But in their professions of continued fealty to the United States, southern unionists misled the North and perhaps themselves. They were anomalies but did not know it. What they did know was that they must avoid having to choose between North and South. And that meant Lincoln must avoid forcing them to confront such a fearful decision. They were intensely suspicious of the president and disbelieved he represented the majority in the free states. They doubted whether he could command enough support even in the North to use force against the seceded states. That was understandable because the diversity of opinion expressed in the press showed there was no unified northern point of view. The North, for its part, failed to understand either the determination of the Confederate States to pursue independence or the quality of Union sentiment in the upper South.

Confederates also feared their experiment would fail without the upper South and redoubled their efforts to convince those states that their future lay with them.[17] Even before they formed the Confederacy, individual seceded states sent delegations to the upper South on a sales mission. One of these men, Judge Alexander Hamilton Handy, a Marylander who had moved to Mississippi, went back to his native state to warn that Lincoln's administration intended to

"overthrow the constitution, and subvert the rights of the South."
By these, of course, he meant the means "by which one man can own
property in his fellow man."[18] The boisterous crowd that jammed
Baltimore's Maryland Institute Hall roared its approval of Handy's
claim that slavery, hardly a sin, enjoyed divine sanction.

Henry Lewis Benning, also a judge, represented his native Georgia to the Virginia convention sitting in Richmond during the secession crisis. An ardent exponent of disunion, he had advocated a
separate southern nation for more than a decade. Like Handy, he
tried to alarm Virginians about the threat that Republicans posed to
slavery. At the end of an impassioned speech, he implored his listeners to join hands with the Confederacy: "Sir, in such a cause, cowards
will become men, men heroes, and heroes gods."[19]

As Americans assimilated Lincoln's address, some of them could
see that despite its ambiguities and appeal to peace, it was not peace
at any price, for it revealed the president's determination to maintain
the whole nation intact. That firmness troubled unionists in the
upper South, and they privately and publicly condemned the suggestion of force in the message. Within a few days of the inauguration,
though, they had stifled their own misgivings and successfully tamped
down secessionist agitation in their region, preventing "hasty action,"
in the words of a Marylander.[20] They fervently prayed that in the
end Lincoln would favor the more pacific ideals he expressed in his
address rather than the hints he might attempt to coerce the Confederate States back into the Union. If so, they had a chance to resolve
the crisis without violence. Certainly throughout March they acted
as if peace, and not war, were the likeliest future for the nation.

If Lincoln had bluntly asserted his intention to use force to preserve the Union, and not cloaked the glint of steel in soothing appeals
for peace, southern Unionists would not have been able to cling to
hopes for a happy outcome as long as they did. The result might have
been an explosion in the upper South much earlier. But even Lincoln
was not sure of the course ahead. He resisted making a decision. His
speech therefore fairly reflected his own thinking in its proffered
mixture of the olive branch and the arrows of war.

RETIRED DIPLOMAT and former U.S. senator William Cabell Rives desired only to spend his declining years on his estate in the rolling Piedmont hills of central Virginia with his horses, and his books, and his plans to write a biography of James Madison, father of the Constitution. He was a short man, dour of countenance but ebullient in his faith in the country's future. He had a familial aversion to disunion to match his constitutional principles; most of his children and numerous grandchildren had made their homes in the North. The national crisis called him out of retirement, and he labored as much as anyone behind the scenes to avert a breakup of the republic he revered. He viewed his state as "the neutral ground between two . . . angry, excited, and hostile portions of the Union." For his pains, the genteel Rives was mocked and dismissed by the secessionist press as a lickspittle trimmer, fit only to "embalm" Madison.[21]

Four days after the inauguration, Rives abandoned his rural solitude and went down to Richmond to address a huge, anxious assembly of fellow citizens. He endorsed the remedies proposed by the Peace Conference, even though they had just failed to persuade a majority of both houses of Congress. Rives's detractors admitted that the elder statesman gave an impassioned and impressive performance. He was most eloquent when he warmed to his favorite theme, the once and future glory of the Old Dominion. He implored his listeners to renew Virginia's role as the leader of the border states. Did they not realize that the commonwealth was the only state that possessed the moral authority to save the Union single-handedly? Despite Congress's rejection, the Peace Conference proposals were acceptable to the states in the middle. They should therefore build on that basis. They could then gradually coax the whole country into accepting compromise.

The anxieties of his state and others of the upper South were painfully apparent in the reported reaction of the audience to the central rhetorical question Rives posed: "Was Virginia, then, when in sight of the promised land, to bolt out and join the seceded sisters of the South? [Mingled cries of 'no' and 'yes']."[22]

CHAPTER 3

TOUJOURS LA POLITESSE

Washington, D.C., Early to Mid-March

There will be no war, it will be all arranged. I will drink all the blood shed in the war.

—James Chesnut Jr.[1]

The new president had reason to be well satisfied with the inauguration and with his address. The event had come off without incident and confounded the rumormongers. General Scott's flying artillery battery had not been required to fire grapeshot down Pennsylvania Avenue at enemies of the Constitution. No assassin showed his hand. Lincoln was glad to have the inaugural ball behind him, too, for he would need all his energy. He had not finished choosing his cabinet, and already a crescendo of pleas from office seekers threatened to overwhelm him.

When he reached his office the day after the inauguration, he was not prepared for the bad news that awaited him. It came in the guise of a lengthy letter written that morning and delivered in person by Joseph Holt, Buchanan's secretary of war. A stern, heavyset Kentucky Democrat, perpetually frowning and increasingly hostile to secession, he once was described as a politician "with none of the milk of human kindness in his veins."[2] Holt was staying on the job until Lincoln's appointee, Simon Cameron, could take office. His

long cover letter introduced a packet of documents received the day
before from Maj. Robert Anderson, commander of the garrison at
Fort Sumter in Charleston Harbor.

The fort had been in the news off and on since Christmas, when
Anderson made a pivotal decision to move his small command from
indefensible Fort Moultrie on the harbor's northern shore to Fort
Sumter out in the channel. There he could withstand attack from a
force far larger than his skeleton garrison. As forts surrendered
across the South, the unfinished citadel in the heart of secession took
on symbolic value. By the time of the inauguration, it and Fort Pickens, near Pensacola, Florida, were the only major military installations still under Washington's control and within Confederate
borders. Lincoln knew that, but he assumed Anderson was well
enough supplied to withstand indefinite siege, if it came to that.

In his latest communication, however, the major informed Washington that his food would run out in less than six weeks unless the
government mounted a massive effort to reprovision him. Shaken,
and also keen to justify himself, Holt told Lincoln that this intelligence came as an utter surprise. Given Anderson's previous assurances of his safety behind the fort's thick walls, the government was
unprepared to meet the "extravagant estimates" that the major now
made for the size of a relief expedition.[3] Indeed, Anderson doubted
such a force could succeed with fewer than twenty thousand men.
The whole army numbered less than that.

LINCOLN THUS had to form his administration in the shadow of a
sudden, specific threat when he had been expecting to have much
more time to defuse the larger constitutional crisis. What was strik-
ing about his choice of cabinet officers was that so many of them had
been rivals for the Republican nomination for president. With the
benefit of hindsight, later writers have cited this as evidence of Lincoln's astuteness, his assurance in surrounding himself with strong
personalities. That he would select men who thought they should be
sitting in his chair said something about his self-confidence. But that
became clear only much later. At the time, the president had done

nothing to prove he was a strong leader or made of sterner or more intelligent stuff than the others.

He later admitted to being "entirely ignorant not only of the duties, but of the manner of doing the business." Unfortunately, he tried to do it all himself. With no one to show the way, he made mistakes. Allowing office seekers to monopolize his time was the worst of them. An "ill-bred, ravenous crowd," they swarmed through the corridors and even had unimpeded access to the president's office. He later admitted he was "fair game for everybody of that hungry lot." John Nicolay, one of his private secretaries, recalled that because of the pressure during those early days, "we have scarcely had time to eat sleep or even breathe." Not long into Lincoln's administration, the press began remarking on how haggard and pale the president began to look under the strain.[4]

The center of activity in the scramble for office was the Willard Hotel, the six-story dormitory of choice for aspiring bureaucrats two blocks from the White House. It so overflowed with patrons that the management put mattresses in the halls. Despite a wealth of spittoons, tobacco juice fouled its passageways. Within its walls that March, wrote a visitor, were "more scheming, plotting, planning heads, more aching and joyful hearts, than any building of the same size ever held in the world."[5] They came from all over the free states, flitting in and out, clutching testimonials of their fitness for appointment.

In light of Major Anderson's surprise, it was puzzling that Lincoln did not make Fort Sumter the centerpiece of the first cabinet meeting, a formal and dull affair on March 6. It was not until they gathered again three days later that the cabinet secretaries heard about the alarming situation in Charleston Harbor. They were astonished to learn that the fort's predicament compelled General Scott to advocate retreat. A letter Lincoln wrote Scott that same day, however, indicated his reluctance to agree. He asked the general if, after further reflection, he had the wherewithal to resupply or reinforce Fort Sumter. If not, what would it take to achieve that objective?[6]

Another indication of the president's thinking came four days later when he received a visit from a former naval officer. Gustavus

Vasa Fox had a plan for Fort Sumter, and his wife's brother-in-law, Postmaster General Montgomery Blair, provided the entrée to Lincoln. Blair, a lean West Point graduate, was the only cabinet officer with a military background. His reedy, weak voice and "rat-like expression" led some people to discount his opinions. Regarding secession, he bluntly told Lincoln that nothing had been done to stop it "or prevent its being regarded at home or abroad as a successful revolution."[7] Only action at Fort Sumter would galvanize the North and demoralize rebellion.

Blair had made it possible for Gus Fox to present his plan to Buchanan in February, but nothing had come of it. Now, hoping to sway Buchanan's successor, Blair enabled Fox to present his idea again. Lincoln later called this enormously energetic sailor-turned-factory-manager "a live man, whose services we cannot well dispense with."[8] Finding such men among the legions who begged him for office and rank would be a crucial task for him in the weeks to come. Not yet forty, the balding Fox sported a luxurious dark beard and mustache that concealed his expression. A bon vivant, fond of rich dinners and good cigars, he bubbled over with contempt for set patterns and old ways.

His plan called for transporting men and supplies to the waters around Fort Sumter in large, seagoing ships and then running them in to the fort on shallow-draft tugboats, past Confederate obstructions in the harbor. The president was intrigued. Wanting to keep all options open, and eager to avoid capitulation, Lincoln invited Fox to present his plan to the cabinet. The majority, like Scott, still favored evacuation, but now a practical, though risky, measure to avoid that course lay on the table.[9]

On March 15, Lincoln asked each of his cabinet officers to give him a written response to one question. He prefaced it with an assumption that suggested the influence of Fox on his thinking. Assuming it was possible to reprovision the fort, he asked, "under all the circumstances, is it wise to attempt it?"[10] Most of them opposed any such effort as likely to lead to war. It was not worth the chance. Attorney General Edward Bates understood the point of honor about holding

Fort Sumter but on balance thought it more prudent to give it up. Salmon Chase, the Treasury secretary, did not want to provoke war but did not think resupplying Anderson would run that risk. He therefore was somewhat inclined to give Fox's scheme a chance. Only Blair unequivocally favored an expedition even if it did lead to fighting.

The divided opinions of his advisers and his distaste for retreat reinforced Lincoln's temperamental reluctance to act. The president was not ready to oppose the majority and so postponed a decision.[11] The rights of slaveholders, the return of runaways, the extension of slavery into the western territories—none of these hot issues that had poisoned the 1850s mattered now that actual secession threatened to produce the long-feared breakup of the nation. How to keep the loyal slave states from leaving and somehow to stitch up the rift with the seceded ones together constituted the main issue for Lincoln's embryonic administration. As much as the president hated deciding what to do about Fort Sumter, the tiny garrison in Charleston Harbor had become the embodiment of that larger problem, and it would not go away.

WHILE LINCOLN ASSEMBLED his administration and wrestled with Major Anderson's plight, the men of Montgomery were building a new nation. Jefferson Davis's first cabinet meeting fell by symbolic intent on March 4, Inauguration Day in Washington. Like Lincoln, the Confederate president already looked haggard from overwork. Tall and dignified, the fifty-two-year-old Davis carried himself with the erect posture of his West Point days, but poor health dogged him. His face was racked by painful neuralgia, and a blinding film covered one eye. The other, however, sparkled with determination and intelligence.

Like his adversary in Washington, Davis displayed enormous self-control and reserve. Unlike Lincoln, however, he lacked tact, failed to compromise, and tended to meddle in the work of subordinates. He was irritable, impatient, stubborn, oversensitive to criticism, and unable to admit fault. Stiff in social situations, he would much rather commune with his letters and official documents. He drove himself and those around him with unrelenting energy born of his commitment to the cause.[12]

Like Lincoln, as well, Davis built his cabinet from a patchwork of former rivals. They knew that they needed a strong central government if their nascent republic was to survive. Yet they also believed they could fashion a polity that would honor their commitment to the sovereignty of each individual constituent state. Their Confederate democracy rested forthrightly on the twin pillars of states' rights and the inequality of men, enshrined in the institution of slavery.

Davis, like Lincoln, needed time. Neither side wanted precipitate action. For him, as much as for Lincoln, the situation in Charleston was fraught with danger. He feared the South Carolinians, reckless and unreliable, would attack the fort before the rest of the Confederacy was ready. Throughout March, he kept in contact almost every day with South Carolina's governor, Francis Pickens. He urged Pickens not to allow some local hotspur to start a war they were unprepared to wage.[13] Davis doubted the prospects for a bloodless separation, and he wanted to give his commanders time to plan. For the moment, both needs, diplomatic and military, demanded caution and delay. For the moment, then, to some degree the interests of Confederate and Union administrations coincided.

DAVIS SENT three commissioners to Washington to treat for a peaceful separation from the federal government and to establish diplomatic relations. He was, as he put it in his letter to Lincoln, "animated by an earnest desire to unite and bind together our respective countries by friendly ties."[14] No matter how thickly he coated his text in the soothing words of diplomacy, there was that one hard phrase: "respective countries." It admitted no compromise on the adamantine difference that separated him from Lincoln.

Within hours of Lincoln's inauguration, Secretary of State Seward learned about the commissioners' desire to meet with him. His answer, conveyed indirectly, disappointed them. A formal meeting would embarrass the administration, still in the process of organizing itself.

A month from celebrating his sixtieth birthday, William Henry Seward had strutted on the national stage for nearly three decades, first as governor of New York and more recently as U.S. senator. Slender, but with stooped posture, he had a long neck, shaggy eyebrows, an aquiline nose, and graying hair that once was red. A raconteur of great personal charm and equanimity, ambitious and worldly, he methodically advanced his presidential aspirations.[15] He was the most prominent antislavery politician in the late 1850s, and he famously predicted an "irrepressible conflict" between free and slave labor. Although that phrase made him suspect in the South, some in his party distrusted him as an opportunist. For that reason, the Republicans passed him over at their nominating convention.

When the Gulf states chose secession as their response to the 1860 election, most Republicans, including Lincoln, dismissed it as bluff. Seward believed otherwise. He saw that the Union was in grave danger, and he meant to save it. He believed the infant southern republic could not survive without the more populous slave states still in the Union. For Seward, the key then was to keep those upper South states from leaving. The most important way to achieve that end, according to his lights, was to remove all points of potential conflict that might force the upper South to choose sides. Withdrawing the garrison from Fort Sumter would be the most important step. This was just what hard-line Republicans feared. With the pragmatic Seward in the cabinet, the most strident abolitionists were convinced the administration "would cave in."[16]

Throughout March, Seward kept up a clandestine correspondence with unionists in the upper South. It is difficult to determine how much Lincoln knew of his secretary of state's overtures. Seward certainly did go behind the president's back in some of them. But he believed he was accurately relating Lincoln's inclination, if not yet his firm conviction, when he suggested that the fort would shortly be evacuated. And just as certainly, by mid-March the president knew about some of Seward's southern contacts and his promise that the administration would remove the sticking point represented by Anderson's garrison.[17] That Lincoln did not squelch such backstairs maneuvering says more, however, about his distaste for making a decision than approval of Seward's position.

On March 15, Seward was agitated. The president had just asked his cabinet officers whether they thought it wise to attempt to resupply Fort Sumter. For the moment, most followed Seward's lead in opposing such a move. With time, the secretary of state thought he could convert that sentiment into the next step, evacuation. Removing the garrison would scuttle any radical agitation in the upper South and, he believed, would bring the seceded states to their senses. But on the same day the cabinet met, the Confederate commissioners were threatening to leave Washington at the slight of not being officially recognized. Such a step would upset Seward's pacifying strategy and might trigger hostilities. While Seward puzzled over what to do, John Archibald Campbell and Samuel Nelson, both associate justices of the Supreme Court, walked into his office.[18]

A tall, commanding figure from Alabama, with a high, intelligent forehead and an enormous capacity for hard work, Campbell was known for long, ruminative walks about town, tugging his bushy eyebrows as he went.[19] It was on one such stroll that day in March that he ran into his colleague on Pennsylvania Avenue and fell into an extended discussion about the crisis. Campbell learned from Nelson that Lincoln had forbade formal contact with the commissioners. The two men decided to call on Seward to encourage him to find some unofficial way to open communications with the southerners. The secretary of state ruefully explained how any contact would embarrass the administration. He also confessed that the unexpected crisis over Fort Sumter was consuming the president's time.

Then Seward floored his visitors by admitting that Lincoln contemplated abandoning the fort. Like everyone else in Washington, for the past week Campbell had heard rumors to that effect. They were just hearsay, but now here was confirmation from the mouth of the secretary of state. At once, Campbell offered to act as intermediary. He would do whatever it took to mollify the commissioners and prevent rash action on their part.[20]

A states' rights jurist, Campbell had earned widespread enmity in the North and was equally distrusted in some southern quarters because he staunchly opposed disunion. He declined to resign from the bench when his home state seceded because he thought the Constitution sufficiently protected southern rights and slavery against anything the Republicans might do. Like many conservative southerners, Campbell believed a reaction would set in against the radicals and force the lower South to return to the Union.

Now, unlooked for, an opportunity to help had come to him and of a magnitude he had not imagined. Immediately after leaving the secretary of state, he went to see Martin Crawford, one of the southern commissioners. Crawford, a tall, blond Georgian known for dry wit and gifted oratory, had helped organize the Confederate States at Montgomery. Campbell urged him against pressing for recognition. At first Crawford refused to be swayed, but he relented in the face of Campbell's offer to put into writing his confidence that the federal government would evacuate the fort. As soon as he extracted Crawford's agreement to give Seward more time, Campbell wrote to Jefferson Davis, confident that the crisis was about to be resolved.[21]

For their part, the commissioners believed time was on their side, so they tolerated the delay in being recognized by Washington. They were confident that Seward's hope for a conservative southern reaction against secession was fruitless. "We are feeling our way here cautiously," one of them wrote to Montgomery. He was content to wait, believing Seward would yet convince Lincoln to back away from confrontation at Fort Sumter.[22]

LINCOLN VACILLATED. He wanted to avoid conflict but even more abhorred surrendering federal sovereignty. Because he was cautious, was temperamentally averse to snap decisions, preferred to react to the actions of others, and above all loathed the possibility of having to give up the fort, he made no public pronouncements on the situation in Charleston Harbor. The press interpreted inaction as a sign of weakness. Even those who meant the president well began to doubt him. Charles Francis Adams, son of President John Quincy Adams and a friend of Secretary of State Seward, concluded that Lincoln was "drifting the country into war, by want of decision." He added that "the man is not equal to the hour."[23] British correspondent William Howard Russell thought the administration looked passive in the face of the dilemma posed by Fort Sumter. To an outsider, he mused, "It seems as if they were waiting for events to develop."[24]

Only a few days after Lincoln learned about Fort Sumter's plight, details about conditions there and the divisions within his cabinet became common knowledge in Washington. So was the fact that the government contemplated withdrawing the garrison. The remarks of a midlevel Patent Office bureaucrat, who learned the broad details two days after the cabinet did, showed how much people understood of the state of affairs. While complaining in his diary on March 12 that Washington was full of strangers angling for political office, he noted, using a common northern spelling error, "It is understood that Fort Sumpter is to be evacuated."[25]

Before the middle of the month, and even before Lincoln asked his cabinet members for their opinions, newspapers broadcast the situation facing them and fairly accurately gauged the options open to the government. Some northern opinion increasingly favored evacuation rather than resupply. According to this view, withdrawing the soldiers from Fort Sumter and thus removing the most contested point would kill secession. Such speculation energized southern unionists. Exponents of secession feared for their cause. But at the same time, a countervailing sentiment in the North strengthened, too. Strident Republicans had always counseled Lincoln to use force. If war was to be the answer, "the sooner it is begun, the sooner it will be over," one opined.[26]

If sentiment in the North had coalesced behind Republicans demanding military action to assert the federal government's authority, upper South unionists would have been forced to choose sides. They would not have been able to persist in their hopes of avoiding such a decision and finding some peaceful solution. An entirely different outcome would have resulted if there had been accelerating

momentum behind the quite substantial sentiment in the North
for letting the Deep South states "depart in peace," to use the familiar formula. But there was no consensus, and the season of drift continued.

JOHN ADAMS GILMER figured more prominently than any other politician in the upper South in the effort to inoculate his region against
secession.[27] A bluff, powerfully built congressman from Greensboro,
North Carolina, he had a round face, a kindly smile, and an appealing
ability as a speaker to captivate his listeners, even bring them to
tears. He labored behind the scenes with Seward to defuse the threat
that more states might join the Confederacy. Seward nudged Lincoln
to offer Gilmer a cabinet post as a token of conciliation to his wavering region. In the end, it did not happen, but the North Carolinian
continued to aid Seward in promoting the administration's hands-off
attitude and keeping the upper South from having to choose sides in
a fratricidal war.

Gilmer, though, represented the limitations of southern unionist
thought. His main idea for preventing war was the now familiar but,
for Lincoln, no less distasteful one: the federal government should
abandon the remaining forts it still held in the Deep South. He
asked of Lincoln more than the president was willing to give. Lincoln
did not believe that surrender was the only way to ensure the continued loyalty of the upper South states. That showed his limitation: an
unwillingness to consider that conceding on the forts might have
been the more courageous path than fighting to keep them. And on
that difference of opinion between very different men hung the fate
of the nation. To Gilmer, a decision to confront the Confederates over
Fort Sumter would be reckless beyond measure. "There must be no
fighting," he pleaded, for in such an event, the unionist majority in
the upper South would "be swept away in a torrent of madness."[28]

CHAPTER 4

CONTRIVANCES OF DELAY

Richmond, Mid-March

Gray is all theory, but green is the golden tree of life.

—Johann Wolfgang von Goethe

Aweek after Lincoln's inauguration, George Summers took the floor of the convention in Richmond, Virginia, that had been called to consider secession. He spoke for five hours. A stout man with a white beard and an aristocratic mien, he possessed the deep, rich voice to overcome the hall's bad acoustics and the powerful oratory to command the attention of his colleagues. Summers was representing Charleston in the northwestern part of the state. He had labored for decades, usually in vain, against the lopsided power of the older, longer-established eastern counties. He accepted responsibility in the twilight of his career, first as a member of the state's delegation to the ill-starred Peace Conference in Washington, then as unionist leader in the convention. Behind the scenes, he labored to keep both the resolute and the more hesitant unionists together and in control of the proceedings.[1]

In his address, Summers marshaled his famous gift for appealing to juries with forceful, almost charismatic language. He argued that to safeguard southern rights Virginians must remain within the

Union and shun the untested new republic in Montgomery. Secession was not likely to be had peacefully. And in the improbable event
that it was, it still would leave Virginia with less protection for slavery than before. Problems with runaways and disputes with the free
states could only increase, with disastrous results.

Sympathetic newspapers hailed Summers's effort a prodigy. One
of them crowed that his words struck "deep into the ranks of the
traitors."[2] Summers had laid out the argument that the conservative
majority would reiterate throughout the convention. In the Union
lay safety, the greatest hope for the upper South and for its continued prosperity based on slavery. The region had no common interest
with the cotton kingdom of the Deep South. The Confederacy's wild
course threatened everything the founding fathers had created.

The president of the convention, tall, courtly, patient, and long-
suffering John Janney, who publicly stood above faction and played
no favorites, privately revealed his delight. Now, he confided in a letter he wrote to his wife, Alcinda, on the evening of Summers's great
speech, "The little pigmy secessionists with their clap-trap nonsense
have been reduced to the size of small mice."[3]

A SPECIAL SESSION of the state legislature in January had called for
the convention that Summers addressed. The unionist sweep of the
election for delegates in February halted the course of secession in its
tracks. For the first time since John Brown had entered Harpers Ferry,
the political tide of dissolution receded, in Virginia and across the
upper South. By electing an overwhelmingly unionist majority, the
most populous southern state reasserted its allegiance to the nation
and pointed the way forward for its neighbors. Optimists thought
Virginia's example might even lead to the eventual return of the
wayward Confederacy.

The Virginia gathering, which convened on February 13, was
important because it was the only state convention that remained in
session from that point on through all of March and April. The
records of its proceedings, dry and formal, nevertheless reveal earnest efforts to persuade opponents and real anguish on the part of

many delegates over what course to take to ensure the rights and safety of the state's citizens. The proceedings thus open a window onto sentiment across the conflicted upper South, still a part of the United States under Lincoln and yet uncertain if that condition should or would continue for long. What the delegates decided would determine the fate of their state, and possibly their region, though the extent of their influence was less than they realized. But they could not know the future, and for a time all eyes were on Virginia.

With forty thousand inhabitants, Richmond in 1861 was one of the most prosperous small cities in the nation. At the rushing falls of the James River, eighty miles inland from the Chesapeake Bay and a hundred miles due south of Washington, the Virginia capital owed its wealth initially to two sources, tobacco and slaves. In the past decade, though, newer economic forces were transforming Richmond at a rapid pace. The smoke and clangor from foundries and machine shops signaled an outpouring of goods that forged ties of commerce and friendship with cities farther up the Atlantic coast, especially Baltimore, Philadelphia, and New York City. By the time the convention assembled in the Mechanics Institute at the base of Capitol Square, a cluster of stylish new churches, public buildings, and mansions looked down the hills on the thriving commercial district that made them possible.

When the 152 delegates gathered in the second-floor hall of the Mechanics Institute, all the groups present favored delay. The secessionist minority knew that the infant Confederacy in Montgomery, which carried their hopes for the future, needed time to organize. They believed that as it did, it would entice more adherents in the upper South. They were content not to push for a vote for their cause just yet. In the meantime, though, their advocates outside the hall railed against "the Presidential Frankenstein" in Washington to whom Virginia made disgusting obeisance.[4] Uncompromising unionists, another minority, also believed that with time they could convince others of the grave costs of secession.

By far the largest element consisted of conservatives who loved the Union, mistrusted Lincoln deeply, but accepted his election. They favored states' rights and slavery, but like conservatives everywhere, they clung to familiar ways and shunned revolution. They hoped that with time they could fashion a Union-saving compromise, just as the nation's leaders had done before whenever sectional differences threatened. Their special hope—evoked by like-minded patriots in every border state from the presidential election until the end of spring—lay in coordinated consultation among the upper South slave states.

The main weapon in the secessionists' arsenal was to invoke the fear of "coercion" by the North. They defined the concept loosely enough to cover any attempt by Lincoln to carry out his duties that would transgress against the seceded states. The most likely possibility for coercion involved the Deep South forts still under federal control, Sumter and Pickens. The continued presence of those small garrisons threatened to become a pretext for fighting. And that, argued southern unionists, was just what the radicals wanted: "They are absolutely agog for it."[5] Shedding blood would play into their hands.

On the floor of the convention, constitutional theory became palpable as face-to-face confrontations gave voice to the issues dividing the nation. Jubal Early had little time for secessionist agitation. A profane, crusty, sarcastic attorney and former army officer of forty-four, he represented Franklin County, in the southwestern Piedmont just east of the mountains. Premature arthritis stooped his posture, and he spoke with a high voice that squeaked, said a friend, like a "Chinese fiddle." But his stern gaze and strong features, and especially his towering, indeed arrogant, sense of rectitude, far outweighed these disabilities. Despite his lack of conventional charm, the force of his personality was apparent for all to see.[6]

Early did not approve of Lincoln's inaugural address. Even less did he approve of efforts to overthrow the Constitution. With an invidious, backhanded comment directed at his fellow delegates, he reminded them that ordinary Virginians, "the real people—the bone and sinew of the State," were at home calmly and quietly following the routines of daily life. They looked to the convention to resolve the issues that threatened to divide the nation and to do so wisely, by legal means, and not by violence.[7]

John Goode, a hot-blooded lawyer from Bedford County, which bordered Early's district, mocked his colleague's caution. He did it with such a contemptuous flourish that the visitors' gallery, packed with secessionist women, erupted in applause and laughter. The president of the convention threatened to eject them from the hall. Early exploded with indignation as Goode provocatively claimed that the farmers of Franklin County, far from calmly going about their chores, were writing fevered letters to Richmond calling for secession. Early denounced him for presuming to know the minds of his constituents. He insulted Goode and implied that he was no gentleman, that he was, in fact, no better than the rabble he incited out in the streets, who tried to threaten the convention with noisy protests. The exchange between these two proud men almost led to a duel before Goode backed down.[8]

Nothing did more to mollify opinion in the upper South than the rumors about evacuating Fort Sumter that began to filter out of Washington shortly after the inauguration. Stephen Douglas suggested as much in a speech that—even if it was wishful thinking on the senator's part—energized southern unionists. Douglas's bombshell on the Senate floor and Seward's back-channel assurances that Lincoln would indeed let the forts go without a fight took the wind out of the secessionists' sails in the Richmond convention. "Virginia is safe," predicted one overjoyed unionist. Surrender of the forts, said another, would "more completely *put to rout* the disunion party, than all the guns and soldiers in the world."[9]

The unionist majority of the delegates believed the purpose of their convention was to devise a grand national compromise, not break up the country. Accordingly, they appointed a federal relations committee, which offered its preliminary report on March 9. The majority pushed their colleagues to accept it, propose it to the nation as a solution to the crisis, and then go home. The debate over the report would take a little time, and they all would have to endure more long-winded speeches. These would undoubtedly address the

constitutional details of the committee's report, but they would also
likely range far and wide across all of the issues that agitated Americans that spring. The unionists, however, were confident of gaining
approval and adjournment by the end of the month. They were willing to tolerate some delay by secessionists as long as they could rely
on Seward's conciliatory policy to continue. He obliged, with repeated
assurances that Fort Sumter would soon be evacuated.[10]

The heart of the majority report presented a complex set of constitutional guarantees. These echoed the Crittenden attempt to revive
the Missouri Compromise line dividing the West into free and slave
territories. These provisions were meant to assuage southerners that
slavery would be protected, but they failed to address the unpleasant
fact of secession. Unfortunately for the compromisers, the Confederate States were intent on building a new nation. They had no interest
in tinkering with the U.S. Constitution, however more favorably it
was amended to satisfy them. Because the committee report only parroted Crittenden, it revealed the limits of the unionists' imagination.
Yet, they sincerely believed the report offered a sound basis for settling all differences and restoring a united nation.

Henry Wise, the quixotic former governor who had been shunned
by unionists and mistrusted at first by advocates of immediate secession, ensured that the debates would be long and rancorous. He was
the most active delegate to the convention and ultimately the most
influential one. No one else spoke as much, evoked as much laughter
from the delegates or from the galleries, or won as much attention.
Leaders of the unionist majority spoke more cogently than Wise,
with the cloying, silken, lapidary phrases of southern gentility, but
none could match his fire. He jested darkly that under Lincoln they
would not be "relieved of our apprehensions," but they would "certainly be relieved of our negro property."[11]

Indeed, he literally engendered the most basic and intimate con-
tradiction of the South—a defender of slavery who, in addition to five
legitimate sons, sired an unacknowledged one of mixed race. Though
he appeared much older than his fifty-four years, he was a figure of
mesmeric intensity. Erratic, slovenly, gesticulating as he spoke, drib-

bling tobacco juice down the front of his linen shirt, contorting his face and waving his hands, Wise in full cry was unmistakable.[12]

Secessionists swallowed their initial misgivings about Wise and gravitated toward him as their spokesman. Despite his labyrinthine, impenetrable arguments, his temperament for obstruction played exactly to their need to thwart a vote on the majority committee report. It, they rightly feared, threatened adjournment without taking the Old Dominion out of the Union.[13] The chairman of the committee complained that Wise made elaborate speeches, proposed nothing, agreed to nothing. Staunch unionist delegates from the western part of the state believed he was behind every rumored radical plot.

Wise achieved his aim of delay and drove his opponents to distraction. John Janney, the convention president, admitted privately that if Wise had not been a delegate, they all could have gone home weeks before. Perhaps Janney exaggerated. But an argument can be made that he fairly assessed Wise's overweening influence. If he was right, and the convention had adjourned, Virginia would have faced the great question of secession in a different context, without this assembly dominated by the state's conservative unionist leaders.

Viewing the world from an entirely different perspective from that of Wise, Waitman Thomas Willey raised an issue that threatened to divide the convention along a fissure that long predated secession—indeed, one that went back decades into the state's past. A handsome Morgantown lawyer with high cheekbones, a prominent forehead, and a firm jaw, Willey was a devout Methodist layman of fifty and a rising leader in the northwestern section of the state. He asked his colleagues to consider the just need of states for equality within the federal Union. He then drew a parallel between that relationship and an internal issue, Virginia's unequal taxation of property.

Here was an old wound that few delegates wished to see reopened, especially at this volatile moment. It was no dry-as-dust point, beloved only of bookkeepers and lawyers, but a divisive, inflammatory threat. The state constitution gave explicit preferential tax treatment to property in slaves. Those under the age of twelve were not

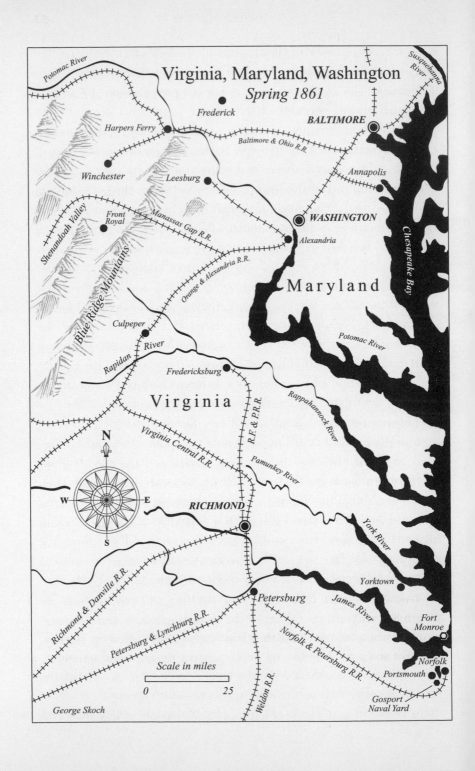

Virginia, Maryland, Washington
Spring 1861

Potomac River

Frederick

BALTIMORE

Harpers Ferry

Baltimore & Ohio R.R.

Annapolis

Winchester

Leesburg

Susquehanna River

Manassas Gap R.R.

WASHINGTON

Front Royal

Shenandoah Valley

Alexandria

Blue Ridge Mountains

Orange & Alexandria R.R.

M a r y l a n d

Chesapeake Bay

Culpeper

River

Potomac River

Rapidan

Fredericksburg

Rappahannock River

V i r g i n i a

R.F. & P.R.R.

N

Virginia Central R.R.

Pamunkey River

W   E

S

RICHMOND

York River

Richmond & Danville R.R.

Yorktown

Petersburg & Lynchburg R.R.

Petersburg

James River

Fort Monroe

Norfolk & Petersburg R.R.

Scale in miles

Norfolk

Portsmouth

0   25

Weldon R.R.

Gosport Naval Yard

George Skoch

subject to tax, and the maximum valuation for adult slaves for tax purposes was a low $300. Why, Willey argued, should his property in slaves be shielded from taxation but not the property of his non-slave-owning neighbors?[14]

By 1861, slightly more white Virginians lived west of the Appalachian Mountains than to the east, but most slaves lived to the east. As a result, the disparity in regional tax burden, long a sore point for westerners, became increasingly acute. Now Willey abruptly injected it into the debate. The speech went off like "a ten inch bomb," wrote one delighted western editor. Secessionists were outraged. They denied the analogy with their own states' rights grievances against the federal government. They could not deny that Willey's speech resonated powerfully with western delegates. This awakening separatist political consciousness in western Virginia warned them all where secession might lead.[15]

In a speech on March 21, John Brown Baldwin, one of the unionist floor leaders, confidently laid out the argument of the largest faction in the convention. Baldwin represented Augusta, a large county in the middle of the state, midway between the increasingly antagonistic east and west and midway down the Shenandoah Valley. He had blazed a brilliant path through the University of Virginia and, at only forty, had become an accomplished lawyer, the owner of ten slaves, and a captain in the Staunton militia. A tuft of dark chin whiskers and small, wire-rimmed spectacles accentuated his unassuming appearance but belied the force of his intellect. He was a man of blunt manners and eloquent speech. His address offered an important statement, the first but not the last or the most crucial instance in which he would play a part in the unfolding national drama.[16]

Baldwin asserted that in the long-running sectional dispute, the South had only one complaint—"the slavery agitation, and the questions growing out of it." He then laid out his justification for slavery, "a right and a good thing—on every ground, moral, social, religious, political and economical." He challenged anyone to deny that the national government had always supported the rights of all forms of southern property. He disputed that "the election of Lincoln, or of any other man, could, in any just sense, be regarded as justifying disunion." Why? Because American liberty was based on the checks and balances provided by the Constitution. The founders had not intended that at the first assault on their liberties—if that was what the Lincoln administration represented—the American people should give up on that constitutional protection.[17]

Baldwin's embrace of slavery did not commit him to secession. On the contrary, it led him to renewed devotion to the Union and its protections for all manner of property. Still sanguine about the future, he saw the prosperity of slave-owning Virginia within the old Union, not the new Confederacy.

Despite the cautious optimism of delegates like Baldwin, and despite the gloom of their foes in the Mechanics Institute, unionists did worry about one unsettling development. They wanted to avoid war at all costs. What if they achieved that end, but the lower South remained independent? That prospect put them in an awkward position. They were arguing for keeping the whole country intact, not peaceful separation. As the weeks passed and the Confederate republic put down roots, the chances for reunion seemed to recede.[18]

It was the insistence of the Deep South on independence that created the insoluble dilemma for upper South unionists, and it hung over all their deliberations throughout the hopeful days of March. The flaw in their position was that, if pressed, they would have acknowledged the theoretical right of secession. What if Lincoln tried to compel the Confederate States to return? If a clash occurred, the unionists would have to choose sides. They did not have to face that circumstance in March, but they could never eliminate the dread possibility of having to make that choice.

Secessionists, for all their violent, exaggerated rhetoric, saw the nub of the matter more clearly. They believed Virginia would eventually have to choose between the North and the Confederacy. Ignoring that likelihood solved nothing. They also were not swayed by Baldwin's argument that the future security of slavery lay with the Union. They favored secession for the very reason that they feared slavery could not withstand the pressure of proximity to free territory. They believed that the institution was already in decline in the border South and that the North threatened southern rights, especially the right to human property.

James Philemon Holcombe, a law professor at the University of Virginia and delegate from Albemarle County, expressed their fears in stark terms. Though his father had advocated emancipation, the younger Holcombe represented the generational shift in an increasingly defensive South. With slavery under assault more than ever before, he, like Baldwin, embraced it as a positive good. Unlike Baldwin, however, he warned the convention that slavery, in an upper South unprotected by membership in the Confederacy, would be forced "like a scorpion girdled with fire, to sting itself to death."[19]

While secessionists under Wise's leadership delayed the federal relations committee's report within the convention, southern rights advocates outside the hall stepped up their agitation. That the Old Dominion remained in the Union under Republican rule was almost more than they could bear. John Moncure Daniel's *Richmond Examiner* denounced the "Federal mummies and masked Abolitionists" who droned on at the Mechanics Institute, that "vast manufactory of froth, soap bubbles, treason and submission." Daniel vowed that for their craven reliance on Seward, a man who "has spent the best years of his life in building up a party whose mission is the overthrow of slavery," these traitors to old Virginia would pay dearly. Once the news spread that Fort Sumter would soon be evacuated, however, the radical press was reduced to impotent anger and fulmination.[20]

Daniel, a small, dark figure, fond of luxurious clothes and incendiary language, often dueled literally as well as rhetorically with his opponents. He had quit his post as American consul in Turin, where he observed the movement for Italian unification, to return to his editorial desk and urge Virginia into the Confederacy. He brought back advanced European notions about revolution and national self-determination, which he blended with the volatile homegrown elixir of states' rights and defense of slavery. His frustration at the hands of the convention, "inexhaustible in its contrivances of delay," enraged him all the more.[21]

Daniel vented his spleen in a celebrated column headlined "Gli Animali Parlanti." It described a mythical parliament of animals deliberating the threat of the new monarch, "an ugly and ferocious old Orang-Outang" named Abe, to subdue the beasts of his kingdom. Readers could not mistake Daniel's cruel description of John Letcher, the moderate unionist governor, as "the Boar of Rockbridge . . . notorious for the large quantity of swill that he could consume." The editor limned other delegates as various timid cats, ponies, and hyenas. And through the animals' debates, a serpent "was gliding silently along from member to member," whispering poisoned promises in their ears: Seward.[22]

For white Virginians in their twenties and thirties, there had never been a time when the sectional crisis had not seemed about to divide the nation. They could not remember a day when a minatory North had not threatened southern rights. Instead of another compromise, like one their elders had brokered in years past, they were drawn by the appeal of a radical break with history. Action and not talk was what was needed.[23] They began to believe people like Daniel who bluntly warned that the North meant to kill slavery and feast "upon the carcass of our defunct and putrescent Republic." He also argued that there was a distinct southern nationality, an increasingly popular notion among southern radicals. He had seen firsthand the Italian struggle for independence against Habsburg Austria, and it led him to write that two nations may live together for a long period, but the day will inevitably come when the oppressed will throw off the oppressor.[24]

Petitions favoring immediate secession, sent to the convention from a series of county meetings in eastern Virginia, testified to the increase in popular feeling for the Confederacy. Or so the petitions alleged. In fact, they exaggerated the strength of disunion sentiment among the electorate, but they were an effective means of exerting pressure. That the majority in the convention still rejected the radicals out of hand, however, only increased their anger.

In frustration, some secessionists began to contemplate extralegal action. Rumors circulated in late March that if the convention did not vote their way, southern rights advocates would take matters into their own hands. People talked openly of a coup against the convention and the state government. Demonstrators in Richmond began to intimidate supporters of the Union and break up their meetings. O. Jennings Wise, the firebrand son of the former governor, threatened that if the convention did not endorse secession, "it ought to be driven from its hall at the point of a bayonet."[25] He was just a young hothead, said his detractors. Even so, it was clear that he was not just letting off steam with his violent words and that he was not alone in his sentiments. If he and his friends had acted on them, they could have pushed Virginia over the brink from constitutional dispute to internal civil war.

By late March, the daily litany of overblown rhetoric in the hall had long passed the one-month mark, with little to show for the effort. So far, though, nothing had happened to disrupt the cautious confidence of unionists that they could eventually find a peaceful resolution. The measure of that hope could be gauged in the rising frustration and stormy rhetoric of their radical opponents. Each faction underestimated the other and deluded itself about what the other side might do. What stands out, however, given the tragic events of the following month, is the strength of the Virginia unionists in their hopes for the future of the United States.

As THE STANDARD-BEARER of northern Democrats, Sen. Stephen A. Douglas had lost the presidential election to his old rival from Illinois. At only five feet four inches tall, the impatient, aggressive "Little Giant" radiated energy and pugnacious devotion to his most cherished ideal, the sovereignty of the American people. He had been the only one of the four presidential candidates in 1860 to wage a national campaign. He faced a cool reception in New England, where he denounced abolitionists as agitators, and even more hostile crowds in the South, where he warned against disunion.

In defeat, he threw himself furiously into the cause of compromise. Right before Virginians voted on delegates to their convention in February, he wrote a public letter that newspapers printed through-

out the state. Douglas declared that all would be well if only the
upper South would stand firm against secession. Like nearly every
other political leader, he thought the Old Dominion was key. "All
depends on the action of Virginia and the Border states," he declared.
"Save Virginia, and we will save the Union."[26]

That was what conservative Virginians told themselves, and that
was what many northern politicians like Douglas believed. But as
March wore on, uncertainty crept in. Those like Douglas who preached
a nostalgic optimism for the country and a faith in the good sense of
the people began to wonder whether the initiative had passed to others less tractable.[27]

Indeed, the unionist majority among the delegates in Richmond did
not admit it, but they were haunted by the passing of influence, the
decline from a position of national leadership of the Old Dominion—
"worn out, prostrate, retrograding Virginia," in the sneering words
of William Lloyd Garrison's abolitionist *Liberator*. Their obsession
with the threats of internal disunity, represented on the one hand by
the awakening separatist sensibilities of the western counties and on
the other by secessionists, accentuated the sense of declension. For
all their grand talk about emulating Virginians of the glorious Revolutionary past, they could not deny that an angry number of their
fellow citizens dismissed them as dabblers in the tomfoolery of an
adolescent debating club.[28]

Despite their apprehensions, though, on balance the unionist delegates, who maintained an impressive majority in the convention,
shared John Baldwin's confidence. Most of them agreed with Baldwin when he likened the state to a lighthouse founded upon rock,
able to withstand, in his words, "the breasting and surging waves of
Northern fanaticism and of Southern violence."[29]

CHAPTER 5

COLLISION COURSE

Late March to Early April

The nation is holding its breath and nerving itself for the shock of war.

—*Philadelphia Daily Evening Bulletin*, April 8[1]

On April 4, after more than a month of numbing speeches, parliamentary intrigue, delays, and diversions, for the first time the strident radical faction in the Virginia convention submitted a straightforward proposal of secession to a vote. They thought sentiment had moved enough in their favor to take a chance. They lost, 45 to 90, an impressive margin of victory for the unionists. If the secessionists dared try another vote, John Janney exulted privately, they were "without the slightest hope of success."[2]

The news lifted the spirits of those in the upper South who all winter had resisted the radical attempt to align their region with the Confederacy. For them, the political climate now matched the rapidly advancing springtime, which by late March had coaxed the fruit trees into bloom and spread warmth and now optimism over their region. In little Harpers Ferry, where the notoriety of John Brown lingered, Union men fired a thunderous salute in honor of the vote. Now, they believed, their state would remain loyal to the Stars and Stripes. It would regain its former glory and give the lead to the rest of the upper South. What cooler heads had been predicting all along seemed about to take place. The secession agitation would gradually die out. In time, even the seven prodigals of the Confederacy would return to the fold, their experiment an abject failure.

Even as this small patriotic fusillade reverberated through the hillside village in northern Virginia, however, rumors hinted that events were moving in an entirely different direction. Indeed, a week before the convention vote, a decision made in Washington put a peaceful resolution at grave risk.

UP TO THE END of March, Lincoln had probably been inclined to accept that Fort Sumter's dwindling supplies would compel him to evacuate the garrison. He hated the thought. It would betray the promise of his inaugural address. But he accepted General Scott's verdict that the army lacked the force either to hold the fort or to relieve it. Still not wanting to make a distasteful decision, he put it off as long as possible. How much he knew about Seward's indirect promise to the Confederate commissioners is disputed, but Lincoln certainly did know of his secretary of state's overtures to the Virginia unionists. In this, Honest Abe was being less than forthright. He was willing to allow the continued hope of evacuation if it strengthened the hand of those who opposed secession in the upper South.

Those southerners interpreted Lincoln's passivity as evidence that the administration meant to pursue a hands-off policy. "Policy," though, is too strong a word to describe the government's failure to come to grips with the issue of Fort Sumter. It therefore increased southern apprehensions that even though Washington made no aggressive move, neither did it show any signs of delivering on Seward's promise as March faded away.

Secessionists were frustrated, too. Like rock-ribbed Republican stalwarts in the North, they prayed that Lincoln would provoke conflict. If he did, he would confirm the stereotype they painted of him as a vicious "Black Republican," bent on humiliating the South. Only when he revealed his true nature, they believed, would the scales fall from the eyes of their conservative fellow southerners, still besotted with the idea of the Union. On the other hand, the longer Washington failed to act, the more solid a foundation the Confederates built for their experiment and the further they moved toward achieving peaceful separation. Lincoln's choices remained as unattractive as ever.[3]

Observers in Washington scrutinized every scrap of telegraphed news to try to figure out how the administration would address its quandary. Justice Campbell tartly described Lincoln's reluctance to act: "The President is light, inconstant, and variable. His ear is open to every one—and his resolutions are easily bent."[4] Campbell was only repeating what Seward had said to him: Lincoln was especially receptive to those who held out hope for Fort Sumter. Both assessments ultimately underestimated the man, but in March they were on the mark, and he did nothing to contradict them. No one would know until later the strength of his commitment to maintain the Union intact. For the time being, Lincoln's vacillation, his reluctance to make a decision, contributed to the sense of an administration adrift.

As time passed, though, it became clearer to Lincoln that inaction might split his own party. Republicans began to doubt the strength of loyal sentiment in the upper South. They began to question whether there was any value in trying to mollify that opinion. They also raised the issue of the economic costs of failing to resolve the crisis, for it had spread a pall of uncertainty over commerce. If reunion was the goal, the means were more sharply disputed than ever. On the one hand, conciliatory Republicans agreed with southern unionists that a fight over Fort Sumter was a mortal threat. It would instantly alienate the upper South. On the other hand, hardline Republicans increasingly believed that reunion could happen only if the administration risked war. An anonymous New Yorker wrote the president, "Give up Sumpter, Sir, & you are as dead politically as John Brown is physically. You have got to fight."[5]

For all anyone outside the administration could tell, nothing had changed since the inauguration. "There is a dead calm here," reported the Confederate commissioners in Washington. Justice Campbell wrote to Jefferson Davis at the beginning of April, "The present desire is to let things remain as they are without action of any kind." That had been true for most of March, but it no longer was so. On March 28, Lincoln ended his hesitation and decided the conciliatory strategy had failed. Pressure from leaders of his own party—reflected in the drumbeat of assertive editorials in Republican newspapers warning against retreat—had its effect. But the decision was his alone, and he had to bear the responsibility for choosing risk and confrontation as much as his opponent in Montgomery.[6]

It disappointed Lincoln that conservative southern unionists continued to argue that he should abandon not only Fort Sumter but also the other bastion still in federal hands, Fort Pickens, as the only way to mollify opinion in their region. The president had let himself nearly be persuaded that giving up Fort Sumter was a military necessity, but there was no military need at all to give up Fort Pickens. In that frame of mind, he bristled when General Scott added his voice to the push to abandon both forts. That the general presumed to give him political advice now fed his doubts about Scott's earlier opinion regarding the situation in Charleston Harbor.

On that same evening, March 28, the president hosted his first state dinner, a glittering occasion to show off his official family. In other circumstances, it would have been an event to savor for the leader of a victorious new administration. Lincoln managed to suppress his anger at Scott's impertinence and charmed the guests with his legendary tall tales. One of the few nonofficial observers that night was the visiting British correspondent William Howard Russell. Himself an accomplished storyteller, Russell recorded with admiration how Lincoln "raises a laugh by some bold west-country anecdote, and moves off in the cloud of merriment produced by his joke."[7]

As soon as the other guests departed, however, the president dropped the mask of bonhomie and kept his cabinet officers behind for an impromptu meeting. Barely containing his temper, he described Scott's effrontery about the forts. All the others agreed the general had stepped over the line except Seward, who found himself alone in supporting Scott. Lincoln announced that the cabinet would meet again in the morning and adjourned the gathering. He did not sleep at all that night.[8]

The president arose depressed from lack of rest and perhaps at the prospect of informing the cabinet of his decision. When they gathered at noon, Lincoln asked each one his thoughts about the two southern forts. At earlier meetings, he had concealed his own opinion while canvassing theirs. This time he let them know he had made up his mind. He would attempt the relief of Fort Sumter—but with a twist. He told them he intended to put a variation of Gustavus Fox's plan into action. He would send supplies to reprovision but not reinforce the garrison and thus maintain the status quo. Only if the supply ships were fired on would they be instructed to add men and arms to Anderson's command.

All but Seward now backed Lincoln. The secretary of state again argued that the attempt they envisioned would risk war. He realized Lincoln had made up his mind, however, and did not press his point. Lincoln did not set an absolute deadline but instructed Secretary of War Simon Cameron and Secretary of the Navy Gideon Welles to have an expedition ready to sail from New York by April 6. The pressure on the president was intense, and it took a physical toll. A severe headache sent him to bed after the meeting.[9]

On that day, a few blocks from the White House, an agitated friend of the Confederate commissioners buttonholed a visiting Englishman in his hotel room and railed against the perfidy of Seward for refusing to meet them. On the same day in Richmond, a unionist delegate told his wife that secessionists were plotting bloody revolution. He assured her his side would stand firm against sedition. On the same day, a New York newspaper described how illegal slave traders in West Africa had just evaded detection and loaded 780 Africans destined for servitude in the New World. Though they were bound for Cuba, they might eventually end up across the Strait of Florida. On that same day, too, in Charleston Harbor Anderson's garrison opened the last barrel of flour in its larder.[10]

Seward recognized that opinion in the cabinet had shifted against

him, but he did not give up. The following Monday he sent the president a memorandum, because, he said, the administration needed
to have a policy to deal with the crisis. He urged a series of aggressive international maneuvers, including threatening foreign powers
against interfering in Mexico, as a way to divert attention from
domestic troubles. As a show of strength, he urged reinforcing Fort
Pickens, though it was not in danger of having to be evacuated. He
continued to urge withdrawal from Fort Sumter in the interest of
reducing tensions.

Lincoln ignored the memorandum. He did inform Seward archly
that the administration had a policy. He had stated it in his inaugural
address when he promised to hold all federal posts still in Union
hands.[11]

On the same day, Seward launched a desperate effort to dissuade
Lincoln from confrontation. He cabled Virginia unionist leader
George Summers that the president wished to see him. Lincoln
apparently was willing to go along with Seward's effort to arrange a
meeting. "Tell Mr. Summers, I want to see him *at once*," a follow-up
message from the president told the Virginian, "for there is no time
to be lost." Summers consulted his colleagues. Because the convention was at a delicate juncture, they agreed that he must remain in
Richmond. In his place, they would send a close associate, John
Baldwin.[12]

Baldwin took the night train north and was in Seward's office the
next morning, April 4. At the White House, he and Lincoln held a
private conference. The president, a reluctant participant in Seward's
negotiations, nevertheless agreed to it if there was a chance of keeping Virginia safe for the Union. For his part, he wanted the unionists
to adjourn the Richmond gathering because he feared it would follow
the example set earlier by other conventions in the Deep South.

Probing, Lincoln asked Baldwin why the convention did not
adjourn. The Virginian replied that unionists like him controlled the
proceedings and would continue to do so. The president could be sure
of that. But he said there was a catch. They would remain in charge
only if Lincoln would remove the two garrisons as points of conten-

tion. His line of argument confirmed Lincoln in his conclusion that he could not rely on the Virginia unionists. The two men were just talking past each other.

Baldwin was ignorant of the president's decision about the relief expedition. In addition to asking Lincoln to withdraw the garrisons from both southern forts as a show of goodwill, he asked him to call a national convention. He argued that only such a body could settle the differences between the sections. He later said that never "did I make a speech on behalf of a client in jeopardy of his life, with such earnest solemnity and endeavor."[13] Like many upper South unionists, Baldwin believed that the crisis was a product of misunderstanding. A gathering of reasonable men could sort it all out, even at this late date.

Lincoln had already concluded that further inaction over Fort Sumter was futile and that risking war was necessary to save the Union. If Baldwin was unrealistic in asking Lincoln to give up both forts, for his part the president showed his own limitations. He was unwilling to consider the potential for disarming the confrontation by removing Anderson's garrison from their untenable position while maintaining the soldiers at Fort Pickens, which could be resupplied by sea with impunity. Such a choice—which Seward advocated—would not have satisfied Montgomery. The Confederates would still have demanded evacuation of Fort Pickens, but removing the Fort Sumter garrison just might have given the upper South unionists a strong enough hand to maintain control in their own states.

A few days after this sterile encounter, the tempestuous Virginia unionist John Minor Botts also met with Lincoln. Nicknamed "Bison," Botts was a giant of a man with commensurate temper and appetites. He would later spend time in one of Jefferson Davis's political prisons. After his talk with Lincoln, Botts charged Baldwin with committing an act of monumental duplicity. He claimed that the president had renewed the so-called fort-for-a-state offer he had allegedly made to William Cabell Rives when Lincoln met with a group of upper South unionists on the eve of his inauguration. On that occasion, according to an account written much later by one of the men present, he had offered to withdraw from Fort Sumter if Virginia would stay in the Union. The excitable Botts denounced Baldwin for not revealing this offer to the convention, as it could only have had an explosive effect.

Baldwin denied that Lincoln made any such offer. He said nothing like it could have been inferred even obliquely from anything the president told him. In fact, both Baldwin and Botts probably gave honest versions of their White House conferences. Sketchy as it is, the evidence points to Lincoln giving Botts a misleading account of his session with Baldwin.[14] He had already made up his mind about Fort Sumter; nothing Baldwin could say would have dissuaded him. But even if he had made such an offer, and Baldwin had taken it to the convention, it was probably too late. Events were in train that would overrun all such diplomatic gambits.

Baldwin left the White House in deep disappointment. He was previously scheduled to give a unionist speech later that day in Alexandria, just across the Potomac. The newspapers reported it as a rousing performance, but his heart could hardly have been in it. That same day, Lincoln authorized Fox's ships to sail for Fort Sumter. It was the same day, too, that the Virginia convention, ignorant of Baldwin's secret mission and of Lincoln's order to Fox, voted 2 to 1 against secession. As Lincoln feared, the convention did not adjourn. Though his order to the fleet was not yet irrevocable, the pieces were now set in motion to produce the result all southern unionists most dreaded.

Until the time Baldwin met with Lincoln, and even beyond, Virginia unionists believed they held the whip hand in the convention. They continued to disparage those they called wild men, intemperate radicals who would throw away the Constitution bequeathed to them by their fathers for the chimera of an untested slave republic. The unionists, a solid majority, were moving deliberately under the protecting shadow of what they believed was the administration's promise to make no abrupt move that might trigger a violent clash. They hoped to call a border state conference later in the summer to devise a solution in concert with the slave states that remained loyal to the

United States. Evidence of their progress came while Baldwin was in Washington, and the motion to secede decisively failed. "That vote decided that Virginia would not commit the suicidal act of secession," exclaimed one delegate in cheerful ignorance of Lincoln's instructions to Fox.[15]

As THE DAYS LENGTHENED, spring crept up the coast. With the returning warmth and sunshine, planting season began, first in the lower South and then in the middle Atlantic states. In the upper South, enslaved and free Americans put in a new crop of corn and tobacco and wheat that would not reach harvest before waves of citizen soldiers began to despoil the region's green farmlands. Outside the federal capital and political circles, the rhythms of life moved at their accustomed pace, undisturbed by great matters of state. "As to public affairs, we are yet in a perfect fog," confessed even a delegate to the Virginia convention.[16] But when newspapers began to report unusual military and naval preparations in early April, unease grew that the simmering crisis might finally boil over. Overnight, inactivity gave way to frantic preparations, which encouraged stories—now not just rumors—of secret orders from Washington dispatching ships laden with soldiers to the South.

The first signs came with an ominous report from the Brooklyn Navy Yard about the navy's most powerful warship. The USS *Powhatan*'s engineers had submitted an unfavorable readiness report, and the ship was slated to be taken out of commission. To the surprise of everyone, however, orders arrived to outfit immediately for an undisclosed new mission. Any southern sympathizer—and in New York, with its commercial ties throughout the South, there were many—who went down to the Brooklyn waterfront could see that this report was no fiction invented by an unscrupulous journalist. With a lag of but a day or two, southern papers quoted details picked up by reporters poking around the New York waterfront. They identified the other ships being readied for action and meticulously described their armaments and crews, even if they did not know where they were meant to sail. That did not stop spectators

from betting on the ships' destinations or badgering the crews for
details.

Part of the activity in New York sprang from confusion within
the navy about its orders, and that was all on account of meddling by
Seward. He had still not given up trying to deflect the administration
from confrontation. He decided to send a naval expedition from New
York to reinforce Fort Pickens, even though it was in no danger of
having to surrender. It could be reprovisioned by ship without risk of
attack from shore batteries. On his own initiative, Seward directed
army and navy officers to outfit this expedition using the *Powhatan*,
which Fox counted on for his. Seward got Lincoln to sign orders for
the Fort Pickens expedition without the knowledge either of Secretary of the Navy Welles or of Fox, who was preoccupied with equip-
ping his own flotilla.[17]

Improbable as it was, for a day, two naval expeditions were being
readied in New York without knowledge of each other. Such a situation could not last for many hours. When the officers discovered the
circumstances, Seward and Welles confronted each other. Together
they rushed to see Lincoln. It was nearly midnight on April 5 when
they arrived at the White House. Welles remembered the president
looking quizzically first at him and then at Seward, stunned by their
news. Lincoln admitted he had given the orders for Seward's expedition, and he immediately revoked them.[18]

In consequence, Seward sent a cable reassigning the *Powhatan*
back to the expedition for Fort Sumter. Further confusion ensued
when the message reached the ship. The captain refused to allow this
latest order to overrule the earlier one. It, of course, bore the president's signature. The new one merely carried the name of the secretary of state. In a quandary over what to do, the ship's captain cabled
Lincoln with thundering understatement that the mixed signal
"complicates matters seriously."[19] Some people later interpreted this
contretemps as another token of Seward's deceit, though in truth it
was just one more among the many botched decisions that week.

On Saturday afternoon, April 6, a curious crowd gathered at the navy yard. They could see the captain of the *Powhatan* receive two sealed packets bearing orders from Washington. He immediately got up steam and, with the aid of a tug, slowly pushed away from the dock and out into the stream. As spectators watched, the warship passed down the East River, without receiving any salute from the harbor forts or the mass of shipping quietly riding at anchor.[20] In London, Lloyds sharply increased insurance premiums on cotton, a sure sign the counting houses of the world feared for their commerce.

The *Powhatan* proceeded to Florida, where it was useless. Fox, who left New York on the *Baltic* on April 9, did not even know until he reached Charleston that the strongest ship intended for his mission had sailed for Fort Pickens instead. He may have had an inkling, though. While waiting for the morning tide to leave New York, he wrote his wife, "I am afraid we are too late."[21]

As the premonitory signs grew, thoughtful voices cautioned against the horrors of internecine conflict. "To what good end shall we inaugurate a civil war?" asked the *Daily Chicago Times*. If southerners no longer wanted to remain part of the nation, how could the North in good conscience compel them? The paper reminded its readers that the Revolution had enshrined the right of self-determination against oppression. The devastation that armed conflict would entail could do no good: "Evil, and evil alone, can come to us by a civil war."[22]

Such sentiments resonated most strongly in the border between North and South—that wide band of states running from North Carolina, Virginia, Maryland, and Delaware in the mid-Atlantic, across the mountains to Tennessee and Kentucky, and across the Mississippi to Arkansas and Missouri. In Nashville, an editor rued the probable resort to violence and lamented, "This is not the choice of Tennessee." But if it came to war, like it or not, residents of the state would have to choose. Fight against their fellow southerners, dissolve their ties with the Union they loved, or perhaps find some independent course between these unpalatable extremes? Hindsight might brand that undefined middle course mere wishful thinking, but in early April the desire for it became stronger and more widespread as the threat of confrontation grew.[23]

In contrast, supporters of resolute action began to take heart as a military conclusion to the standoff looked more likely. In Montgomery, Confederates welcomed the prospect of a fight, though many still thought Lincoln would avoid it. In New Orleans, word of martial preparations in Washington and New York "produced an unwonted excitement." From Charleston came the defiant claim, "We . . . are now ready to receive our enemies, come as they may." There was even a renewed threat that private citizens would assault Fort Sumter if the Confederate government delayed action much longer.[24] On the other side, an Illinois newspaper anticipated conflict and warned against the notion that the president was subordinate to Congress and therefore powerless to act alone. This was a pernicious error, the editor warned, for the president uniquely was the defender of the Constitution.[25]

Wall Street lawyer George Templeton Strong typified the sentiment of moderate Republicans as they anguished over the government's apparent indecision. Modest, witty, and urbane, a devout Episcopalian layman and successful lawyer, he captured New York culture and national politics in a voluminous diary that stands as a primary document of his times. He had admired the firmness of Lincoln's inaugural address but in the following weeks regretted the administration's drift. Strong ruminated morosely over the gossip about secessionist threats to Washington, D.C., but, he fretted, "would even this aggression stiffen up the spiritless, money-worshipping North?" Like Charleston, New York lived on commerce, and the uncertainty over Sumter was beginning to affect trade. Some businessmen greeted the sudden bustle of naval activity with approval. Anything was better than continuing the agonizing suspense. On a visit to the Brooklyn Navy Yard, where he saw immense activity and learned that warships had just sailed on an undisclosed mission, Strong was exhilarated. The prospect that Lincoln would not give up Sumter without a fight renewed his hopes.[26]

Despite the signs of growing resolve that Strong purported to see, sentiment in the North for letting the Confederacy depart the Union in peace gathered strength in early April. Many northerners feared the cost of forcible action to undo what the men of Montgomery had wrought. Even a paper in Illinois sympathetic to Lincoln cautioned the president that "the sooner we cut loose from the disaffected States," the sooner the crisis would end without bloodshed.[27]

IN THE FEDERAL CAPITAL, gossip among Washingtonians fed on every hint that could be gleaned from official sources. Horatio Nelson Taft, a new resident, was a New York attorney who had given up a struggling law practice for a well-paid post as examiner in the Patent Office. After more lobbying for the job than he had reckoned on, Taft moved his family of six to a house at 15th and L streets and began to record the foibles of Washington society in his diary. He periodically reported rumors about the impending evacuation of Fort Sumter. As March turned into April, he noted increasing unease as that prediction kept being postponed and talk of troop movements and mysterious naval expeditions overwhelmed tales of bureaucratic intrigue. Taft's anxiety mounted as word circulated the first week of April about a coup against Washington by secessionist plotters. Fearing the worst, one night after he tucked his sons into bed he decided he had better clean his revolver.[28]

Taft reflected the skittish mood of the District of Columbia. Two days after he cleaned his gun, the *Evening Star* reported that someone in Richmond had mailed Lincoln a paper box full of poisonous snakes. If true or just a wild rumor, the president paid it no mind. With the die cast and the small fleet en route to Sumter, he even found time to deal with the minutiae of some of those political appointments that Taft observed from the sidelines. But he was not oblivious to the gamble that the expedition represented. On April 8, the day Fox's first ships left New York, Lincoln sent a laconic cable to Gov. Andrew Curtin of Pennsylvania: "I think the necessity of being *ready* increases. Look to it."[29]

Perhaps nowhere else outside Charleston and Montgomery was

the spring of tension wound so tightly as in Washington that first damp week of April, when office workers kept the fires going all day to ward off the chill. The sound of brass bands and tramping boots gave the federal city an unaccustomed martial tone. For a week, General Scott had been reporting to the president "that machinations against the Government & this Capital, are secretly going on, all around us." Scott took the rumors seriously. He recalled the few regular U.S. Army units he could spare from the West, mainly dismounted cavalry and artillery from Texas and Minnesota. As reports of their maddeningly slow progress toward Washington trickled in, he admitted that the reinforcements "may be too late for this place."[30]

In the meantime, he relied on a few companies of D.C. militia volunteers. The response of these men to their orders, however, gave Scott and his subordinates a shock. Several companies that reported for duty were so under strength that they were useless. Among the others, many of the men who did show up then proceeded to fall out of line and refused to take the oath swearing them into federal service.

The assistant adjutant general, Irvin McDowell, discovered that many of the men feared they were being converted to regular army status and refused the oath for that reason. This blunt, abrasive, and efficient protégé of Scott, who would lose the first great battle of the coming war, tried to explain to the men that they were being asked only to defend the District of Columbia. He did not intend to send them beyond its borders. The swearing-in took place in front of the War Department, where despite a driving rain a throng of Confederate sympathizers tried to disrupt the proceedings. McDowell strove in vain to clear the enclosure of onlookers. He worried about the chances to reverse the situation. "It remains to be seen to-day," he wrote on April 11, perhaps buoyed by the clearing skies, "what will be the effect of the defection of yesterday—whether it will be spread among the others or will rouse a contrary spirit."[31]

Happily for McDowell and Scott, the next day most of the companies reported with sufficient strength. A local newspaper editor breathed a sigh of relief that these citizens had stepped forward to defend the government, "the true ark of civil and religious liberty." The day before the dubious militia companies were called up, a New Yorker wrote the president offering to recruit black men to serve "in the present crisis, and distracted state of the country." Though people now worried that war would come, few imagined that in two years' time African American volunteers would swell the armies of the Union and even provide the margin for ultimate victory.[32]

The Confederate commissioners had been under observation for their own recruiting efforts in the District of Columbia. Some federal officials believed these emissaries from Montgomery intended their recruits not to go south but to capture Washington for the Confederacy. Charles Pomeroy Stone, the inspector general for the District, was convinced the expected attack on Fort Sumter would give the signal for these men to "seize and hold the Capital until the Southern army could reach here." Up to the day they planned to leave D.C., their diplomatic mission a failure, the Confederate commissioners continued buying northern arms and powder for the South.[33]

COMMODORE MATTHEW FONTAINE MAURY spent early April crafting a proposal for international maritime cooperation. The task helped distract the superintendent of the U.S. Naval Observatory from worrying about what to do if his native state seceded. For nearly two decades, he had labored to build the reputation of the observatory, located six blocks west of the White House. He collected data from around the world to aid navigation. A renowned scientist in his own right as author of *The Physical Geography of the Sea*, the short Virginian with the high forehead and pronounced limp had established the field of modern oceanography.

While Fox's expedition was en route to South Carolina and the capital was abuzz with rumors of war, Maury busied himself by sending all the diplomatic missions in town his proposal for an international expedition to the Antarctic. On April 11, he sent the secretary of the navy a briefer commentary, not about exploration or winds

and tides but about a celestial event. Maury reported the astronomi-
cal details of a new comet discovered earlier that month. In more
primitive times, people would have viewed the sighting as an ominous portent. Given the traumatic events soon to unfold, some might
make the same fearful attribution in 1861. But Maury was a man of
science and paid no heed to such superstitions. Yet unbeknownst to
him, on the day after he announced the comet to his superior, the
thunderous denouement at Fort Sumter would convulse Maury's
life and that of all his countrymen.[34]

CHAPTER 6

FLASH POINT

Charleston, April 12

Out of the south cometh the whirlwind.

—Job 37:9

Through newspaper accounts, Maj. Robert Anderson learned the consequences of moving his command from Fort Moultrie to the formidable, if incomplete, bastion in Charleston Harbor. Three months after that decision, his black speck of rock loomed as the chief remaining symbol of U.S. authority in a contested land. By moving there, he had ensured that his tiny garrison would be that lightning rod, even though it was the last thing this gentle, temperamentally pacific Kentuckian wanted. Fort Sumter now became an annoying impediment to Confederate territorial integrity and, in consequence, the likely target of assault.

As a son of the border, Anderson personified his divided country. A close friend of General Scott, he had also known Jefferson Davis since their time as cadets at West Point. Though the record is unclear, it was possible he had sworn in Abraham Lincoln for his short service in the Black Hawk War on the Illinois frontier. Anderson was determined not to start a fight. He had refused a violent response when southern cannon fire turned back a supply ship in January.

Years before, he had written his wife, "I think that killing people is a very poor way of settling National grievances."[1]

Deeply religious, tactful, and courteous, he had served the army conscientiously for thirty-five years. Anderson's eyes, framed by dark, thick eyebrows, radiated a weary, almost sad appearance. His close-cropped iron gray hair and strong nose and jaw accentuated his restrained but forceful soldierly bearing. As the sectional dispute intensified, he admitted that "my sympathies are entirely with the South." At one time he owned slaves. Perhaps because of his background and because he had pessimistically advised the president it would take twenty thousand men to relieve Fort Sumter, Lincoln did not entirely trust him.[2]

The president, however, did not yet know the depth of Anderson's devotion to the Union or his distaste for war. Nor did he realize how abandoned by his government this loyal soldier felt, watching a hostile world from his island prison for weeks on end without a word of guidance from Washington. Later, Anderson said of the experience that he felt like "a sheep tied watching the butcher sharpening a knife to cut his throat."[3]

SOUTH CAROLINA'S SECESSION in December 1860, the catalyst for other states of the Deep South, did not erupt spontaneously in reaction to Lincoln's election. The ground was laid over the decades by determined radical theorists who preached state sovereignty, fear of federal authority, and the need to protect the institution of slavery. These "fire-eaters" held out secession as the only sure means of reaching the promised land of southern independence. For years, their extremism repelled most conservative southerners. But the animus of the Republican Party toward slavery gave the fire-eaters increasing credibility. In the eyes of many white southerners, the American constitutional system seemed impotent to stop abolitionism. When the Republicans took the White House, the fire-eaters no longer appeared so wild.[4]

South Carolina nurtured their most devoted acolytes. That it was the first state to secede was no surprise. The vote in the convention was unanimous. It reflected the state's near universal loathing for the once cherished Union. One Charleston resident who formerly supported it now called it "a dead carcass stinking in the nostrils of the Southern people." Not for nothing did Judge James Louis Petigru, said to be the last Union man in Charleston, famously decree, "South Carolina is too small for a republic and too big for a lunatic asylum."[5]

Charleston's near tropical climate suggested a languor that belied reality. For the font of secession was no decayed backwater dreaming of past glory when it had been the hub of the richest colony before independence. When it left the Union, it throbbed and bustled with the distilled wealth produced by the state's teeming plantations of slaves. It held out brash hopes that the new southern nation would soon outshine the United States. As bad luck would have it, by a fluke of geography the strongest federal fort in the South lay within sight of the Charleston waterfront. Local patriots would not tolerate that insult for long. Already, cautious shippers were beginning to prefer Savannah to avoid sailing past the guns of Fort Sumter. A commercial price compounded the symbolic slight of the Stars and Stripes flying over sovereign South Carolina territory.[6]

Built on a small but expensive artificial island, the pentagonal fort boasted the latest military design, with thick concrete and brick walls and three tiers of guns. The citadel was incomplete, however. Only some of its cannon were in place, and the garrison numbered barely a tenth of the full complement. Since the beginning of their tenure there, Anderson's men improvised as best they could. Using makeshift riggings, they installed some of the cannons in the lower levels and positioned others to contest an amphibious landing. Life for the 128 officers, soldiers, and civilian workmen narrowed to a tedious routine. As they watched, swarms of South Carolina militiamen and impressed slaves methodically built artillery emplacements aimed at them. Still no word of instruction came from Washington.

Francis Pickens exuded the best and worst traits of the small, tight-knit planter elite that dominated South Carolina politics. A stout, heavyset man, imperious and charming, the governor had taken office on the eve of secession. Overnight he became chief executive of an independent republic in the heady days leading up to the formation of the Confederacy. As one of the South's wealthiest slave owners, he imbibed the fashionable hostility toward all things northern. He displayed the tetchiness of southern gentility, almost a caricature in his hair-trigger readiness to take offense at perceived slights to honor. "I believe it is my destiny," Pickens opined, "to be disliked by all who know me well."[7]

Pickens's insistence that South Carolina possess Fort Sumter as quickly as possible troubled Jefferson Davis. The Confederate leader could not ignore the alarming talk making the rounds of Charleston parlors. These rumors said local patriots would launch an attack without waiting for approval from Montgomery. Davis was no less concerned that a prolonged federal presence at the fort would undermine southern claims to independence, but he was content to bide his time.[8]

In early March, he took the militia units surrounding the fort out of Pickens's hands and placed them under national control, with Gen. Pierre G. T. Beauregard in command. A magnetic, vain officer of faultless uniforms and manners, Beauregard was a talented career soldier who knew how to keep his men on a tight leash. When Major Anderson, who had taught Beauregard at West Point, learned of his appointment, he assured Washington it meant a cool head would prevail, with "the exercise of skill and sound judgment." Had Pickens remained in a position to cause mischief, a clash might have come sooner, with unpredictable results. Rash action by Pickens might have driven a wedge between the lower South Confederacy and the hesitant upper South. At the least, the course of conflict would have taken a different path had the South Carolinians attacked on their own.[9]

LINCOLN HAD PROMISED not to change the status quo at Fort Sumter without first giving notice, but when he kept his word it was a blunt formality. To announce that he intended to resupply the garrison, he sent a messenger not to Davis in Montgomery but to the South Carolina governor. He thus slighted not only Davis but also Pickens, because he sent the message by a lowly clerk in the State Department.[10]

Robert Chew left Washington on the evening of April 6 and after a bone-rattling train ride arrived in Charleston within forty-eight hours. Granted an interview with the governor, Chew did as instructed and read aloud the message from Lincoln. It consisted of one long sentence, clear despite the misspelling and full of portent: "I am directed by the President of the United States to notify you to expect an attempt will be made to supply Fort-Sumpter with provisions only; and that, if such attempt be not resisted, no effort to throw in men, arms, or ammunition, will be made, without further notice, or in case of an attack upon the Fort."[11] When he showed the governor the paper, it was evident to Pickens that Lincoln was flouting all diplomatic niceties, for there was no salutation. In fact, the document was addressed from Secretary of War Cameron to Chew. Pickens's name appeared nowhere on it. To drive home the slight, when Pickens asked about a response, Chew, the glorified messenger boy, cut him off. He was authorized only to deliver the missive, not to accept a reply.[12]

A few hours earlier, the Confederate commissioners in Washington had received a belated answer to their request for an audience. When their secretary arrived at the State Department, he received a blank envelope that contained Seward's unsigned memorandum finally responding to their original overture. The Lincoln administration would not deal with them as representatives of an independent nation. Their mission now confirmed a failure, they prepared to leave town, "in disgust, protesting that they have been humbugged and deceived." They had good reason. Seward had indirectly promised them more than Lincoln would offer. As a parting shot to cause maximum embarrassment, the commissioners gave copies of their correspondence to foreign diplomats.[13]

Seward's intermediary, John Campbell, would soon have angry words of his own with the secretary of state about dissembling and bad faith. Each of them—Seward and Campbell—had let an inflated sense of his power to influence events convince him he could single-handedly avert a clash, a misperception they now both bitterly came to appreciate.[14]

A month before, Davis and Lincoln had both wanted delay. Now Lincoln had made his decision, and Davis would have to make his. Lincoln in effect offered Davis a continuation of the status quo. Supplies to Anderson would let the standoff continue, without resolution, to be sure, but without violence or capitulation. Lincoln believed this effort to reassert federal control over Fort Sumter would likely lead to conflict, but if it did, the onus would be on Davis. Lincoln's move is often cited as a clever one, even genius, for putting Davis at fault in the eyes of the world. But it might be said as well that Lincoln acted with unimaginative rashness. For he invited hostilities rather than attempting to avoid or at least postpone them by retreating from untenable Fort Sumter while retaining unassailable Fort Pickens as a symbol of federal authority in the South. That he chose risk over caution would have momentous ramifications, especially in the upper South.[15]

On April 8, the Confederate president received the bad news both from his commissioners in Washington and from Governor Pickens. He knew his response would be a test of credibility for his government and his personal leadership. How could he trust that Lincoln was sending only food? Like Lincoln, he had suffered from severe headaches of late, the result of the immense pressure. Like Lincoln, too, he faced a growing demand for action. With exaggerated fear, a Mobile editor cried that "the spirit and even the patriotism of the people is oozing out under this do-nothing policy."[16]

The nearly simultaneous telegrams from Pickens and the commissioners promised hostile intent. Davis had been willing earlier to negotiate compensation for federal property in the South. Now it was too late. Fort Sumter was no longer just a symbol but an actual threat to Confederate independence. In his eyes, for the United States to remain there constituted an act of war. He urged the members of his cabinet to demand that Anderson evacuate the fort, with an ultimatum that would expire before the relief expedition arrived. They agreed. While they deliberated, a short distance away down by the riverside, a calliope played "Dixie."[17]

Davis's secretary of war was as little suited to the role as Lincoln's Simon Cameron. A lean, angular secessionist with an impulsive manner, Leroy Pope Walker telegraphed the cabinet's decision to Beauregard on April 10. He must demand immediate evacuation, insisted Walker. If refused, he must proceed to assault the fort "in such manner as you may determine." Davis did not expect Anderson to surrender, any more than Lincoln expected his resupply effort to be received peacefully. A visitor later recalled Davis saying, "They mean to compel us into a political servitude we disown and spurn."[18]

Either president could still have stood down and avoided a clash, but the one who did would have paid a high political price. Both men feared to be seen as weak in the face of what each chose to define as a mortal threat. Both therefore shared the blame for moving the crisis across the clear and dangerous threshold from standoff to violent confrontation.

On his island, Anderson felt the pressure mount. On April 7, Beauregard informed him of orders to cut off all communications between the fort and Charleston, except for mail. Up to this point, the garrison had received periodic deliveries of fresh food from vendors in the city to supplement its diminishing store of army issue salt pork. Now it could count on nothing but letters. The next day, Beauregard cut them off, too.[19]

The residents of Charleston had lived with the potential for confrontation for months. Now that the prospect finally was about to be realized, people flocked to the waterfront and strained to see any sign of activity out in the harbor. "The Battery is crowded with people who wait in anxious expectancy," wrote a northern reporter on the scene. Soldiers from militia companies around the state and beyond poured into town. Businesses suspended operations.[20]

On April 11, Anderson knew his prayers would not be answered. Before dawn, a small boat arrived bearing three of Beauregard's aides and the ultimatum. The major received the aides with correct formality and withdrew to share the demand in private with his officers. They all refused it. As he escorted the aides back to the jetty, Anderson asked if Beauregard would give further notice before opening fire. When told that was unlikely, he made a startling reply: "I will await the first shot, and if you do not batter us to pieces," he confessed, "we will be starved out in a few days."[21]

Beauregard hastily cabled this glint of hope to Montgomery. The reply came back that if Anderson would fix a date to withdraw, Beauregard should hold his fire. His aides rowed out to the fort a second time. Anderson said he would leave at noon in three days' time, unless he received help or orders from his government. Here was a last-second chance to avert violence. It was not enough. The Confederates knew Fox's fleet was approaching and would arrive before three days passed. Beauregard's aides told the major that hostilities would begin in an hour.

In March, Edmund Ruffin had left his native Virginia for the more congenial politics of South Carolina. The thought of living in a state that recognized Abraham Lincoln as president disgusted him. With a wild, flowing gray mane, the dour agrarian reformer looked the part of a biblical patriarch dispensing justice with fire and brimstone. At sixty-seven, this irascible prophet of disunion had despaired of ever seeing his dream fulfilled. Four years later, he would put the muzzle of a rifle in his mouth and use a forked stick to depress the trigger. But that last act of an unrepentant rebel lay hidden in the future, for in spring 1861 the crisis rekindled his baleful hope.

Ruffin, revered for his long-standing advocacy of states' rights, was given a place of honor with the Palmetto Guards. They offered him the chance to fire the first cannonball from their battery. His moment came shortly after 4:30 a.m. on April 12, an hour and a half before sunrise. At that moment, he spotted the prearranged signal shot fired from a mortar. It arced high over the harbor, trailing a parabola of sparks, and burst in the darkness, a fleeting pyrotechnic omen of woe. One by one, the batteries ringing the fort began firing, and when it came his turn, Ruffin greedily pulled the lanyard on the sixty-four-pound cannon under his command.

"And the war came." So Lincoln would famously reflect in his second inaugural address, tersely eliding complexities of cause and motive. But that cryptic remark four years later conflated events terribly. In April 1861, no one could see where the furious cannonade would lead. For several more tumultuous weeks, in fact, many Americans still hoped and worked to avert a full-scale civil war. For all the hostility, noise, and anger released in Charleston Harbor, the shape of the prospective disunion of the country, like Edmund Ruffin's fate, still lay hidden in the unknowable future.

FORT SUMTER'S POSITION astride the most direct channel from the ocean into the harbor also put it within range of artillery emplacements on the mainland and three nearby islands.[22] At the signal to commence action, in turn each southern battery opened up until their firing became an almost continuous rumble. It was an unequal contest. The Confederate artillerists outgunned Anderson. They had mortars, which the U.S. soldiers lacked, to send plunging shells into the fort. They fired red-hot solid shot, which began to set fire to the wooden buildings in Sumter's courtyard. To make the inequality worse, Anderson's men could fire only solid cannonballs because their ample supply of shells lacked fuses. To cap off the disparity in firepower, Anderson ordered his men to stay in the more protected lower levels and avoid the exposed upper deck of the fort, where their largest-caliber Columbiad artillery pieces therefore languished for lack of crews. The imbalance in weaponry was overwhelming.

The Confederates felt cheated when the fort made no reply to their assault. In fact, Anderson's men did not begin to fire back until they had endured nearly three hours of bombardment. But gradually, the fort's guns added their own thunder, less vigorous than their foes yet steady and determined. In the early afternoon, soldiers watching out to sea shouted that the fleet had arrived. Emboldened by the prospect of succor from Fox's ships, the men serviced their guns with renewed hope. The barracks were ablaze, and the impact of thousands of solid shot gradually began to tell against the thick masonry walls. But the navy was coming to the rescue.

It did not come, however, and still the shells rained down. They battered the main gates and chipped away at the masonry. Fire spread in the interior wooden parts of the fort, igniting the barracks and threatening the main powder magazine. Before they had to abandon it, work parties moved some barrels of powder to safety. When fire threatened even the salvaged powder, Anderson ordered the men to throw most of it into the water. With no food left and little ammunition to keep up more than a desultory return fire, prospects were bleak. On the morning of April 13, with no help apparent from the sea, Anderson decided he had done enough to defend honor and the flag.

At that point, Louis Wigfall, violent marplot and former U.S. senator from Texas, appeared as if from nowhere. Brandishing his sword with a white cloth tied to it, he presented himself to a startled Major Anderson. When he saw that Sumter's flag was down, Wigfall had ordered a black oarsman to row him across the channel, while cannonballs arced overhead. He was there on Beauregard's behalf, he claimed grandly, to accept Anderson's surrender. The major was ready. He said he would accept the terms Beauregard had originally offered: the men could take their arms and private property; they could salute their flag on leaving; they could take passage to a northern port.

Wigfall had sown confusion at a delicate point. He had no mandate to represent Beauregard or to offer or accept terms. The general had also seen Sumter's flag come down and flames appear to engulf the fort. He sent three aides to Anderson, who was angered to learn from them that the grandstanding Wigfall had come of his own volition, without authority. Distraught, Anderson was ready to send the aides back and resume firing, but they convinced him that further fighting was useless. They agreed that Beauregard would stand by the terms Anderson had accepted from the bogus emissary.

GUSTAVUS FOX'S FOUR navy ships had weighed anchor and departed New York for South Carolina on April 8 and 9, with three tugs to follow. On top of the muddle caused by Seward's competing expedition to Pensacola, they had to fight the elements. A raging coastal storm buffeted them all the way down the Atlantic seaboard. It was the same tempest that delayed the rejected Confederate commissioners' departure from Washington. Fox reported "constant steady bad weather and heavy sea."[23] Seasickness prostrated the crews. Fox's ship, the *Baltic,* arrived before dawn on April 12 at the rendezvous ten miles east of the Charleston lighthouse. The storm blew two of the tugs far off course. The third never left New York. Without them, Fox would have to improvise if he was to have any chance of landing supplies. When the sun rose, he could see and hear that the fort was under an intense barrage from all sides and enveloped in thick smoke. The first of his goals—reprovisioning Sumter peacefully—was no longer possible.

In consultation with his captains, he decided to wait until nightfall and attempt to run in a few of the ships' small boats packed with supplies. The heavy seas were against them, though, and then fog rolled in toward morning. In desperation, one of Fox's captains commandeered a passing ice schooner with the intent of sailing it to Sumter on the following night. But by then the fort had surrendered. Fox later admitted that Confederate guns would have blown the frail sailing vessel to pieces.[24]

Sunday morning, April 14, dawned bright and clear. Small craft filled with sightseers dotted the harbor. Already, enterprising boatmen rowed paying customers out for a good look at the battered fort. Before the smoke had cleared, a venturesome Charleston cameraman clambered over the ruins to take stereoscopic views that he put on sale in two days' time.[25] Anderson was allowed to contact Fox's ships to arrange transport home. He was particularly keen to conduct an elaborate farewell ceremony honoring the flag he had defended against fearful odds. Beauregard generously granted him that request.

Anderson insisted on a thunderous one-hundred-gun salute from the cannons on the top deck of the ruined fort. The men not servicing the guns stood at attention down on the interior parade ground as their comrades slowly lowered the Stars and Stripes from the flagstaff. For the soldiers, the terrifying emotions induced by being shot at for a day and a half had given way to relief at surviving the bombardment and the conflicting feelings of pride at withstanding a superior force and regret at the inescapable outcome. Nearly halfway through the process of firing and reloading, a pile of cartridges accidentally caught fire and exploded, killing one U.S. soldier outright and mortally wounding another. Throughout the whole cannonade of thousands of solid shot and exploding shells, no one on either side had been killed. Now, in a macabre coda mocking that fluke of good fortune, two men died in an accident during surrender formalities.

The tragedy cut short the salute. In the afternoon, Anderson's men marched out of the fort, with drums beating and the band playing "Yankee Doodle." The major, subdued, heartbroken, and exhausted from his ordeal, carried the fort's singed flag under his arm. Sailors ferried him out to Fox's ship for the voyage to New York.[26]

AT THE HEIGHT of the attack, Confederates as well as defenders had seen numerous vessels hull down on the horizon. To untrained eyes, it looked as though the whole U.S. Navy had come to rescue Anderson. In fact, only a pitiful few belonged to Fox. But a number of commercial steamers and brigs, not wanting to be caught in the conflict, stood out to sea. As they waited out of range, to distant observers they appeared to swell the numbers of the relief force.[27]

Even if they all had been Fox's ships, and even if Seward's Pensacola expedition had not hijacked the *Powhatan*, it would have made no difference. Fox could have done no more than delay the inevitable. He could, with great theatrics, have run the gauntlet and landed supplies and reinforcements, just as he had proposed to Lincoln. But they would have put off the surrender for only a short time. Even so, Fox dearly wished he had had that opportunity rather than watching helplessly as the Confederates pummeled Anderson into submission.[28] As he waited for the garrison to be transferred to the *Baltic*, his anger and frustration almost overwhelmed him.

Though he could not have changed the military outcome, he and Anderson had applied the fatal spark in Charleston Harbor. The opposing objectives of Davis and Lincoln may have led to blows any-way, but Anderson's move to Sumter fixed the place and Fox's plan of rescue the timing of the explosion.

Without Fox's stratagem, more cautious army officers, who be-lieved that there was no way to save Sumter, might have carried the day. If Lincoln had accepted their opinion rather than the gamble offered by Fox, and if Anderson had abandoned his command with-out a cannon fired, a political uproar likely would have ensued in the North. Even so, such a decision by Lincoln would have avoided the fireworks at Fort Sumter. Conflict, though still likely in some form, would then have come at a different place and time. As long as there was no fighting, the unionists of the upper South could keep their states from seceding. They, and people in the North who thought like Seward, could keep alive the hope that some solution short of war was still possible. But the fighting at Fort Sumter was now a fact, and that was what Americans had to react to.

CHAPTER 7

TIDINGS OF WAR

April 12 to 15

Out of the crooked timber of humanity no straight thing can ever be made.

—Immanuel Kant

For planters in northeastern North Carolina, the Roanoke River was lifeblood, their connection to the outside world. It allowed steamboats to venture deep into the interior and take crops down to Albemarle Sound and then up the eastern seaboard. But this April, swollen by heavy rains, the river overflowed its banks and threatened the rich bottomland. Small farmers and large ones faced ruin. Among them were the Edmondstons, who with nearly two thousand acres counted as the elite of Halifax County. In the midst of spring planting, with dogwoods in bloom and the corn and melon seeds already in the ground, they had to divert all of their slaves to reinforce an earthen dam against the floodwaters.

Catherine Ann Devereux Edmondston was distracted by other matters, however, as she freely admitted. At thirty-eight, this brusque, confident woman of strong opinions and sharp features deftly managed her family's assets, including nearly a hundred bondsmen. Rivaling her concern for the plantation was "a feverish anxiety, a longing" to know about affairs beyond Halifax. "Fort Sumter occupies all our thoughts," she wrote in late March. Edmondston shared the secessionist faith of her Charleston-born husband, and she broke sharply with her own father, a courtly lawyer who feared for North Carolina if it left the Union. She mocked her sister's naive devotion to the flag. "Who cares for the old striped rag," she sneered, "now that the principle it represented is gone?" The rift within her family reflected the divide in households across the region. Once the fighting began, she cheered for Confederate victory. When it came, after a day's bombardment of the fort, she hoped the sections might still separate peacefully. In any case, she concluded, war or not, "the Union is gone."[1]

IT HAD ALL COME so suddenly. At least it seemed so at the time, no matter how predictable it appears in the easy omniscience of hindsight. Americans had lived with sectional tension for decades and the secession crisis for months. But at the beginning of April, the glacial pace of events abruptly accelerated at a vertiginous pace. Ultimately, a part of the upper South would break away from the Union. On the weekend Fort Sumter fell, however, the precise division of the country was not at all apparent. Indeed, it was not yet decided. It would take weeks before the contours of the split revealed themselves, and not completely even then.

Davis and Lincoln had tried to make each other appear the aggressor. Each believed he succeeded. To an extent, each had. Lincoln said he meant only to send food to a tiny band of hungry men. To give bread, not arms. An attack on the national flag ensued. For his part, Davis denied the legitimacy of Anderson's garrison, camped as it was within sovereign Confederate territory. Any attempt to prolong that presence was an affront. He had offered compensation and had been rebuffed. Honor demanded that he act. He would later justify himself, stiffly but not entirely without logic, by saying, "He who makes the assault is not necessarily he that strikes the first blow or fires the first shot."[2]

Within a month, the two presidents would both achieve something close to the second-best goal each desired—if not peace, then a

more united North and a more united South supporting their respective causes. But despite the assertions of patriots on both sides that
each section was instantly united by the news from Charleston, that
was not at all the case. It compresses events to say that all the states
that would join the Confederacy coalesced suddenly, uniformly, after
Fort Sumter. In fact, the fighting there contorted the upper South in
a spasm of anguished indecision. Unionists were distraught. Even
after Anderson furled his colors, many of them still resisted having
to make a choice. Despite all that had happened, they still found it
hard to embrace the breakup of the country. If they could not contemplate taking up arms to put down the Confederacy, they were
equally not yet ready to fight for it.

That spring, the networked system of telegraph lines and daily
newspapers that plugged Americans into a flood of instant reportage
came into its own. As soon as the first cannon fired in Charleston,
that network spewed a torrent of lurid details about the fighting and
the reaction to it. Unlike in the days of their grandparents at the
nation's founding, Americans in 1861 could follow momentous events
unfolding nearly at the same time they happened. And their reactions, as recorded day by day in the newspapers, revealed that though
the fighting at Fort Sumter electrified the upper South, great uncertainty persisted over the course the region should and would take.

The next key event came when Lincoln announced his response
to Fort Sumter. Therefore, it is important to look closely at the period
between April 12, when news of the fighting flashed across the
nation, and April 15, when the president's reaction to it was broadcast. In this brief span, the telegraph and the daily newspaper told
everyone about the Confederacy's military action. In the words of
one editor, the news traveled "on the wings of lightning to the most
remote corners of the land."[3] But no one knew yet how Washington
would respond. Until it did, upper South unionists still hoped to prevent their states from seceding. The plume of smoke rising above
Charleston Harbor need not mark the funeral pyre of the Union.

The terse cables between Charleston and Montgomery, transmit-
ting the ultimatum to Anderson and his reply to it, appeared in

newspapers verbatim almost as soon as the original recipients of the telegrams could read them. When the message arrived announcing the beginning of hostilities, Montgomery erupted in congratulatory excess. As soon as the Confederate president learned that Anderson would surrender, he wired heartfelt thanks to Governor Pickens in Charleston: "All honor to the gallant sons of Carolina."[4]

A crowd gathered in front of Montgomery's Government House to shout their cheers for Davis and Beauregard. They fired cannons and demanded the president give them a speech. He, however, remained closeted with his cabinet. Distorted accounts of the fighting coursed through the streets with the revelers. In the evening, thousands of well-wishers, their euphoric faces lit by a sea of blazing yellow torches, followed a brass band, chanting their demand that Davis come out and speak to them. Exhausted, the president sent his apologies and his war secretary to assuage the crowd. Davis deplored the frivolity of speechifying. There was so much work to be done. The carousing of the mob long into the night offended his conviction that they now faced a future filled with danger.[5]

Though he might deprecate the revelry in the streets, it was the precise result that he and his colleagues had anticipated: attacking Fort Sumter would energize the Confederacy and convince more states to join it. That prospect had motivated their ultimatum, and they were proven right. In the eyes of the Confederates, Fox's mission to Fort Sumter revealed Lincoln's deceit. The blame, bellowed a Louisiana commentator, rested wholly on "the low cunning and cowardly duplicity of the miserable pretenders who now fill the high places in the once respectable Government of the United States."[6]

For several days after their famous victory, armed men swaggered and sang in the streets of Charleston, with the "hot oxygen which is called 'the flush of victory' on the cheek." Ordinary southerners in places far removed from the conflict were caught up in the euphoria. In Goldsboro, North Carolina, where "all was noise, dust and patriotism," a revolutionary ecstasy transported both men and women. They cheered and waved and danced themselves to exhaustion. In New Orleans, swelling bands of citizen soldiers filled city streets with drum and fife music and exuberant tributes to southern patriotism. Besides eliciting this giddy Confederate response, a local observer concluded, Lincoln's futile efforts at Fort Sumter had betrayed the benighted character of his administration, "irreligious, spasmodic, and superficial; the blind impulse of a misguided mob . . . nothing but pitiful imbecility."[7]

The artillery duel in Charleston galvanized the North with equal if opposite intensity. The identical cry of newspapers across the country was that nothing like this had occurred within living memory. More thoughtful commentators throughout the free states tried to reflect on what was happening, but they were as caught up in the tumult as their neighbors who poured into the streets to demonstrate their patriotism.

In Philadelphia, crowds thronged newspaper offices for the latest bulletins from the South. In response to discouraging reports about the battering Anderson's men were receiving, a printer ran up the national flag outside. At nearby offices and shops, others caught the spirit, and "each successively ran up its colors like a fleet of ships on the eve of action."[8] The same story repeated all across the North. Agitated citizens, not knowing what to do in the face of sudden cataclysm but determined to do something, put out flags and more flags until there were no more to be had.

In Pittsburgh, concern about the outcome at Fort Sumter suspended commerce for two days. The *Post*'s editor conceded that the South had struck the first blow but predicted it would unite the North. The time for recrimination about what could have been done differently to avoid fratricide was past. Nothing remained to be done but to stand by "The Flag of Our Country—the glorious Stars and Stripes must be supported and defended by every American."[9] Behind that cry lurked a threat—hidden for the moment but not for long—that no dissent would be tolerated.

In Chicago, the excitement and the crowds equaled the scenes in eastern cities. Throughout the weekend, contradictory telegrams about the fate of Anderson's garrison stoked communal anxiety and dominated the comments of ministers on Sunday. At the First Congregational Church, the Reverend William Weston Patton chose as his text a verse from the Gospel according to Matthew: "And ye shall hear of wars, and rumors of wars; see that ye be not troubled." Patton, who in four years' time would walk in triumph through the burned ruins of Confederate Richmond, exhorted his parishioners to see the hand of God in the tumult. He assured them that providence often chose the destruction of war to overthrow tyranny and oppression. Patton said the time had come to defend the Constitution, for "the present struggle is one in which every Christian may *rise from his knees, and shoulder his rifle.*"[10]

Kindred sentiments echoed in the Brooklyn church of Henry Ward Beecher, where an overflow crowd gathered to hear one of the North's most eloquent preachers. A man of large, dreamy eyes, he excelled in a brand of hypnotic pulpit oratory that gained him a wide following. Like his sister, Harriet Beecher Stowe, he fervently embraced abolition. Though he preached a romantic, genial Christianity of love, on that Sunday Beecher thundered like an Old Testament prophet. Better to let war come "than that slavery, with silent corruptions should be permitted longer to fester in our body politic." A messenger burst in to interrupt the service with word that Anderson had been relieved. The church erupted in cheers. Beecher warned that even if that report later proved false, the nation called on its youth to enlist. He invoked the contemporary surge in Europe for national self-determination and freedom among Italians, Poles, and Russians. The service ended with a robust singing of "My Country, 'Tis of Thee."[11]

Beecher's abolitionism stirred few northern hearts, but saving the Union did. They rallied to defend the Constitution, not to free the slaves. Most white northerners, like their president, were willing to let African Americans languish in perpetual bondage if that was the cost of preserving the Union. Frederick Douglass's journal was exultant: "The slaveholders themselves have saved our cause from ruin! They have exposed the throat of slavery to the keen knife of liberty."[12] That was a clairvoyant judgment, but in spring 1861 it was also grossly premature.

More typical of northern reaction was New York lawyer George Templeton Strong's. He snapped up the extras hawked by newsboys on Friday evening with headlines screaming about the bombardment of Fort Sumter. He doubted the Confederates had been so rash as to attack, but the next morning's confirmation lifted his spirits. "So Civil War is inaugurated at last," he wrote. "God defend the Right." By that he meant defense of the Constitution and Union. Already he saw manifold signs of a stiffening northern backbone. Strong, a Republican, marveled at the patriotic reaction of Democrats to the assault on the flag.[13]

For a few days, however, the partisan spirit that had divided northern opinion throughout the secession crisis persisted. Newspapers that had opposed Lincoln in the presidential election blamed him for starting open warfare—"willfully, wantonly, and maliciously"—and dashing hopes of reconciliation.[14] According to an upstate New York paper that had supported Douglas, if the action at Fort Sumter had been a worthy attempt to restore the Union, all Democrats would have rallied around. But the administration's action had no such effect: "It cannot restore; it can only destroy." The editor implied that Lincoln's purpose was to stir up hatred between the sections and kill any chance for peace.[15] In Maine, another editor claimed that Lincoln's "egregious mistake" had snuffed out all hope for compromise and had embroiled the nation in war over an unimportant bastion that could have been evacuated without dishonor. The writer tried to wish away the conflict: "The war has been begotten by extremists in both sections. Let them fight it out."[16]

Only a few voices spoke with anything approaching detachment. In Newburyport, Massachusetts, an editor lamented with resignation the lack of restraint on both sides and concluded it was too late to ask who started the fight: "We have chosen war or been forced into it; and it makes no difference which."[17] In the Midwest, another newspaper decried the shameful fact of "deadly strife between men of the same country . . . between *friends*." The realization that such a calamity had finally befallen the nation was depressing: "Who does not sicken at the thought of all this?"[18] Such reflection on the dramatic turn of events was in short supply.

These sentiments were quickly overwhelmed by the outrage that swept the North. Many Democratic editors, so used to telling their readers how to interpret events, misjudged the patriotic response of the northern public. Seeing their error, they rushed to denounce "the drunken minions of Jeff. Davis and his slave Oligarchy." They warned northerners that whoever was not for the flag was against it: "There is no middle ground." The Confederates may have defeated Major Anderson, but at the same time they converted even sympathetic northerners into enemies. By firing on Fort Sumter, "they have completely shot off the legs of all trimmers and compromisers." That outcome hinted at the enforced unanimity of sentiment that a nation at war would demand of its citizens, at the cost of liberty of expression in both North and South.[19]

These reactions show that by the way Lincoln chose the confrontation in Charleston Harbor, he did more than encourage the Confederates to fire the first shot and thus bear the onus for starting a hot war. When Davis elected to accept that burden, Lincoln achieved the result that was most likely to bring northern Democrats along with him.[20] The first reaction of some of their most partisan newspapers, cited earlier, denouncing Lincoln for causing war, was quickly overwhelmed by indignation at the insult to the flag. That tide washed over the North and swept nearly all along, Democrats as well as Republicans, in support of Lincoln's initial war aim of putting down rebellion and defending the Constitution.

IN THE UPPER SOUTH it was different, at least for a time. Secessionists were overjoyed and energized, confident that their cause would finally prevail in the slave states that so far had remained in the Union. But many unionists there still felt torn between conflicting allegiances—fealty to the Constitution purchased by their Revolutionary grandfathers' blood versus loyalty to their southern roots and institutions.

They greeted the first reports of violence with dismay. It mattered to them which side fired first. They were ready to blame either Lincoln or the South Carolinians for starting a war—or both. For a day or so, the desire to get the facts straight about which side shot first was important to the cautious men in between. They learned the facts soon enough, but even then, whether they chose to blame Lincoln for provoking the confrontation or Davis for ordering the assault, they still drew back from secession. Many Americans along the border believed that with their region lay the responsibility for preventing the fighting from becoming a generalized war. "Their position between the extremes of the contending parties," observed a Washington newspaper, "gives to them the post of honor, of duty, and of danger."[21]

North Carolinian B. F. Moore captured the southern unionists' despondency when he sorrowfully wrote to his daughter, "Civil war can be glorious news to none but demons, or thoughtless fools, or maddened men." In Kentucky, Tennessee, Arkansas, and Missouri, others like Moore faced renewed secessionist demands for immediate action in the wake of Fort Sumter. The disunionist *Louisville Courier* declared that civil war had begun, blamed Lincoln entirely, and demanded to know of Kentuckians, "For whom will you fight—an Abolition Administration . . . or for your brethren of the South?"[22]

In Maryland, the *Baltimore Sun* pleaded with residents not to succumb to passion, but to oppose the horror of civil war and "insist upon a peaceful adjustment to the cause of strife." With political sentiment divided among its citizens, Baltimore had more to lose than communities farther to the north or south that were less riven and farther from the expected front lines. The news of Fort Sumter first reached town Friday evening, and on Saturday crowds gathered at the newspapers just as they did elsewhere to make sense of the contradictory telegrams that poured in. For the moment, a majority seemed overwhelmed with sadness and curiosity rather than exuberance. Just in case, the police came out in force, alerted to head off any confrontation. A hailstorm on Saturday afternoon probably did more to dampen hostile feelings. The next day, the crowds reappeared but then diminished once people believed Anderson would indeed surrender.[23]

In Virginia, the fissure between east and west that had been developing for decades had been papered over but was never fully sealed. The secession crisis agitated this intrastate fault line, and the news from Fort Sumter now cracked it wide open. In Wheeling, the *Daily Intelligencer* had been forthright in condemning disunion. The news from South Carolina did not surprise the editor, and Lincoln's firmness in sending the relief force pleased him. "We have a Government now," he proclaimed, "if we only stand by it like men."[24]

Across the Appalachian Mountains to the east, and a world away in sentiment, John Coles Rutherfoord also welcomed the clarification brought by the outbreak of fighting. It gave an uncharacteristic elation to the morose, perennially depressed planter in the Piedmont region west of Richmond. Rutherfoord gloried in his role as an early advocate of secession. He blamed his state for a supine course that emboldened Lincoln's "desperate policy of coercion." Now the guns of Fort Sumter would unite North and South against each other and demonstrate to all the world that two distinct and incompatible nationalities existed in the former United States of America.[25]

In Richmond, crowds surged through the streets to cheer the news from Charleston. They set fires that blazed until midnight, while "the city looked like an immense hive." On Capitol Square, they fired cannons a hundred times to salute southern victory. Nimble young men climbed to the top of the Capitol and replaced the Stars and Stripes with a Confederate banner. Bonfires, fireworks, and brass bands playing "La Marseillaise" and "Dixie" gave the city a carnival atmosphere and cowed unionist delegates to the convention, who scrambled to caucus about what strategy to take in their continuing opposition to secession. They cannot have been encouraged by the evidence of their eyes and ears: triumphant speeches by southern rights advocates, incessant and exuberant toasts to the Confederacy, and noisy parades that choked the streets of the business district.[26]

One party of revelers headed for the governor's mansion on Capitol Square and called for John Letcher to address them. Like other unionists, the governor labored under tremendous pressure. A weak leader, Letcher was an optimistic moderate, more comfortable with the middling professional classes than with the state's plantation elite. His balding dome and wire-rimmed glasses unfortunately did nothing to enhance his appearance or mitigate his tedium as a speaker, and he made an easy mark for his enemies. A few days before, the *Examiner*'s fiery editor, John Moncure Daniel, cast another slur at the drinking habits of the "bibacious" Letcher and claimed that Lincoln had bought him "with buckets of his swill." The governor came out to respond to the crowd, but they hissed him and moved on, disappointed by his low-key, cryptic platitudes about Virginia doing its duty when the time came. When they left, he gave orders to take the Confederate flag down from the Capitol.[27]

Though their ranks were diminished, Virginia unionists scorned the excitement. Some of them were more determined than ever to resist secession and to convene a border state convention. They thought it folly for Virginia to leave the Union when it was surrounded by loyal states. Consultation with the rest of the upper South was the only safe way forward. It might even lead to a middle confederacy between the South and the North. Whatever resulted, safety lay in numbers, to stay in concert with the other states of the border. These conservative sentiments enraged secessionists who could not believe the convention had failed to join the Confederacy the instant word of fighting came from Fort Sumter. Ignorant of the lack of combat casualties, a South Carolina reporter covering the meeting noted sardonically that it meant to show everyone "that the wholesale murder of their Southern brethren was not to disturb the tranquility of great minds."[28]

In the convention, on the Saturday that brought hourly updates about the firing in Charleston Harbor, delegates spent four hours debating constitutional amendments to resolve the sectional dispute. When they turned to discuss the effect of Fort Sumter, the contempt of the factions for one another could not be concealed. The exaggerated courtesies of southern gentility that normally marked debate vanished, parliamentary victims of the deluge.

Prickly and scornful of his opponents, Jubal Early still stood up boldly for the Union. No one who heard him speak that weekend would have predicted that he would soon put on Confederate gray. He said his heart was full of sorrow, not so much because Anderson, a friend from army days, had been forced to bow to superior numbers but because his fellow Virginians so gleefully cheered that defeat. He angered the secessionists by charging that to exult over the "dishonor to our flag" brought no glory to the Confederate cause. Rather, he said pointedly, "it has placed a gulf between them and the people of Virginia." He twisted the knife more when he accused secessionists of betraying states' rights because they urged the Confederacy to march its army across Virginia without permission and attack Washington.[29]

Thomas Goode of Mecklenburg County, a bulldog of disunion, took immediate offense. He was a cousin of John Goode, who had nearly challenged Early to a duel in March, and he welcomed the chance to revive the bad blood between Early and his family. Thomas Goode charged that Early had impugned his honor and, in microcosm of the conflict to come, echoed his cousin by threatening to call Early out to duel. This time it was Early who backed down. Perhaps he decided there were greater issues that demanded his energy than a spat with yet another angry Goode. The tide was moving against people like Early in the upper South, but as long as they resisted secession, the outcome in those states remained uncertain.

Alternatively, if the upper South unionists had caved in immediately rather than continuing to resist secession, they would have swept Virginia into the maelstrom sooner. They might then have created a surge of disunion along the border greater and earlier than actually occurred. But they did not instantly capitulate at the news from South Carolina.

On April 13, residents of the federal capital gathered around the newspaper offices and hotels to learn the latest telegraphed news from the South. They had heard about the opening guns the night before. Now they hung on every alarming cable updating the world about the artillery duel in South Carolina. Local secessionists had kept a low profile since the inauguration, but the news emboldened them. Republicans nervously scoffed at the credibility of telegrams sent by rebel operators in Charleston. Scuffles and street fights broke out between partisan hotheads. A company of volunteer militia in the District denounced the expedition to Fort Sumter and declared its solidarity with secession.[30]

In contrast with the excitement outside, within the White House the Saturday routine was little changed. The president's staff took their cue from Lincoln, whose phlegmatic demeanor set a calming tone. Like Davis, he knew that once he had made his decision, the next steps were in the hands of others. When he learned the result at Fort Sumter, he would announce the next move. The cabinet assembled, but there was little to deliberate because the military outcome was not yet determined. There was one exception to the routine, however: the arrival of a delegation from the Virginia convention.[31]

The alarms triggered in early April by reports of unusual activity at the Brooklyn Navy Yard had perturbed the moderate unionists in the Richmond convention who still hoped Lincoln would avoid force. Some delegates wanted to send a mission to Washington to find out the administration's intentions. Others were suspicious of the idea, fearing it was a trick to provoke Lincoln, but a majority approved.

The convention chose three delegates from among their number. William Ballard Preston was a onetime congressman and secretary of the navy under Zachary Taylor. Formerly a moderate unionist, he now inclined toward secession and had proposed the idea of calling on Lincoln. George Wythe Randolph, a Richmond secessionist described by enemies as "a tall, ghastly-looking man, with red whiskers and a weak voice," had no interest in compromise.[32] Alexander Hugh Holmes Stuart, a handsome man with a round, clean-shaven face more youthful than his fifty-four years, was the sole staunch union man among the trio. He was the brother-in-law of John Baldwin, whose clandestine meeting with Lincoln a week before was still a secret.

It was an ill-starred mission from the outset. Heavy rains from the same storm that buffeted Fox's fleet on its way to Charleston also washed out the rail connection between Richmond and Washington. When the storm finally abated, the delegates made their way to Norfolk and took a steamer on its passage up the coast to Baltimore. They reached Washington nearly a week later than expected. Another passenger on the same ship was Robert Chew, returning from South Carolina after delivering his message to Governor Pickens.[33] His mission was over; the Virginia delegation's more daunting one lay ahead of them.

Their appointment with the president took place on the unfortunate Saturday when the whole country was fixated on the latest news from South Carolina. By then Lincoln's hopes for upper South unionists had curdled. He received the delegation coolly. Rather than engaging in an open discussion, he stiffly read to them from a written response he had already prepared. The text, composed that morning and given to the newspapers to print the following day, left no doubt, no diplomatic ambiguity, about his direction.[34]

He confessed that he was surprised anyone still found his purpose unclear because he had spoken plainly in his inaugural address. He then quoted to them from it about his intent to "hold, occupy, and possess, the property, and places belonging to the Government." This was a bit disingenuous, because the clarity of that point was obscured by conciliatory passages elsewhere in the address. Further, his government's hands-off stance during March was reason enough for people to infer he did not want confrontation.[35]

Lincoln went on to say that if the cables from Charleston were borne out, and it was indeed the fact that southern gunners were firing on Major Anderson, "I shall hold myself at liberty" to retake not just Fort Sumter, but any other federal property that had fallen to the Confederates before he took office.[36] It is impossible to know if Lincoln would have been more receptive if weather had not delayed the Virginians. If the meeting had occurred before the violence at Fort Sumter, he might have been less dismissive. But it is unlikely there would have been a different outcome. For by April he had decided to risk confrontation, and no delegation was likely to have dissuaded him, as his earlier meeting with Baldwin suggested.

In light of their frosty reception, the three men excused themselves from their engagement to dine with Seward and hurried back to Richmond.[37] The republic was breaking apart before their eyes, and there was nothing they could do to stop it. Indeed, two of the three no longer wanted to stop it. When Stuart, the sole, solid unionist of the three, returned to the convention, he said he found Lincoln's remarks "in the highest degree unsatisfactory," but even then he hoped the president did not mean to wage war.[38]

AFTER HIS fruitless meeting with the Virginians, Lincoln received the text of a cable scribbled on the notepaper of the Magnetic Telegraph Company, whose Washington office was a short walk down Pennsylvania Avenue. The same intelligence received by the president was soon broadcast North and South: "Fort Sumter has surrendered [and] there is nobody Hurt."[39] Embedded in the major news was the hopeful detail about casualties. The unfortunate explosion during the ceremony when Anderson lowered his flag claimed two lives, but that was an accident. By some remarkable stroke of good fortune, there had not been a single combat death.

In Montgomery, Jefferson Davis received this same news with joy. "Fort Sumter is ours and nobody is hurt," he exclaimed.[40] Some people dismissed the report as absurd. How could there have been a furious artillery duel for a day and a half without anyone on either side being killed? Others, clutching at hopeful straws, viewed the report as a sign from above, "as if the hand of Providence were visibly outstretched to stay the progress of the plague which . . . is without precedent in the annals of history."[41] In Baltimore, the metropolis of divided Maryland, an editor called the lack of combat casualties the one happy circumstance "in this mournful event" and ventured the sanguine thought that peace might still be possible.[42]

CHAPTER 8

CHEATED AND DECEIVED

April 15 to 17

The prologue to our country's tragedy has ended. Fort Sumpter has surrendered.

—*Baltimore American*, April 15

The thunderclap from Charleston that reverberated through the telegraph wires on April 12 filled John Janney with foreboding. Even so, letters that the president of the Virginia convention wrote over the next two days revealed that he and his fellow unionists kept a cautious hope alive. They still believed they could restrain the stampede toward secession. It would not be easy. The clash at Fort Sumter energized prophets of disunion in the upper South as nothing had done since the inauguration. Then, they had to sift through Lincoln's ambiguous words to find martial hints they could exaggerate. Now, they could point to actual conflict, even if no combat deaths had resulted and no matter that Confederates had started the shooting. Still, there was hope for the Union in the upper South.

On the next evening, April 13, Janney told his wife that as he wrote to her, all around his Richmond hotel he could hear cannons firing and strident crowds cheering about Fort Sumter. It was shameful, he said, to learn of the disgrace to the nation's flag. He put little stock in the convention's delegation sent to meet with Lincoln and was angry with the president for not withdrawing the garrison. But he was angrier still at the Confederates for opening fire. Alcinda Janney agreed. It was clear to her who started the fight: "I only wish S Carolina had to bear the whole weight. . . . I only feel contempt and am sorry she is in N America." She shared a common upper South disdain for both Lincoln and the secessionists. The question was whether the fine balance of that scorn would endure much longer. The convention, her husband vowed, "still stands fast and all the news today had no effect upon it." He concluded, however, "We know not what a day will bring forth."[1]

Janney's words reflected apprehension throughout the upper South and across the political spectrum. In North Carolina, though the Roanoke River inundated her newly planted cornfields, secessionist Catherine Edmondston was obsessed with the conflict. She freely admitted that "outside matters occupy us so that tho' [the flood] is a heavy blow . . . we do not regard it as ordinarily we should. Public affairs absorb all our interest; the desire [is] to know what next Mr Lincoln will do!"[2]

On the border between the slave and free states, the editors of the unionist *Baltimore American*, with reluctance, almost unwilling to say it, sorrowfully predicted "the prologue to our country's tragedy has ended." With fervent, trembling hope, the paper printed the words to "The Star-Spangled Banner" on its front page the day news arrived to answer Janney's and Edmondston's question: How would Lincoln respond to Fort Sumter?[3]

WHILE MAJOR ANDERSON prepared to take down his flag, armchair strategists on both sides began to speculate about what would happen next. Once the garrison surrendered, some people thought that act would remove the main point of contention between Montgomery and Washington. Some thought that meant the two sides could then negotiate a peaceful separation. At the least, if fighting continued, perhaps it could be contained within the seven-state Confederacy. But the shock wave that battered the upper South that weekend raised the question anew whether those states would finally give in to the pressure they had so far resisted. Would they throw in their lots with the Confederacy, or would they continue their fence-sitting in hopes of avoiding conflict? Would they act together or piecemeal?

On Sunday, April 14, the president and his cabinet met at the White House to articulate the details of the government's response. Despite misleading reports to the contrary, they now knew for certain that no good news would come from Fox's expedition. Anderson would surrender that day. In his own hand, Lincoln drafted the text of a proclamation. In flat, legalistic terms, the crucial passage rang the dreaded tocsin of civil war: "Therefore, I, Abraham Lincoln . . . hereby do call forth, the militia of the several States, of the Union. . . ." He requested loyal states to supply seventy-five thousand soldiers for three months' service. He asked citizens to support the Union, gave those in rebellion against it twenty-five days to disband, and called a special session of Congress to meet on July 4.[4]

Lincoln based his assertion of authority on the 1795 militia act. He would be criticized for invoking that law irregularly, but he argued he was responding to an emergency when Congress was not in session and believed the safety of the republic demanded commensurate measures. His old adversary Senator Douglas came to the White House for a long private interview. The president shared the draft proclamation with him. Douglas, who for so long had counseled compromise, now demanded a resort to overwhelming military force. He personified the transformation of many, though by no means all, wary northern Democrats into advocates of all-out war against secession. Though he had no inkling, the Little Giant had less than two months to live. With his old enthusiasm, he pledged unwavering support for Lincoln. Asked about Washingtonians with Confederate sympathies, he replied, "If I were President, I'd convert them or hang them all within forty-eight hours."[5]

Lincoln made minor editorial changes to the draft of his proclamation, and the cabinet endorsed it. He originally had titled the document "To the People of the United States of America" but crossed through that line and wrote instead the more assertive heading "By the President of the United States A proclamation." Though written on April 14, it was dated the following day, copied, and sent to newspapers for publication on Monday, April 15.[6]

While the president summoned Americans to the colors in broad terms, Secretary of War Cameron sent the details to the governors. By telegraph, he enumerated the quota of regiments being requested. He identified the towns where each state's units should gather, where a U.S. Army officer would administer the oath of loyalty and muster the soldiers into federal service. The secretary asked each governor to notify him when the requisitioned forces would reach their rendezvous sites.[7]

The printed table of regiments distributed with the proclamation reveals that it did not request troops from all loyal states or in proportion to their population. There was no quota for California and Oregon because they were so far away from the seat of trouble. The War Department also notified governors of some of the smaller states that their troops could reach the rendezvous points as late as May 20.[8] Their numbers were too small to make a difference for the present emergency.

The most crucial part of the proclamation concerned the upper South. Given the overwhelming response from the free states, Lincoln could easily have raised his seventy-five thousand men just from them alone. There was no military necessity to seek troops from the upper South. If he had not done so, unionists there would have faced less of an outcry from their opponents. They might have retained their shaky control over their states. But Lincoln did not choose that path. Of the ninety-four regiments requested, twenty-one were to come from the eight slave states still in the Union. He asked Maryland, which had half the population of Virginia, to furnish four regiments, while its neighbor to the south had a quota of only three. The fact that he asked for any regiments at all from them or the other slave states that were still nominally in the Union was enough to confront them with the great choice they feared: to reaffirm or renounce their loyalty.

Replies from the governors came within a matter of hours, thanks to the telegraph. There were no secrets. Newspapers printed the text of the cables as soon as possible, coupled with reports of public reaction. The typical newspaper ran pages of short paragraphs summarizing the response to the proclamation in dozens of cities and towns in both sections. Within days, therefore, the whole country could see the developing pattern and what those answers might mean for the outbreak of war and, indeed, for how the nation was splitting apart.

Northern governors replied with overwhelming enthusiasm. "We will furnish the largest number you will receive. Great rejoicing here over your proclamation," declared Ohio's normally cool and aloof William Dennison.[9] "The people of Maine of all parties will rally with alacrity to the maintenance of the Government and of the Union," echoed Israel Washburn Jr., the quick-tempered governor who eight years before had convened the antislavery meeting that founded the Republican Party.[10] Others demanded that Lincoln increase their quotas. Indiana's Oliver P. Morton, soon to become the most energetic midwestern war governor, offered ten thousand men, more than double the strength requested.[11] Andrew Curtin, Secretary of War Cameron's sworn enemy in Pennsylvania politics, rushed to tell his erstwhile opponent that volunteers were flocking to the colors. He would send them on at once to Washington, even without arms or ammunition.[12]

News of the proclamation scythed through unionist feeling in the upper South and cut it off at the ground. Overnight, public opinion shifted radically. When it came down to it, having to choose between fellow white southerners and the North was no choice at all.

With the exception of Thomas Hicks, the timorous unionist governor of Maryland, straddling a powder keg of divided sentiment, leaders of the upper South expressed unanimous outrage. Gov. John W. Ellis of North Carolina had long feared for states' rights and slavery if the Republicans took the White House. He angrily replied to Cameron the same day, saying, "I can be no party to this wicked violation of the laws of the country." The governor of Kentucky, Beriah Magoffin, echoed Ellis: "I say emphatically Kentucky will furnish no troops for the wicked purposes of subduing her sister Southern States." Isham Harris of Tennessee also rejected Cameron's request outright. His state would "not furnish a single man for purpose of coercion, but 50,000, if necessary, for the defense of our rights and those of our Southern brethren."[13]

Virginia's John Letcher had long endured the calumny of radicals for his defense of the Union. He told Cameron he doubted the request's authenticity because it was so outrageous. When he realized it was not a fabrication created by an agent provocateur, he denounced it as strongly as the other southern governors: "Your object," he accused, "is to subjugate the Southern States."[14]

In North Carolina, the proclamation destroyed once vigorous unionist strength. Just before Fort Sumter, an editor complained that the South had been "cheated, imposed upon, and deceived" by Lincoln for not evacuating the garrison and predicted that his failure to do so would drive the upper South out of the Union.[15] That prophecy, however, represented a pitifully small minority opinion before mid-April, for North Carolina unionists expected the North's hands-off attitude toward the Confederacy to lead to gradual reunification of the sections. Unlike in Virginia, here there was little agitation for secession before Lincoln's proclamation.

Now, however, the majority for remaining in the United States was suddenly overthrown. "We loved the Union," swore the *Greensboro Times*, "but we love honor more."[16] The day after the proclamation, a pro-Union candidate for Congress reversed himself and called Lincoln's act a declaration of war. William Holden had been a dominant figure in the Democratic Party and a states' rights man during the 1850s. Even so, he feared secession would destroy the South and urged giving Lincoln a chance. He argued that if the president had asked for soldiers only to defend Washington, unionists in the upper South would have approved. "But he 'crossed the Rubicon,'" argued Holden, "when he called for troops to subdue the Confederate States."[17]

North Carolina state senator Jonathan Worth mourned the lost opportunities to save what was now forsaken. The son of Quakers, a devout Whig, and an indifferent speaker, the plain and sober Worth was an atypical southern politician but nevertheless personified common southern contradictions. He profited handsomely from owning slaves, yet he denounced secession as insanity. He believed a majority in his state remained solid for the Union, even after Fort Sumter. But, he lamented, with his proclamation "Lincoln prostrated us. He could have devised no scheme more effectual than the one he has pursued, to overthrow the friends of the Union here." With sorrow, Worth accepted the Confederacy and would serve as wartime state treasurer. "I think," he grieved, "the South is committing suicide."[18]

The proclamation smote moderate upper South opinion a terrible blow. "The news paralyzes the people here, and they have not yet recovered," read a telegraphic dispatch from Louisville.[19] Nowhere was it more apparent than in an article that appeared in George Prentice's *Louisville Journal*. Known far beyond Kentucky for his sarcastic, witty style, Prentice had built a reputation as one of the country's most brilliant newspapermen. He was an old Henry Clay Whig, and in 1860 he had supported the Constitutional Union Party in the border South's attempt to find a middle way between sectional opponents.

On hearing the news from South Carolina, Prentice wrote an impassioned essay that denounced Confederate "revolutionists" for firing on Fort Sumter. He believed the fighting could be contained if Washington responded with prudence and forbearance. But as the paper was going to press on April 15, Prentice learned to his dismay about Lincoln's proclamation. "Struck with mingled amazement and indignation," he inserted a last-minute emendation that denounced the president for betraying the conservative men of the South.[20] In the end, though he criticized Lincoln, Prentice did not opt for the Confederacy. Many other southern unionists did, and they used the proclamation as an excuse to rationalize their decisions.

Some voices still called for calm. A day after the proclamation, the *Baltimore American* argued that Lincoln had to reply to Confederate provocation. He could not meekly accept aggression without a response. The paper maintained that peace was still possible. If not, civil war would condemn Maryland to terrible suffering, "from the bare contemplation of which the heart recoils with unspeakable dread." Down the street, however, the *Exchange* reflected a different local sentiment and accused the administration of "a wicked and desperate crusade . . . against the fundamental American principle of self-government."[21]

Across the mountains, a Tennessean advocated a separate border state confederacy as the only way to maintain "strict neutrality between the mad men of the sections."[22] Only in hindsight was it also madness for southern unionists to champion such a solution and think they could still thwart the breakup of the Union. The fact that many still hoped for border state consultation or even a middle confederacy—some third way between Lincoln and Davis—suggests that in their minds the outcome was not decided with Fort Sumter, or the proclamation, or even after. Indeed, the proof of that attitude is embedded in the often neglected fact that almost as large a portion of the upper South did resist secession as the portion that rebelled.

WAR DID NOT come to America in a vacuum. It came after decades of slowly building anxiety, mistrust, and animosity between North and South. But when the crisis did come, it ignited that accumulated fund of hatred with a thunderous explosion of emotion. The lower South and, after April 15, a large swath of the upper South could see only a hostile, hateful, aggressive North attempting to impose its will and destroy their way of life. A Richmond paper received the text of the proclamation by telegraph just before going to press. There was no time to write a detailed reaction, but the editors, already committed to the disunion cause, demanded that the only proper response was to rise up and "fight to the death for our altars and firesides."[23]

"All disguise is thrown aside at last," proclaimed the *New Orleans Picayune*, "and the result is—war." The fire-eaters' dream was realized. The belief that the North was the aggressor demanded that southerners defend themselves against an alien power, no longer their own government but a foreign oppressor. "Slowly but surely," exulted the *Charleston Mercury*, "time has lifted the veil from the hideous and loathsome features of Abolitionism enthroned in Washington."[24]

For their part, northerners began to view the whole South as a traitorous region that meant to pull down the temple of the republic. The increasingly violent rhetoric of the past decade fed this outburst of intersectional hatred that boiled over in the middle of April and fueled outrage on both sides. When both were sustained by such elemental emotions—defense of hearth and home on the one hand, defense of the Constitution on the other—the prospects for putting out the fires before a tremendous bloodletting had occurred were dim.

The upper South began to split apart. But it would not fracture neatly, and exactly how and where the fault lines appeared were not foreordained. They were not even completely clear before the end of the month. The response to Lincoln's call, however, would lead to violence long before then and in a place no one expected. Fort Sumter rallied the seven-state Confederacy to the common cause. It did so, too, for the North because of the assault on the nation's flag. It was the proclamation three days later, however, that was critical for the reaction in the upper South among those hoping to stay in the Union even after Fort Sumter.

AFTER MAJOR ANDERSON surrendered and Lincoln responded, champagne flowed and jaunty martial music pulsated through the crowded parlors of Montgomery's hotels. The Confederate elite, many of them dressed in the gaudy colors of disparate militia uniforms, toasted their success. Throughout the southern states, in towns and villages even more remote than Montgomery, people gathered to echo the celebrations in the parochial national capital.

Stiff, imperious, and humorless, Davis shunned such frivolity. He was weighted down with the knowledge that his work was just beginning. His hopes that a clash over Fort Sumter would energize the South seemed borne out. He had shown Lincoln that his government meant to defend its independence. But would the North relent once the impediment of Fort Sumter had been removed? The answer came when Lincoln's proclamation showed he meant business, too. It extinguished any hope that the North might back down in the face of Confederate steel.

As urgent as the task of building a new government had been before Fort Sumter, it now took on a more frenetic character for the Confederate leaders as the prospect of war exploded before them. They expected Lincoln would declare a naval blockade to accompany his call for volunteers. With that in mind, Davis's cabinet endorsed a request to the states for additional volunteers. They approved letters of marque and reprisal to authorize privateers to harry northern shipping. The normally equable attorney general, Judah P. Benjamin, chagrined at his ignorance of how to compose the wording of such a document, corralled a visiting Briton for help. Like Lincoln, Davis called his Congress back into session.[25]

Although he understood that building military power was important, Davis knew the most crucial task was a diplomatic one, to convince those eight wavering slave states in the upper South to join him. Nearly two months after his inauguration, he had not persuaded a single one. Now Fort Sumter gave him a powerful new argument, and he immediately sent emissaries to entreat them. He wanted them to know where they fit in the Confederacy's distinction between "alien friends" and "alien enemies."[26]

Fort Sumter alone, however, was not enough. Lincoln's response to it, though, gave the Confederates greater hope. The flood of encouraging telegrams from the border in response to the proclamation heartened even Davis's anemic, irritable vice president, Alexander Stephens, a diminutive conservative intellectual from Georgia. Almost as quick-tempered and self-righteous as Davis, "Little Aleck" was jollied out of his usual pessimism by the sudden turn of events. "I *think* the whole South will consolidate," he let himself hope on April 17.[27] The prize, of course, was Virginia. If they could pry the Old Dominion loose from the Union, the whole upper South might join the Confederacy. From the perspective of Montgomery, when Lincoln announced his proclamation, all the signs looked good. But still no one knew exactly how the upper South would respond.

CHAPTER 9

GIVE THE OLD LADY TIME

Richmond, April 15 to 17

*Sir, I know what is before me; I know that an Ordinance of
Secession is war, a cruel, bloody, civil war.*

—John Janney, April 17[1]

Roger Atkinson Pryor, an intense, pugnacious Virginia newspaper
editor and congressman, took his politics seriously. He had
fought duels over them and once nearly demanded satisfaction from
a House colleague who dared question the morality of slavery. Like
Edmund Ruffin, he could not abide the thought of his state accepting
Lincoln as president. In protest, he resigned from Congress the day
before the inauguration. Also like Ruffin, the young fire-eater was
drawn to Charleston by the standoff over Fort Sumter. Shortly before
the cannons fired, he addressed an adulatory crowd from the porch of
his hotel. They had come to lionize this hot-blooded darling of southern rights for showing his solidarity with them.

After the jubilant throng of well-wishers had serenaded him,
Pryor gave them the rhetorical fire and brimstone they expected. His
dark, brilliantined hair, combed straight back from a high forehead,
formed a long mane that he tossed back and forth as he denounced
Lincoln and heaped scorn on anyone who hoped for a pacific solution. He apologized for his state's recalcitrance in the cause of south-

ern independence. "Give the old lady time," he begged his audience with mock humility. "She cannot move with the agility of some of the younger daughters. She is a little rheumatic."[2]

SINCE EARLY APRIL, the unionist majority in the Virginia convention had faced a mounting deluge of rumors, intrigue, and menace. Pressure grew as petitions from radicals in the heavily slaveholding eastern counties demanded immediate secession. Paranoid accounts of suspicious northern characters being accosted on the railroads with forged papers had the same effect. Newspapers circulated bogus reports that black men had applied for government jobs in the North and intimated the same would happen in the South under Lincoln. Unionists feared to walk the streets of Richmond after dark because of roving bands of secessionist thugs. Slave traders with plenty of cash to burn were widely rumored to have paid them in gold to intimidate their opponents. Radicals openly threatened violence if the conservative leaders of the state did not submit to their wishes. "Bands of men are arming & organizing in this city, ready for revolution," warned a unionist delegate. Despite these ominous signs, the convention's unionist majority held firm.[3]

This was the climate when, on April 8, thanks to the courtesy of the legislature on its adjournment, the delegates moved from the bad acoustics of the Mechanics Institute up to the chaste, white, colonnaded Capitol. Designed by Thomas Jefferson, this first neoclassical building in all of America, a Roman temple on a hill, manifested the ideals of the republic in brick and stone. An austere marble statue of Washington, said to be the finest sculpture in the land, stood in the rotunda. Dominating the square outside, a more flamboyant equestrian figure also honored the father of the country, the founder of the Union that some delegates now strove to undo. Both sides invoked Washington's name, either to preserve his Union or to resist tyranny and fight a second revolution for freedom.

At Metropolitan Hall, a notably less refined institution two blocks from Capitol Square, a self-proclaimed Southern Rights assembly, also called the People's Spontaneous Convention, was scheduled to meet on April 16. It was hardly spontaneous. Newspapers had announced it weeks in advance. Attendance was by invitation only; notices had been sent only to known secessionists. Instead of blackface minstrel shows, the hall now resounded behind closed doors to cries for disunion.

Prominent among these voices was that of O. Jennings Wise, son of the former governor and reckless editor of the *Richmond Enquirer*. Sixteen months earlier, he had offered John Brown the consolation of a clergyman on the day of his execution. It must have annoyed him when Brown spurned the offer, saying he would rather be comforted by barefoot slave children than a Virginia minister.[4] Outside the hall, the younger Wise harangued sympathizers, who flooded the streets in braying, torchlit parades. Not for them the craven mummery of devotion to the Union.

Some of the men inside Metropolitan Hall advocated a more sinister agenda than noisy protest. The rumors whispered that they would take illegal measures. These were not just the idle fears of skittish unionists. The day before the attack on Fort Sumter, John Beauchamp Jones, a pro-southern editor who had fled to Richmond from his home in New Jersey, learned how the assembly intended to pressure the official convention. "If the other body persisted in its opposition to the popular will," he wrote with unseemly anticipation, "the most startling revolutionary measures would be adopted, involving, perhaps, arrests and executions."[5]

If exaggerated, this assessment nevertheless accurately gauged the undertone of dread felt by conservatives who feared that events might turn violent. Henry Wise cryptically told the excitable and credulous Jones not to leave town for a few days because the Spontaneous Convention "might do something." Wise's letters to likeminded men confirm his obsession with extralegal force in the cause of southern rights. More than a month before, one of Wise's conspirators admitted, "I am afraid we shall have a war amongst ourselves."[6]

Behind the bombast that inflamed delegates at Metropolitan Hall, a coterie of activists plotted the revolution that Wise hinted at to

Jones. They planned to arrest Governor Letcher and disrupt the official convention, using brute force if necessary. After overthrowing the state's elected authorities, they intended to set up a "provisional revolutionary government" and ally with the Confederacy.[7]

That was where matters stood when the authorized convention at the Capitol began its debate on the day Major Anderson agreed to surrender. At first, delegates were uncertain which side had started the fight in Charleston Harbor. Whichever it was, Robert Conrad, representing Frederick County in northern Virginia, told his colleagues that their neighbors in the western counties and the Shenandoah Valley, and even many in the east, "will not consent to have the Union dissolved either by Mr. Lincoln or the Southern disunionists, at their pleasure."[8]

Former congressman Jeremiah Morton, a delegate from Orange County, bordering the eastern slope of the Blue Ridge Mountains, ridiculed Conrad and his associates for their touching faith in Virginia's power to influence events. To him, their hopes for peace were pathetic. To him, the guns firing on Fort Sumter announced the incontrovertible fact of Confederate independence. These were the realities they faced. Despite them, he charged scornfully, some delegates acted "as if Virginia was the first power on earth; as if her voice was peace or war; as if it is only necessary for her to speak and the Confederate States must bow and the North must yield to her." The press took up Morton's charge. "What the Convention does, or what it leaves undone," railed the *Dispatch* in an echo of a familiar passage from the Book of Common Prayer, "is no longer a matter of the slightest importance . . . it can no longer do mischief or do good."[9]

Morton and the *Dispatch* were right. The majority of delegates did believe Virginia wielded disproportionate power in the affairs of the nation. It was easy to understand their state of mind. As the most populous slave state and the one to which the others looked for leadership, Virginia would indeed greatly influence events, though not in the expected manner. Many in the North shared that overestimation. The *New York Times*'s correspondent in Richmond asserted,

"Virginia is unquestionably the pivot on which the fate of the Union will turn."[10]

Initiative, however, had passed to the incendiaries of the lower South. Their quest for independence assured a confrontation with the North, no matter what Virginia did. Contrary to what all those observers who regurgitated the conventional wisdom thought, Virginia had ceased to be master of its destiny. The new southern republic and the newly steeled determination of Lincoln to uphold his inaugural oath cut away the ground from beneath unionists in the upper South.[11] They could not prevent a collision between determined antagonists. Yet from this eroded base they still could influence the outcome by affecting the time and course of dissolution, if not its fact.

The convention reassembled on Monday morning, April 15. After an invocation of divine favor, it turned to the report of the members sent to meet with Lincoln. Their return coincided with publication of his proclamation calling for volunteers, which instantly undermined the unionist faction. Its leaders still believed they could command a slight majority in favor of a border state conference instead of immediate secession. But their rapidly dissolving control of the convention, and the sudden shift in popular opinion outside the hall, put that hope in doubt. Still, no one could say what the assembly would decide. "The public mind of old Virginia is to-day boiling like one of the ocean's great whirlpools," observed a perplexed northern journalist sent to ferret out the delegates' intentions.[12]

Henry Wise demanded they go into secret session and hinted darkly at his reasons. He wanted to attack federal installations within the state before secession passed, but he dared not reveal his purpose before the convention agreed to secret proceedings. The tumult outside the Capitol began to seep inside. After a disturbance in the galleries, President Janney threatened to clear them at the next outburst.

Parliamentary decorum could barely restrain emotions in the debate over whether to go into secret session. Some denounced the proposal. They feared it would only stoke the fires of rumor. One delegate who was for it, sensing the gaping rift among his colleagues and between the sections of the state, pleaded, "In the name of God, let us have the family quarrel to ourselves, and not before the face of the world." Disgusted by debate, Wise demanded action: "Sir, for God's sake quit talking. . . . The time for action has now come." The number of times delegates invoked the Deity testified to the shortened fuses and bad tempers in the hall.[13]

The unionists' anguish was apparent to Joseph Churchill, who watched the proceedings with the clarity of an outsider. In Virginia, he was an exceptional rarity, indeed, a visiting Massachusetts Republican and a spectator to the debates. On the day word reached the delegates of Lincoln's proclamation, Churchill believed the unionist majority, "a patriotic & conservative body of men fighting unaided," would still have kept control of the Old Dominion were it not for the shocking news from Washington.[14] John Janney, too, was afraid the proclamation fatally undermined the majority. He now expected an ordinance of secession to pass, but he clung to the technicality that it would have to be approved by the voters before it could go into effect. "I have always believed," he sorrowfully wrote his wife, "that national sins are punished in this world and we have committed some of so deep a dye that I fear there is no escape for us."[15]

On Tuesday, April 16, the convention finally agreed to a closed session and heard from the three men it had sent to meet with Lincoln. William Ballard Preston, a former unionist who had gone over to the other side, spoke for "some hours." George Wythe Randolph of Richmond, a secessionist from the beginning, took much less time. The moment of decision had arrived, he insisted, and he flung into the teeth of his colleagues the portentous question: "You have got to fight—and the question is, which side will you fight with?"[16]

The sole staunch unionist of the trio, Alexander Hugh Holmes Stuart of Augusta County, faced a more difficult task. Devoted to both his state and his country, "Sandy" Stuart grieved at the direction Virginia appeared to be taking. All spring he had endured abuse from the lips of detractors. The radical press crowed that in debate Henry Wise had "pinned him to the wall, as a game-keeper would a

John Brown electrified the nation with his abortive attempt to spark a slave rebellion at Harpers Ferry, Virginia, in October 1859. *(Library of Congress)*

When asked by John Brown to join his attack on Harpers Ferry, Frederick Douglass declined, saying it would be like "going into a perfect steel-trap." *(Library of Congress)*

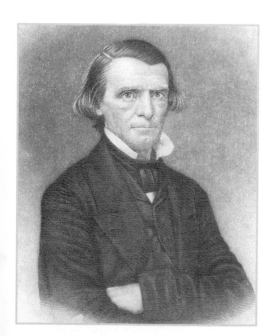

Erratic, conceited, mercurial, a figure of mesmeric intensity, Governor Henry Alexander Wise of Virginia recognized a sense of affinity with John Brown but hanged him anyway. No other delegate to the Virginia convention wielded more influence or bore more responsibility for the secession of the Old Dominion than Wise. *(Virginia Historical Society)*

When Abraham Lincoln took the oath of office on March 4, 1861, seven lower South states had seceded, but there was no war. The most populous slave states in the upper South remained nominally loyal to the national government. How would Lincoln interpret his oath to "faithfully execute" the office of president and defend the Constitution against rebellion? *(Library of Congress)*

Below: The unfinished dome of the Capitol, symbolizing the precarious state of the republic, towered over Lincoln's inauguration ceremony. *(Library of Congress)*

New York newspaper baron Horace Greeley described members of the Peace Conference in Washington as "political fossils, who would not have been again disinterred" were it not for the sectional crisis. *(Library of Congress)*

At his inauguration as provisional Confederate president on February 18, 1861, Jefferson Davis vowed that "our true policy is peace," but it could be purchased only by killing the Union, the outcome the conservative unionists of the upper South most dreaded. *(Library of Congress)*

A northern cartoon, quoting from a speech by Jefferson Davis, ridiculed him on the gallows saying, "O dear! I don't really want to secede this way— I want to be let alone." *(Library of Congress)*

In partial secrecy, and without explicit authorization from their states, delegates from the lower South states created the Confederate republic in less than two weeks in Montgomery, Alabama. *(Library of Congress)*

Chief Justice Roger Taney of Maryland administered the oath of office to Lincoln, though he feared the sixteenth president represented a grave threat to states' rights. *(Library of Congress)*

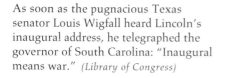

As soon as the pugnacious Texas senator Louis Wigfall heard Lincoln's inaugural address, he telegraphed the governor of South Carolina: "Inaugural means war." *(Library of Congress)*

The champion of northern Democrats, Senator Stephen A. Douglas of Illinois, the "Little Giant," thought the Old Dominion was the key to keeping the upper South loyal. "Save Virginia," he declared, "and we will save the Union." *(Library of Congress)*

Secretary of State William Henry Seward conducted secret discussions with upper South unionists throughout March to prevent further secession and urged Lincoln to avoid confrontation over Fort Sumter. *(Library of Congress)*

An associate justice of the U.S. Supreme Court, John Archibald Campbell thought he could help prevent war by serving as a go-between to establish unofficial channels of communication between the Lincoln government and the Confederate commissioners sent to Washington to negotiate separation. *(Library of Congress)*

A leader of northwestern Virginia, Waitman Thomas Willey represented a part of the Old Dominion that would not countenance secession. *(Library of Congress)*

A profane, crusty former army officer, Jubal Early denounced secessionists in the Virginia convention for trying to overthrow the Constitution. He nevertheless followed his state out of the Union and, shown here in his Confederate uniform, he never looked back. *(Library of Congress)*

Even after the artillery duel at Fort Sumter on April 12–13 in the harbor of Charleston, South Carolina, many upper South unionists thought they could keep their states from seceding. Lincoln's call for volunteers on April 15 fatally undermined them. *(Library of Congress)*

The tiny garrison at Fort Sumter posed problems for both Davis and Lincoln. It represented a symbolic threat to Confederate sovereignty, and its rapidly dwindling food supply forced Washington to choose between resupply and evacuation. *(Library of Congress)*

At Fort Sumter, Major Robert Anderson said waiting for his garrison to be attacked reminded him of "a sheep tied watching the butcher sharpening the knife to cut his throat." *(Library of Congress)*

A former sailor, Gustavus Fox captured Lincoln's attention with an intriguing plan for sending supplies to relieve the garrison at Fort Sumter. *(Library of Congress)*

A moderate unionist, Governor John Letcher of Virginia endured the taunts and threats of radical secessionists all spring. But then he too endorsed disunion and denounced Lincoln for his proclamation calling for volunteers to put down rebellion in the Deep South. *(Library of Congress)*

The debates of the Virginia convention reached their tempestuous climax a week after the delegates moved into Thomas Jefferson's neoclassical Capitol in Richmond on April 8, after the state legislature adjourned. *(Library of Congress)*

Typical of many moderate upper South unionists, William Ballard Preston shifted during spring 1861 from tentative support for the Union to reluctant endorsement of secession. The former congressman proposed the ordinance of secession to the Virginia convention on April 17. *(Library of Congress)*

The sole staunch unionist among the Virginia delegation sent to see Lincoln on the eve of secession, Alexander H. H. "Sandy" Stuart grieved at the direction his state was headed after the president's call for volunteers to put down rebellion. *(Library of Congress)*

Silhouetted in the darkness against blazing fires at the Harpers Ferry arsenal, townspeople lost no time in carting off military equipment after the U.S. garrison retreated. *(Library of Congress)*

At the confluence of the Shenandoah and Potomac rivers, Harpers Ferry sprang to notoriety during John Brown's raid in 1859 and again when militiamen captured the town the day after Virginia's convention passed the ordinance of secession. *(Library of Congress)*

The first blood of the Civil War to be shed in anger was spilled on April 19 in Baltimore, Maryland, in the Pratt Street Riot. *(Library of Congress)*

The timid unionist governor of Maryland, Thomas Hicks, seemed to satisfy no one, neither the Lincoln administration nor Maryland secessionists, as he tried to steer a course to keep his state from exploding. *(Library of Congress)*

Clara Barton joined the anxious throng of Washingtonians that greeted the train bearing Massachusetts soldiers just after they had battled secessionists in the streets of Baltimore. *(Library of Congress)*

The grizzled superintendent of the Washington Navy Yard, Marylander Franklin Buchanan, resigned his commission when his state seemed about to leave the Union. When he asked to be reinstated after Maryland did not secede, the navy struck him from its rolls, and Buchanan joined the Confederate navy. *(Library of Congress)*

Quarrelsome, vain, and overweight, but still possessing a keen mind, General Winfield Scott, the hero of the Mexican War, commanded the defenses of Washington in the days when residents feared attack by hostile secessionist neighbors in Virginia and Maryland. *(Library of Congress)*

If secessionists overwhelmed the District of Columbia, the Lincoln administration planned to make its last stand at the massive stone Treasury building. *(Library of Congress)*

These jaunty Pennsylvania troops were among the thousands who eventually answered Lincoln's call on April 15 for volunteers to defend the capital and suppress the Confederate revolt. *(Library of Congress)*

Below: Without exaggeration, New York newspapers called the monster patriotic rally in Union Square on April 20 in support of the Lincoln government's war effort the largest gathering that had ever taken place in North America. *(Library of Congress)*

Above: Though the U.S. Navy's demolition effort on April 21 produced dramatic pictures of ruin at the Gosport Navy Yard, the Confederates salvaged a formidable stock of munitions and repairable capital ships. *(Library of Congress)*

Secretary of the Navy Gideon Welles inherited a dispirited service, with many vessels unfit for duty and many southern officers preparing to resign. He convinced Lincoln to attempt the defense, and if that was not possible, the destruction, of the Gosport Navy Yard near Norfolk, Virginia. *(Library of Congress)*

Unable to rescue any of the ships at the Gosport Navy Yard that the feeble, intimidated superintendent had scuttled, the navy burned them at their moorings. Here the USS *Pennsylvania* lights up the predawn darkness as fire consumes it. *(Library of Congress)*

Militia general Benjamin Franklin Butler commanded the northern volunteers who relieved Washington by way of Annapolis after the capital had been cut off from the outside world for a week in April. With hooded eyes, the balding, jowly Massachusetts attorney looked the part of the corrupt official, a reputation that dogged his later military career. *(Library of Congress)*

weasel." Stuart, they sneered, liked nothing better than "to wriggle upon his belly into Lincoln's presence."[17]

Stuart told his colleagues that he considered the president's response to the delegation provocative and unsatisfactory. But he begged them to take counsel with the other states of the border and not rush into the arms of the Confederacy. Secession would only bring war to Virginia. "Yes, sir, you bring it home to your own fair cities and families."[18] It meant more, he accurately predicted: "Secession is not only war, but it is emancipation; it is bankruptcy; it is repudiation; it is widespread ruin to our people." It meant something worse in his mind than even disruption of the Union—it meant the dissolution of the Old Dominion. For by then, everyone in the convention believed the northwestern counties would refuse to follow the eastern ones out of the Union.[19] For good reason, they trembled for the future of their state.

Preston then offered the ordinance of secession. With their majority collapsing, many unionists believed Lincoln's action impelled them to side with the lower South. But they made one last stand in favor of consultation with Virginia's neighbors instead of outright disunion. Robert Eden Scott, an eloquent attorney from Fauquier County in northern Virginia, who would be killed two years later by northern deserters, proposed a statewide referendum in place of Preston's motion for secession. The referendum would give voters a choice— either immediate secession or conferring with the other border states.

The referendum offered no stout endorsement of the United States of America. The choice was between secession now and coordinated action, possibly including secession, in concert with neighboring states later. Scott, unfairly characterized by his opponents as a political invertebrate, empty of substance, refuted the charge that civil war already existed. They still had a choice. The fighting had been contained to Fort Sumter. The border states had unanimously rejected Lincoln's call for their militias. Solidarity with them would provide a buffer between the Confederacy and the North. Such a barrier could succeed only if they stuck together. They could do so if they approved Scott's substitute for Preston's ordinance and the people then agreed to confer with their neighbors. Scott called for a consultative convention of upper South slave states to meet at Frankfort, Kentucky, on May 27.[20]

In the debate that followed, Jubal Early denounced secession. "I have felt," he warned, "as if a great crime was about [to be] perpetrated against the cause of liberty and civilization." It would bring "war as this country has never seen, or, until recently, has never dreamed of." Samuel Staples, from Patrick County in the mountainous southwest, had voted against secession on April 4. But he represented the hemorrhage of conservative opinion in the past two weeks. It was the Lincoln government, he argued, that had deceived the people: "That Administration has 'let slip the dogs of war.'"[21]

The convention adjourned for the night. It took up debate again on the morning of April 17 with a reading of Governor Letcher's telegram rejecting Lincoln's call for volunteers. Outside the hall, demonstrators could not believe the convention still had not voted to leave the Union. That knowledge drove them mad with indignation. What would it take to force Virginia into the Confederacy? Inside, delegates' remarks reflected the general expectation that Scott's amendment would fail, clearing the way for Preston's ordinance. One week before, they were all completely calm, one of them rued, "and now we all are upon the very brink of revolution."[22]

The air in the hall was suffused with hatred, hatred of the North and hatred of their fellow Virginians who voiced a contrary opinion. Against sulfurous denunciations of northern perfidy, calls for moderation had no effect. A delegate said, "I feel to day more like being in the midst of a funeral cortege, than being in a Convention. . . . I feel that we are now about to destroy this great nation, which was the hope of the oppressed."[23]

After this supercharged debate, Scott's motion lost, 64 to 77. A switch of seven votes would have altered the state's course dramatically and, in consequence, the nation's. If the unionist majority had held, it would have set Virginia on a course for a referendum rather than immediate secession. In the intervening weeks before the vote, passions might have cooled, and even if they did not, the unionists would have taken heart from defeating the radicals. Other upper South states, especially North Carolina, Tennessee, and Maryland, would have been given a strong example for restraint. The delay before the referendum could take place would have given the upper South several more weeks of breathing space.

Moreover, if the electorate had endorsed Scott's convention of border slave states, they would have given life to that great hope of upper South unionists, consultation among the states caught in the midst of the national nightmare. If events had taken that turn, the option for a middle way—some alternative to the Confederacy and the North—might have been given a chance and in retrospect not seem the chimera that it did when Scott's motion failed.

The vote on the motion, however, showed the surging power of the disunionists, once a scorned minority, and it paved the way for the ordinance of secession.

Long mistrusted on all sides, gaunt, intense, and mercurial, Henry Wise craved vindication. He would not be denied. Though he looked prematurely old and was bedeviled by a hacking cough, a renewed sense of purpose belied his mocking self-description as a has-been. Now it was as though his eyes were lit by the demonic political fires that possessed him. The ordinance of secession would pass. Everyone in the hall now knew that. But Wise meant to smash any lingering opposition. Above all, he meant to initiate military action even before the people ratified the ordinance by referendum.

He bided his time and allowed his colleagues to express their opinions. When he spoke, it was only briefly, but it made an impression no one in the hall would ever forget. As he rose to speak, his sense of the dramatic was unimpaired, for he reached into his coat and pulled out a large pistol. With a menacing flourish, he placed it before him for all to see. They could also see that he was highly agitated. "With glaring eyes and bated breath," an opponent recalled, the former governor threatened the assembled leaders of the state "in the most violent and denunciatory manner."[24]

Though the jejune official records say nothing of Wise's demeanor and drain his voice of emotion, the power of his words shines through.

"His features were as sharp and rigid as bronze," an eyewitness reported. "His hair stood off from his head, as if charged with electricity." Wise revealed the plot to attack the federal presence on Virginia soil. Then, with a deliberate gesture, he took out his pocket watch—making it as much a symbol of intimidation as the gun—and announced that "blood will be flowing at Harper's Ferry before night." With a drumbeat of repetitive, declarative sentences, he outlined one by one the military plans unfolding for capturing the arsenal in northern Virginia and the navy yard near Norfolk.[25]

These extralegal steps were necessary, he insisted, because Governor Letcher refused to approve action even though war menaced the state. This was not an idle threat, he assured his colleagues. The night before, by the light of gas lamps in his hotel room, he and others had perfected their plans, sending telegrams to dispatch militia companies and marshal the railcars to transport them. The die was cast, the time for words at an end. Why, he demanded of the delegates, did they continue to talk the issue to death? "We are here indulging in foolish debates," he shouted, "the only result of which must be delay, and, perhaps, ruin."[26]

When John Baldwin rose to denounce the revolutionary violence Wise meant to unleash, the former governor impugned his loyalty to the state. With the riptide of sentiment in the hall now surging in his favor, Wise seized the moment to crush his opponent. Baldwin did not have the temperament to repay Wise's savagery in kind. He ended his remarks with sorrowing, elegiac resignation. "The future," he said, "looks dark—dark and dreary." If Baldwin halfheartedly tried to stand up to Wise, others did not attempt even that and literally slumped in dismay. George Summers, the unionist floor leader who had been in secret communication with Seward, was devastated. Under Wise's verbal assault, an eyewitness recalled, the stalwart Summers looked "white and pale as the wall near him."[27] Sometimes brashness speaks with golden words while prudence is tongue-tied.

With this brief, brutal, dazzling show of oratory, which to the ears of many delegates exceeded any speech he had given as governor, Wise mesmerized his colleagues, transfixing them on the sharp points of his words. He was, in the bitter words of a unionist delegate, a "Red Republican . . . who misleads the rash, and blinds the reckless."[28]

Shortly before the fateful vote, the dignified president, John Janney, stepped down from the chair for a moment to speak as an individual delegate. He invoked historical precedents to illustrate the horrors that war would visit upon Virginia. The Potomac River would become the American Rhine, its banks "saturated with human blood," just as in Europe. He warned his colleagues that their decisions were "pregnant with the issue of human freedom all over the globe." He continued, "I believe that if [the United States] fails there is no hope left for representative government and liberty regulated by law. I believe that the dark night of universal despotism will settle down over the whole globe, upon the failure of this great experiment of ours."[29]

When everyone who wished to speak had done so, Wise called for the vote. The convention approved Virginia's secession, 88 to 55. It would become official when the electorate approved it in the required but perfunctory referendum on May 23.

The delegates thus exercised the power they believed they possessed to undo the state's adoption of the federal Constitution. Even after the ordinance passed, rancorous argument continued between Wise and Baldwin, who maintained that secession was not legal until the voters approved it. He bitterly opposed the former governor's attempt, in his words, to raise expediency above the Constitution. In Wise's grim, pragmatic calculus, however, extraordinary times demanded commensurate measures. He had no patience for Baldwin's conservative constitutional niceties, "a mere stickling upon a point between tweedledum and tweedledee."[30]

Jubal Early had fought the secessionists all the way, but now he bowed to practical reality. A straightforward country lawyer who delighted in acknowledging that he lacked conventional charm, Early agreed with Baldwin's constitutional principles. Even now he poured scorn on the People's Spontaneous Convention for trying to intimidate the regular convention. Even though he accepted the fact of secession, he gave a blunt, prescient warning: "I would call upon gentlemen to recollect, that it often happens that those who begin a revolution do not end it."[31] He conceded, however, that with war imminent, Virginia could not afford to wait for the electorate's approval in late May before taking active measures of defense, even of preemptive attack. Though bent by arthritis, the prematurely aged former army officer would now devote his full energy to fighting the Union he had struggled so hard to save. He never looked back.

The hopes of secessionists were realized: the upper South was beginning to crack. The radicals were proven right. When forced to choose between sections, upper South unionism largely vanished overnight, to be replaced by solidarity with the Confederacy. The ambiguities of the Constitution bore palpable and lamentable fruit. The fundamental law of the nation, by its silence on a crucial point, allowed for different interpretations of the Union and for men who cherished it to believe they could leave it.[32]

The Civil War began without the upper South, but its decisions determined the scope, locus, and intensity of the struggle. If the coup considered by extreme Virginia secessionists had taken place, the outcome might have been radically different. It might just have been possible that unionist sentiment would have been emboldened in the face of extralegal violence. And if the pro-Confederates overreached in their proposed coup, they might have given Lincoln an opportunity to appeal to more conservative Virginians with a quite different call for volunteers, one to defend their own state against revolutionaries. Perhaps, then, Virginia would not have seceded or would have split apart differently from the way it ultimately did. Those different outcomes in that one state would have given the Confederacy a different northern border and produced a vastly different war for the Union.[33]

The mirage of a border state confederacy entranced upper South unionists throughout the crisis, right up to the Virginia vote and far beyond. It may have been delusional for them to expect they could fashion a middle way between the extremes of the cotton republic and the North. But it was delusional only in retrospect. At the time, it seemed perfectly plausible to reasonable men. All the delegates in the convention sensed that northwestern Virginia would never leave the Union. They suspected that eastern Virginia was about to secede, whatever the convention did. They could see that the Shenandoah Valley, caught between these extremes, was divided. Even if Virginia and the rest of the upper South had managed only what many unionists wanted—to meet and decide collective action, even if that action eventually resulted in collective secession—the course of events would have been vastly different. Precisely how Virginia joined or refused to join the Confederacy would influence the timing and even the location of the strife to come.

At Metropolitan Hall, delegates to the irregular People's Spontaneous Convention impatiently awaited word about the vote up the hill at the Capitol. Most of them were ready to overthrow the official convention if it did not decide as they wished. The wave of emotion generated by their fears that the southern way of life was under attack swept them up in righteous outrage. Though the result of the vote on the ordinance was supposed to be kept secret, the instant it passed, Lt. Gov. Robert Latané Montague rushed down the steep path through Capitol Square to spread the word to the other convention.

A few minutes later, Henry Wise arrived in triumph at Metropolitan Hall to prolonged applause and shouts of exultation. He entered arm in arm with former president John Tyler, an ardent secessionist, and strode "down the center aisle amid a din of cheers, while every member rose to his feet." When the huzzahs subsided, the feeble, exhausted former president spoke, though only briefly. For he was merely the conjurer's assistant and quickly yielded the floor to Wise. The former governor spoke no longer than Tyler, but in the effusive words of an admirer, he "electrified the assembly by a burst of eloquence, perhaps never surpassed by mortal orator." During the pauses in his remarks, the chamber was so silent that delegates could hear the slightest breathing. Tears filled the eyes of many. What Wise desired had come to pass. The time of deliberation, doubt, contemplation, and reason had passed. The same eyewitness wrote, "It was now Independence or Death."[34]

CHAPTER 10

JOHN BROWN IN GRAY

Harpers Ferry, April 17 to 18

Events transpire so rapidly now that it is useless to speculate two days ahead.

—Alexander Stephens, April 17[1]

Ever since Lincoln's proclamation commanded the headlines on April 15, jittery Washingtonians feared for their safety. Some said rabid secessionists with murderous intent were about to descend from the surrounding Virginia and Maryland countryside. Calmer residents discounted these tales. All the same, the government's friends would rest easier when trains brought in enough soldiers to garrison the District of Columbia adequately. Thanks to quirks of geography and the state of the railroad industry, only a single, vulnerable ribbon of track, operated by the Baltimore & Ohio, connected the capital to the outside world in 1861. From the depot at the intersection of New Jersey Avenue and C Street, near the site where Union Station would later be built, the line ran northeast and forked at the Relay House Junction just outside Baltimore. One short branch continued on into that city, where travelers could make a connection to the middle Atlantic and New England states. The other branch ran west. It threaded the green mountain valleys of the Appalachians in a marvel of modern engineering and eventually reached the Midwest.

The news on Thursday, April 18, frayed nerves already throbbing from a week of alarm and the sinking feeling that war and all its concomitant horrors was about to envelop the country. For on that day, unarmed Pennsylvania militiamen arriving in Washington spoke of "taunts and provocations heaped upon them by the secessionist rowdies" as they marched through Baltimore to change from one train station to another.[2] On the next morning, April 19, came news of a greater threat on the main B&O line to the west. Once again, as it had done eighteen months before, with menace and foreboding Harpers Ferry exploded into the capital's consciousness.

WHILE HENRY WISE harangued delegates behind closed doors at the Virginia convention, his radical coadjutors outside the hall were not idle. In the last days before disunion triumphed in Richmond, this clique of strident southern rights men plotted to overthrow the state government and, in the words of a delegate, "break up the Convention, by violence."[3] The continued reluctance of Virginia to join the Confederacy, even after Fort Sumter, embarrassed and infuriated them. Just as they were about to act, Lincoln stunned them with his call for volunteers. Less extreme secessionists, queasy about spilling southern blood, cautioned the plotters to delay. If the president's proclamation shifted enough sentiment in the convention their way, they might not need to risk a coup that could alienate more conservative Virginians.

The conspirators agreed to defer their putsch. Instead of overthrowing Gov. John Letcher, however, on April 16 Wise and his friends badgered him to take action as though a state of war existed between Virginia and the national government. He should call out the militia and seize the navy yard near Norfolk and the federal arsenal at Harpers Ferry, two of the most vital military installations on the East Coast. It may have been only a coincidence that the leading lights among the conspirators, like Wise, had all watched John Brown hang by the neck until he was dead. But the fact that they had been eyewitnesses meant that they had seen firsthand the strategic importance of the arsenal he attacked. Perhaps that shared experience lay behind their desire to take violent, preemptive steps. Whatever their motivation, in the eyes of the federal government, their attempt to seize Harpers Ferry would be no less treasonous than Brown's had been.[4]

Letcher resisted. The convention had not yet approved secession or authorized the use of deadly force. In any case, the terms under which the convention sat dictated that the electorate must approve any decision for it to be binding. Unwilling to brook opposition, and utterly dismissive of constitutional propriety, Wise and his friends acted. They called out sympathetic militia companies in the Shenandoah Valley and found railroad executives willing to transport them north to capture the arsenal. If the governor and the convention would not bend to their will, they intended to commit a private act of war against the United States government in order to stampede their fellow Virginians and rally them to the banner of secession.

A month before, such rash plans would have horrified the conservative majority in the state. But in the intervening time, the political climate had changed swiftly, irreparably. Lacking the foresight of prophecy, unionist leaders reasonably believed in early April that they controlled events in their state. Only a few days later, however, by the middle of the month that expectation precariously rested more on illusion than fact. They could dismiss as a mere claque the secessionist ruffians who prowled the streets of downtown Richmond. But they only fooled themselves by ignoring reality. And that reality was the incontrovertible fact that in the countryside throughout Virginia east of the mountains, the white populace increasingly embraced secession not just as an abstract right but, especially after Lincoln's proclamation, as a practical duty and necessity.

Northern journalists reporting on the convention could sense the sea change. "Secession is a foregone conclusion," one of them wrote for his New York readers on the day of the vote. "Men, mostly young men, with slick, glazed caps and juvenile attempts at moustaches, dashing up and down, and fairly dancing for joy," spread rumors of imminent attacks on federal installations. However condescending, the reporter's words nevertheless captured the febrile excitement of young Virginians over the prospect of joining the Confederacy. More important, the willingness of senior militia leaders and other community officials to take matters into their own hands demonstrated how far beyond mere political bombast the secessionist movement had come. Wise may have been unpredictable, but he was making no idle threat when he promised that blood would flow at Harpers Ferry.[5]

Though Union sentiment remained strong in the Shenandoah Valley, the contrary tide sweeping eastern Virginia rolled over the Blue Ridge and into the valley. Even Staunton, the principal town of Augusta County, which sent unionist stalwarts John Baldwin and Alexander Stuart to the convention, began to shift. "Lincoln's Proclamation settled the matter," one observer there asserted with flat finality. The Augusta volunteer militia responded to Wise's conspirators and made ready to entrain for Harpers Ferry. They did so even as Baldwin and Stuart pleaded in the convention for restraint and cooperation with the other upper South states rather than take irrevocable steps that might bring war to Virginia.[6]

The governor finally bowed to pressure. On the morning the convention voted to secede, though hours before the actual vote, he endorsed the military action that Wise's conspiracy had already put into play. "You are to go to Harpers Ferry," Letcher cryptically telegraphed a militia officer who was in on the plot.[7] The unstated purpose was to make war on the federal government. Once he accepted the inevitability of secession, the no longer timid governor even made an appearance at the People's Spontaneous Convention the night the ordinance passed. There he acknowledged cheers from "the very men who, two days before, would gladly have witnessed his execution."[8]

By the evening of April 17, though the convention's vote to secede was still a secret, Augusta militiamen boarded a train for Harpers Ferry in the midst of a communal celebration. Events like it were about to take place in communities throughout the fracturing nation. It was an emotional scene never to be forgotten, an observer remarked in words soon to be echoed by chroniclers in hundreds of towns. Before the train pulled out with two volunteer companies, the local Baptist and Methodist ministers led prayers for their safety. Soon, men of the cloth of all denominations, on both sides and in every state, would beseech God in similar gatherings for protection and for victory and in many cases for divine punishment to be rained down on the evil men who opposed them. Militia officers, bursting with pride, addressed the ardent throng of their Staunton neighbors and vowed "that they and their men would do or die."[9]

The town of Harpers Ferry perched on the steep slopes of the mountain that rose up sharply from the point where the Shenandoah and Potomac rivers flowed together, a location that Thomas Jefferson had hyperbolically praised as one of the most sublime in North America. There, at the confluence of the rivers on the border between Virginia and Maryland, the United States government had been fabricating weapons for its army for sixty years. The armory workshops and the arsenal to store the firearms numbered in all more than two dozen buildings strung along the narrow strip of riverfront land below the town. Three hundred skilled craftsmen turned out a greater output of weaponry there than at any other southern arms manufactory.

The B&O Railroad ran along the Potomac and crossed it at the point where the Shenandoah flowed into it. The tracks offered ideal access to the armory's factories. A spur that veered off toward Winchester opened up the granary of the Shenandoah Valley to eastern markets. Bearing coal and flour, arms and passengers, the B&O gave tiny, mountain-bound Harpers Ferry access to the wide world beyond.[10]

Alfred Barbour, a lawyer and former state legislator, had been appointed armory superintendent ten months before John Brown's raid. More recently, he had won election as a unionist delegate to the Virginia convention. A month earlier, he had told William Cabell Rives that his impassioned plea for the Peace Conference compromise was the ablest speech he had "ever heard from mortal man."[11] Barbour voted against secession on April 4. But he, like so many, changed his outlook in two weeks' time and would not have voiced the same opinion at the crucial vote on April 17, if he had been present.

As it was, he missed that decisive moment because he was with Wise's conspirators. He hurried back to Harpers Ferry to persuade armory workers to stay on the job when the state took possession. Fatigued by his overnight journey from Richmond, and by one account more drunk than sober, he botched his appeal to the artisans. With the armory workforce and the town politically divided, he managed only to inflame matters. Fistfights broke out. Rioters smashed up shops and bars, nearly wrecking Harpers Ferry.[12]

In the meantime, the militia companies from Augusta County had almost reached their objective. Though these valley men were prepared to take action before receiving the governor's blessing, farmers in the countryside they passed through were not so sure the time had come for a resort to violence. "The people generally received us very coldly," one of their officers admitted candidly afterward. At Charles Town, the county seat six miles from Harpers Ferry, Col. William Allen hastily assembled the local militia regiment on command from Richmond. Given the short notice and doubts about the legality of their orders to seize the arsenal, some men were understandably nervous.[13]

It helped when they learned that the convention had finally endorsed secession and Governor Letcher had approved their action. But the electorate would not vote on the ordinance until late May, and that gave pause to some of them. Even so, they stifled their reservations and marched toward Harpers Ferry. One officer who had no doubts feverishly cabled Henry Wise in the mistaken belief that the U.S. Army was reinforcing the arsenal: "Send on the Richmond regiment immediately & come yourself. We intend to fight now if we all perish."[14]

Lt. Roger Jones commanded forty-two U.S. soldiers guarding the arsenal and armory. Thirty-one years old, he had passed most of the decade since graduating from West Point fighting Indians on the Texas frontier. On the day of Lincoln's proclamation, he declined an offer of reinforcements from Washington. Two days later, as he listened with mounting alarm to Barbour harangue the armory's civilian workers, however ineptly, Jones knew he had made the wrong decision.[15] Brawling in the streets between secessionists and unionists heightened his dread of being overrun. When he heard that the county militia had mustered at Charles Town and was headed his way, he posted guards on the roads leading into town. At about the same hour that day, beyond the western terminus of the B&O, the governor of Ohio nervously cabled Washington, "We hope Harper's Ferry is safe."[16]

Each side feared its opponent intended a violent confrontation. Colonel Allen's militiamen hesitated in their advance when they encountered Jones's pickets outside town. They assumed most of the armory workers had joined the U.S. soldiers. If so, the defenders would have almost as many men as they did—and more than enough modern guns, too. Jones knew otherwise. Only several dozen workmen joined his ranks. He expected only one outcome if the reports were true about the size of the force approaching him.

Jones sent a last, desperate telegram to army headquarters in Washington about 9:00 p.m. on April 18. In it, he told his superiors about the militia gathering in the surrounding countryside. The lieutenant anticipated an assault that night and vowed "to *destroy* what I cannot defend."[17] Only massive, nonexistent reinforcements could ensure control of the arsenal. He was on his own. Just as he finished composing the message, a picket rushed in to report the approach of the hostile militia.

In fact, the nervous Colonel Allen still assumed that the townspeople supported Jones. Instead of attacking, he sent a messenger under a flag of truce to find out the lay of the land. The man also carried a note from Allen's superior officer commanding Jones in the name of Virginia to surrender the armory.[18] It was dark now, and the colonel did not want to make a misstep in assaulting a federal installation. While Allen hesitated, Jones ordered his men to carry out their plans for demolition. They set fire to two arsenal buildings to destroy the thousands of boxed small arms stored there. They next lit fuses to burn the armory workshops.

Once the fires were set, Jones marched his men to the bridge over the Potomac River, which John Brown had crossed when he had entered the town a year and a half before. A few miles beyond, across the narrow Maryland panhandle, lay Pennsylvania and safety. The lieutenant estimated that within three minutes of setting the torch, all the buildings were alight. An angry crowd of armed townspeople followed the soldiers part of the way across the bridge, but they relented when Jones drew up his men in a skirmish line and prepared to fire.[19]

As the militia officers conferred outside town on their next step, the sky lit up with a tremendous flash. It turned the river valley into daytime. Seconds later, the sound echoed against the mountainsides like a summer thunderclap as it rumbled toward them. Mounted militiamen galloped forward to reconnoiter. They found the armory buildings on fire. By the time they reached town, Jones and his soldiers had made good their escape across the Potomac bridge. Silhouetted in the darkness against blazing fires, townspeople lost no time in carting off guns and other military equipment. An eyewitness lamented the consequences and feared for the future of the nation with a forlorn query: "Brethren, what has forced this fatal necessity upon us?"[20]

After a thirty-mile forced march overnight and then a short train ride, by the next afternoon Jones's exhausted command, minus two deserters, reached Carlisle Barracks, Pennsylvania. The lieutenant telegraphed Washington to say, correctly, that he had destroyed the arsenal. A grateful president sent his personal thanks. Lincoln might have been less appreciative when he learned a few days later that Jones had overestimated the damage. His explosive charges blew out factory windows and showered broken glass over the town but did not ignite the fires he wanted. In fact, only three of the many workshops in the armory complex burned.[21]

The Virginians salvaged the machinery for making weapons and within days began shipping it south to work for the Confederacy. The more proximate danger to Washington, however, was implicit in Jones's telegram: the B&O line to the west was now in the hands of a hostile force. Still euphoric from their success, the more aggressive among the Virginians urged greater action. With the sounds of railcars squealing in his ears as the armory machinery was hauled off, one of the Virginians declared, "Nothing can save us from a long and bloody civil war, but the prompt seizure of the Fedl. Capital."[22]

———

THE DAY AFTER militiamen occupied Harpers Ferry, the tension pent up in the Virginia capital after weeks of intrigue finally exploded. Secessionists had planned a mass parade to celebrate the fall of Fort Sumter as a means of pressuring the convention. They put it off temporarily when a vote on disunion seemed likely. Now, two days after the ordinance passed, a great torchlight procession filled the streets of Richmond with revelers glorifying Confederate victory, both more distantly at Fort Sumter and right at home with Virginia's decision. Now they could extol triumph at Harpers Ferry, too.

Ten thousand men and boys, a quarter of the city's population, streamed clamoring through the center of town after sundown, in "a mile-long river of fire." They were accompanied by brass bands and were saluted all along their route by residents who lit candles in their windows. The constant report of firecrackers and skyrockets created a spectacle the city had never before witnessed. One of the many lighted signs read: "Resistance to Tyranny is Obedience to God." It was the largest and most demonstrative parade in the city's hundred-year history, a surging mass that "lighted up with its lurid glare every object with almost the brightness of day." A secessionist approvingly described the events in his diary, but on the subject of all those cannons being fired up on Capitol Hill, he archly observed, "I think they had better save the powder, etc. At night. We have a gay illumination. This too is wrong. We had better save the candles."[23]

The residents could not know it, but four years later, before dawn on another April day, even greater pyrotechnics from exploding munitions and fires in the business district would punctuate the end of Confederate Richmond. The Roman candles and bonfires of 1861 to mark its beginning, however, were innocent enough tokens of joy. "Nothing that ever transpired here has served to infuse so much enthusiasm in the people of all classes, conditions and colors," cried the *Richmond Dispatch*.[24]

The writer exaggerated in assuming such unanimity, especially among people of color. But the excitement of the moment was real enough. It heralded the quest for solidarity that communities North and South would strive for from that point forward, even those in the border states that had been of painfully divided minds. That process began the day the ordinance passed, though unionists, still in shock, and instantly reduced to mere wraiths of their former strength, might not have realized it.

Among the disoriented was Robert Young Conrad, a fifty-six-year-old devout Presbyterian lawyer and father of nine from Frederick County, near the northern border of Virginia, not far from Harpers Ferry. He had sought the chairmanship of the convention's federal relations committee back in February to urge reconciliation and peace. A man of dreamy eyes and unkempt hair, he had a sharp mind and abundant faith in the capacity of ordinary Americans of all sections to overcome the partisans of disunion. Through a torrent of letters to his politically astute wife, Elizabeth, he recorded the agitated course of the convention. Conrad rose with the sun every morning and walked four miles before breakfast to relieve tension and maintain stamina for the day ahead. He did not mind the grueling schedule, where debates sometimes lasted fourteen hours, and jokingly compared himself to a drone toiling in a Dickensian factory. The threat of revolutionary action by secessionists, even physical violence, did not intimidate him.[25]

Neither he nor others like him could hold back the surge of emotion that swept over the convention. Conrad grieved at "the now near prospect of civil, fratricidal war in our country, so young, so prosperous, the pride of our people, the hope of the world." With Lincoln's call for volunteers, however, he reached the limits of his unionism, for he denounced the proclamation as an illegitimate assault on the states. In the wake of secession, Conrad moved as if in a trance. A feeling of impotence depressed him. He had to face the facts, though. Not only had opinion in much of the upper South turned toward the Confederacy, but also the hostility of ordinary northerners toward the South was now undeniable. "I feel without the least power," he regretted, "to do any thing to avert the calamity of civil war." Though he voted against secession, he resigned himself to accept Virginia's separation from the Union if the electorate endorsed it. That did not prevent him from warning his son to remain at home and "take no part" in the attack on neighboring Harpers Ferry.[26]

On the night of April 19, Conrad walked bemused through the streets of Richmond, observing the spectacle of fireworks and cheers for the Confederacy. He shook his head at the frivolity. After enduring weeks of acrimony in the convention, he witnessed his world finally collapse, replaced by this surreal revelry. To his mind, it celebrated nothing less than a coming apocalypse. The setting jarred with his morose frame of mind. In the course of his walk, he came upon one skeptic who offered the heretical thought that such exuberance would be more appropriate if it cheered peace and not war. It was, Conrad ruefully observed, "the only echo I heard to my own feelings."[27]

CHAPTER 11

BURNING BRIDGES

Baltimore, April 17 to 19

Shall Maryland, conservative, Union-loving, patriotic Maryland . . . be made the battle ground of contending sections? That is the Great Question.

—*Baltimore American*, April 18

On the day before Lieutenant Jones abandoned Harpers Ferry, two telegrams that arrived in Washington presaged the next explosive episode in America's embrace of fratricide. They were but two among many that the harried secretary of war, Simon Cameron, fielded on April 17 in the wake of Lincoln's proclamation. It was a hectic day for the skittish and confused secretary, a man whose thin, sharp-featured face bore a constant look of worry. Dogged by a reputation for graft in Pennsylvania politics—an opponent once called him the "very incarnation of corruption"—he owed his post to a cabinet-balancing compromise. Despite his talent for juggling lucrative business deals, Cameron was proving to be an inept manager at the War Department.[1]

The first of the premonitory cables came from Maryland, the second from Massachusetts. Thomas Hicks, the governor of Maryland, sought reassurance about mustering his militia regiments. Could the government guarantee that they would not serve outside their state or the District of Columbia? A timid unionist, Hicks feared what the divided sentiments of loyal, slaveholding, anxious Maryland might spark. He could endorse sending troops to guard public buildings in Washington. But he dreaded the proclamation's explicit goal of putting down rebellion in the seceded states.

When he read Hicks's request, Cameron was about to be overwhelmed by the demands that mobilization would place on his antiquated bureau and his meager talents. For a moment, though, he must have taken heart from the second telegram, sent from Gov. John Andrew of Massachusetts. It promised that one regiment of volunteers would board a train for Washington immediately. Others would soon follow. Here was a state leader without the Marylander's qualms. To reach the capital, though, the Bay State volunteers would have to pass through Thomas Hicks's Maryland.[2]

AT THE HEAD of the Chesapeake Bay, forty-five miles north of Washington, Baltimore was the northernmost city in the slave states and the largest, with a population well over two hundred thousand. It easily topped New Orleans, the largest Confederate city, and it dwarfed Washington and Richmond by a factor of three or more. A bustling port and rail links north and west drew an expanding hinterland under Baltimore's economic sway.

More than the large element of free blacks, it was Baltimore's even greater numbers of free white workingmen and its notoriously rambunctious politics that alarmed secessionists and fueled their mistrust of large cities. In the 1850s, the rule of law had nearly collapsed in the city. Political gangs brutalized public life. Reacting to the turmoil, a civic reform movement wrested control from these violent factions, but it only masked the underlying partisan hatreds. Reformers attracted some Know-Nothing support but relied mainly on old Whigs and pro-slavery Democrats to purge the city administration of their opponents. The legacy of the disruptive 1850s gave Baltimoreans a heightened fear of disorder and, for some of them, a highly sensitized animus toward interference by external authority.[3]

At first, extreme politics in 1861 made little headway in the city, perhaps because it straddled the border between the sections. Advocates of free labor and of slavery coexisted, as did the systems they championed. Slavery in Baltimore, though, looked very little like the bound labor on plantations in the Deep South. In fact, it was slowly receding from Maryland. The proportion of free African Americans was much higher than farther south. On the surface, the city appeared to have put its unsavory past behind it, as evidenced by its tolerance of competing clubs, newspapers, and demonstrations by advocates of both states' rights and Union. For the moment, most Baltimoreans said they supported the Constitution. Like many in their region, they looked favorably on calls for consultation among border states to thread a path between the antipodes of secession and coercion.[4]

The city could not isolate itself from the unrest brewing around it, however. Proponents of disunion become more vocal. The city forbade its police from attending political meetings, but the marshal, George Kane, flaunted his secessionist sympathies. Before heading to Charleston, the ubiquitous Louis Wigfall even set up a recruiting station for the Confederate army in Baltimore.[5]

The firing on Fort Sumter sent a shiver through town. Residents were keenly mindful of their exposed position between potential combatants. Despite their affinity for the South, many of them blamed the South Carolinians for making trouble. Cannon fire in Charleston Harbor produced no instant groundswell for secession. Lincoln's proclamation, however, struck a raw nerve. It was not just vocal states' rights advocates who saw a threat in the president's invocation of military power. After the proclamation, fistfights broke out as crowds gathered for the latest reports outside newspaper offices. Mayor George Brown issued a statement on April 17 imploring citizens to avoid inflammatory speech or acts. To no avail. "I cannot flatter myself," he later recalled with rueful understatement, "that this appeal produced much effect."[6]

Marylanders were anxious to know what their larger neighbor to the south would do. Each day, new rumors that Virginia had seceded percolated through town. Even more important was the reaction of Governor Hicks, who had been worried for weeks that affairs in Baltimore were "in a very unsatisfactory condition."[7] He had resisted

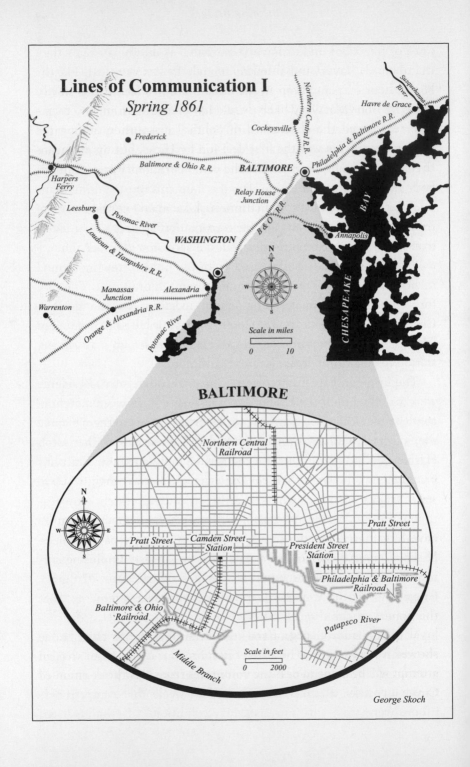

Lines of Communication I
Spring 1861

Susquehanna River

Havre de Grace

Northern Central R.R.

Cockeysville

Philadelphia & Baltimore R.R.

Frederick

Baltimore & Ohio R.R.

BALTIMORE

Harpers Ferry

Relay House Junction

B & O R.R.

BAY

Leesburg

Potomac River

WASHINGTON

Annapolis

Loudoun & Hampshire R.R.

Manassas Junction

Alexandria

Warrenton

Orange & Alexandria R.R.

Potomac River

CHESAPEAKE

N
W   E
S

Scale in miles

0   10

BALTIMORE

N
W   E
S

Northern Central Railroad

Pratt Street

Pratt Street

Camden Street Station

President Street Station

Baltimore & Ohio Railroad

Philadelphia & Baltimore Railroad

Patapsco River

Scale in feet

0   2000

Middle Branch

George Skoch

the Democrats' demands to recall the general assembly, correctly fearing that many legislators intended to endorse secession. In doing so, Hicks showed his stubborn streak and his unionist leanings. If he had given in, Maryland very likely would have left the Union and therefore rearranged the chessboard of political dissolution among the border states. This was the first decision by Hicks, but by no means the last, that could have turned the course of history in a dramatically different direction.

After receiving the proclamation, Hicks hurried to Washington to confer in person with Lincoln, but he temporized about the president's call for volunteers. The governor begged him to appreciate the danger of asking Maryland to fight rebellion in other southern states. He secured a promise that Secretary Cameron later reiterated by cable: the four regiments of volunteers requested from Maryland would have to go only as far as the District of Columbia to guard public buildings against attack. Yet Hicks still issued no orders for his militia to assemble. He satisfied no one.

On the day of Brown's plea urging calm, Hicks issued his own appeal. To allay fears of external pressure, he pledged that no troops from outside the state would cross Maryland except to defend the nation's capital. He ended with an equivocal request that Marylanders resolve their differences in the forthcoming special election for Congress—"to express their devotion to the Union, or their desire to see it broken up."[8]

Such pained, tepid unionism, no better than neutrality, hardly gave Lincoln confidence. The next day, his secretary of war cabled Hicks to restate the government's concerns. Washington had just heard that Marylanders might try to prevent the transit of U.S. troops. An alarming message from a railroad executive confirmed the gravity of the situation. It said he had received a decidedly disloyal query from George Kane, the Baltimore police chief. Kane showed his colors when he asked the railroad if it was true "that an attempt will be made to pass the volunteers from New York intended to war upon the South over your road to-day?" The president discounted some of the menacing anonymous letters he received, but he could not ignore more credible threats like this one.[9]

The passage of soldiers through Baltimore now became the paramount issue. On the morning of April 18, city officials learned they should expect several companies of U.S. artillerymen and some regiments of unarmed Pennsylvania militia, en route to defend Washington. Though they tried to keep that intelligence a secret, word leaked out. A crowd gathered at the Bolton Street station, where 550 soldiers detrained in the afternoon and began marching across town to a different station to board another train for Washington.

A large force of police accompanied them and kept them separated from the crowd. Even so, catcalls, insults, cheers for Jefferson Davis, and a few stones greeted the soldiers. One rock struck the face of Nicolas Biddle, a black Pennsylvanian who had attached himself informally to one of the regiments. As the soldiers boarded the Washington train, men clambered onto the roofs of the cars and continued to taunt them. The police kept order, though, and the soldiers ignored the insults and the stones. A supporter of the Union wrote that it was humiliating to watch as police, "half of whom are rebels," deigned for the moment to protect unarmed militiamen in their march through town.[10]

After the soldiers had passed, jostling throngs of partisans gathered to cheer their respective causes. The streets echoed with braying, clashing stanzas of "Dixie" and "The Star-Spangled Banner." One group tried to fire a hundred-gun salute in honor of Virginia and South Carolina, but after the third discharge, a larger band of unionists grabbed their single cannon and rolled it into the harbor. Secessionists won similar little victories in other altercations. From morning until late at night, the police struggled to prevent violence.

Former congressman John Pendleton Kennedy, a cultured Virginia native and novelist, fretted as he watched his adopted city edge toward anarchy. Ever since the secession crisis erupted, he damned extremists on both sides, "a miserable array of charlatans, and make believe statesmen, and little clap-trap demagogues." With the news of Major Anderson's surrender, he damned Lincoln's misadventure as a "wretched display of incapacity" unexcelled in history and worried that unionists in the Virginia convention would "fly into revolution." On the day his fellow Baltimoreans jeered the Pennsylvania troops, he predicted that "we are on the verge of some violent outbreak."[11]

WHILE BALTIMORE OFFICIALS worried over their predicament, on the evening of April 17, as promised by Governor Andrew, the 6th Massachusetts Regiment left Boston. Under the command of Col. Edward Jones, it was composed of companies drawn from the mill towns of Lowell and Lawrence. The morning before leaving, in a sentimental ceremony full of emotion and expectation, they adopted Jones's daughter of twelve, Lizzie, as "Child of the Regiment." Later at the State House, thronged with people, Colonel Jones accepted the Massachusetts ensign from the governor's hands with the earnest pledge, "So help me God, I will never desert it."[12]

The next morning, the regiment arrived to a tumultuous welcome in New York. Flags flew everywhere; crowds wildly cheered the Bay State volunteers. "My eyes filled with tears," wrote one overjoyed citizen, "and I was half choked in sympathy with the contagious excitement. God be praised for the unity of feeling here!"[13] On the same day, the city greeted the returning *Baltic* as it steamed into New York Harbor bearing Major Anderson and his band of heroes from Fort Sumter. The coincidence was a sign, people said. Surely the Massachusetts volunteers would avenge brave Anderson's surrender.

In the evening, thousands of Philadelphians lined the streets of their city to greet the regiment as it continued southward. The hotel where the soldiers spent the night draped a large flag over its front portico decorated with the words of Daniel Webster's celebrated nationalist motto: "Liberty and Union, now and forever, one and inseparable."[14]

After leaving Philadelphia, Colonel Jones learned that a different kind of reception awaited his regiment in Baltimore. As a precaution, he ordered ammunition distributed. He then made his way through the swaying railway cars to explain to these young men, hardly more than occasional weekend soldiers, what was expected of them. They had been farmers and clerks two days before. Now they might be only minutes away from a violent encounter. "You will undoubtedly be insulted, abused, and, perhaps, assaulted," the colonel warned, "to which you must pay no attention whatever." If fired upon, however, they must obey their officers' order to return fire. But they must take care not to shoot indiscriminately into crowds of civilians.[15] However prescient, Jones's advice could hardly have prepared them for what they faced on the cobblestone streets of the Baltimore waterfront.

In many cities even smaller than Baltimore, by 1861 a transportation revolution had flung rail lines snaking into the center of town from multiple directions. In most cases, though, no direct connections linked the terminal stations of these competing railroad companies. That lack of coordination complicated the movement of passengers and goods from the trains of one line to another, though it enriched the drayage firms whose wagons bridged the gaps.

Baltimore illustrated this common inconvenience in transportation. Travelers from central Pennsylvania came into town at the Bolton Street station, as did the unfortunate militiamen on April 18. Passengers from the northeastern corridor came in on the Philadelphia, Wilmington, & Baltimore Railroad terminating at the President Street station. For transit farther south to Washington, the company uncoupled the locomotive at the station and attached teams of four horses to each carriage, which then pulled them one at a time on a line of track for about a mile along Pratt Street to the Baltimore & Ohio's Camden Street station. There they reversed the process and reattached the cars to an engine headed toward the capital.

This was the procedure that the 6th Massachusetts attempted to follow, with unfortunate results. Though forewarned of potential mischief, neither the officers of the regiment nor those of the rail line trusted city officials enough to alert them to the exact time of arrival. After the previous day's disturbance, it was clear that following the usual routine for transit between stations invited trouble. A safer course would have been to detrain and march together through the streets as one large and intimidating body rather than make the journey in more vulnerable, smaller units, company by company. Such a tactic might have averted the explosion that followed. As it was, one at a time the first seven companies made the transfer successfully to the Camden Street station, despite the menace of a "large and angry crowd."[16]

After the seventh company had reached the station, however, a multitude of people blocked the tracks they crossed. The regiment's band and several remaining companies, about two hundred men, had to leave their rail carriages and march on foot. The route took them along Pratt Street, past the teeming docks of Baltimore's harbor, the congested heart of the commercial district, pungent with the tang of salt air and the scents of exotic cargoes from around the world.

Before the men had gone far, a surging mass of civilians crowded around them and began to hurl insults, then cobblestones. As the soldiers picked up their pace to escape, the throng, perhaps thinking they would not fire or had no ammunition, pressed its assault. Pistol shots rang out. One soldier died; others were wounded. The officers ordered their men to fire. They killed several civilians. Henry Stump, a judge who witnessed the fight, wrote the next day that "the soldiers bore the pelting of the pitiless mob for a long time under a full trot" before they returned fire. Southern partisans swore that the soldiers fired into the crowd without provocation, repeatedly, indiscriminately.[17]

Mayor Brown had gone to the Camden Street station to monitor the soldiers' passage. He was concerned that his police had not received adequate warning of the regiment's arrival. He knew enough about the volatility of public sentiment to fear trouble. In the confusion at the Camden Street station, Brown learned that not all of the soldiers had made their way there from the President Street station. As he hurried down Pratt Street toward the remaining companies, he found the tracks blocked by anchors dragged from nearby docks.

A short distance farther, he met the remaining Massachusetts troops struggling to outpace their assailants, who howled at their heels. Brown joined the officer leading these harried soldiers. His presence momentarily cowed their pursuers, but not for long. Soon the rocks and bullets began to fly again. Into this melee plunged the police marshal, George Kane, with about fifty officers. They formed a line between the soldiers and the mob. With their revolvers drawn, the secessionist Kane and his men fended off the attack and enabled the soldiers to reach the Camden Street station.[18]

When the police heard that another group of men planned to tear up the rail line toward Washington, they sent a party of constables to clear the tracks. As each company of soldiers boarded the cars at Camden Street to wait for a locomotive, Colonel Jones ordered the blinds lowered to avoid eye contact with the locals. But angry civilians crowded in and renewed their stoning. Only with great difficulty was Jones able to prevent his men from jumping off the cars and avenging their fallen comrades. After another provocative volley of stones, some soldiers poked their guns out the windows of the stationary train's last carriage and fired. They killed Robert Davis, a popular Irish-born dry goods merchant, whose friends claimed he was an innocent bystander. Jones later regretted the shooting of Davis but argued that "the men were infuriated beyond control."[19]

By then the situation was so far out of hand that no individual leader, whether of the police, the militia, or the mob contesting the soldiers' march, could control it. Residents in the vicinity of Pratt Street who heard the commotion ran toward the sound. They assumed soldiers were attacking civilians without cause and swelled the numbers of the assailants. Each side inferred the worst of the other's actions.[20] A party of mostly unarmed soldiers remaining at the President Street station, who had not tried to make their way down Pratt Street, attracted the wrath of the mob before their train could return to Philadelphia. The British consul, an appalled eyewitness to the riot, said the crowd attacked them and "hunted them down like terriers after rats" before the police could rescue them.[21]

At about 1:00 p.m., two hours after the Massachusetts volunteers arrived in Baltimore, their train pulled out of the Camden Street station and slowly, uneventfully, made its way toward Washington. The "Pratt Street Riot" was over. Three soldiers and twelve civilians died. Dozens were wounded. The first blood of the American Civil War to be shed in anger had been spilled. The mute tongues of the dead on Pratt Street would not lack for surrogates on both sides crying out for vengeance.

NEWS OF THE CLASH raced through town, and in the repeated retelling, its scope mushroomed out of all proportion with reality. The riot had been spread out along Pratt Street. Probably at no one point did it involve more than a couple of hundred soldiers and several times that many civilians. It was all over, according to a local paper, "[before] most of the citizens even within three or four squares of the place knew anything of it." Though reports inflated the mob to number ten thousand or more, they did not exaggerate the volcanic eruption of outrage among Baltimoreans at the perceived invasion of their city by northern "Black Republican" soldiers. The killing of the popular Davis especially incensed members of the business community.[22]

Publisher William Wilkins Glenn strongly favored a pro-southern interpretation of the events, but he did not overstate things when he recalled, "The news spread like wildfire through the town. . . . Everyone was for resistance." To many of them, on that day Lincoln came to embody a military despotism inimical to all their hopes for the republic. "In such a crisis as this," opined the unionist *Baltimore American*, "all other considerations must give way to our duty towards one another, and to the State and city."[23]

Mayor Brown ordered an express train to rush three emissaries with a letter to the president. In it, he swore that authorities had done their best to protect soldiers and civilians alike. Had it not been for their bravery, more would have died. The people were "exasperated to the highest degree." They opposed any more troop movements through their city. That was a fair enough account of what had happened and how most Baltimoreans reacted. He concluded that it was not possible for more soldiers to march through town "unless they fight their way at every step." Trying to wash his hands of any liability, he ended his letter, "If they should attempt it the responsibility for the bloodshed will not rest upon me."[24]

Stragglers and wounded from the Massachusetts regiment who were left behind found aid at the hands of the Baltimore police and especially from local Freemasons. For the present, intersectional passions had not swept away the bonds of affection among the Masons from states on different sides of the widening divide. For the moment, the streets of Baltimore became quiet again, but calm did not descend and fear still ruled the day.[25]

The city was out of control. Brown knew he had to allay the anxieties begat by the violence. If he did not, civil war might break out at home, never mind what happened in other states. He made a snap decision to hold a mass meeting at Monument Square that afternoon at 4:00. Newspapers immediately chalked up his announcement on the bulletin boards outside their offices. Word spread so quickly that an immense throng gathered an hour before the appointed time and only a few hours after the soldiers fled the stoning on Pratt Street.

The site Brown chose was both practical and fitting. Since 1829, a stout stone column, surmounted by a marble George Washington, dominated the city skyline from a location that originally was on the edge of town. By 1861, the four park squares of Mount Vernon Place, laid out in the shape of a Greek cross surrounding the column, had sparked a building boom that produced the most fashionable town houses in Baltimore. The statue represented the father of the nation resigning his commission as commander in chief. True Baltimoreans were later said to be those born under the shadow of Washington's outstretched hand. Now the stone figure of the first president would preside over the most important public meeting in Baltimore's history.

Some accounts charge George William Brown with secessionist leanings, and Lincoln later jailed him for political reasons. But the mayor's actions on that day of supreme crisis for his city and during the coming week suggest he did not want to align Baltimore with the Confederacy. Instead, he wanted to maintain a neutral stance. That, however, put him as much at cross purposes with Lincoln as if he had embraced Jefferson Davis outright. Above all, he wanted to keep the divided opinions of his fellow Marylanders from bringing ruin down on their heads. He knew a civil war within the city was possible.

A short, clean-shaven man with a high forehead and dark but receding hair, the forty-nine-year-old mayor stood at the pinnacle of his career. He was the quintessential civic leader, always in demand to serve on the boards of charities and schools. Brown had led the municipal reform movement that restored a veneer of decorum to Baltimore affairs, though it had not solved the underlying tensions and partisan rancor. Elected mayor in 1859, he now faced the greatest test of his public life.

By the time he reached the platform at the monument's base, thousands of agitated men, many of them armed, had elbowed their way into the crowded square to hear him. In an emotional appeal, he reminded his listeners that he had acted "at some personal risk . . . to preserve the lives of strangers, but of our own citizens as well." He promised them that the city's authorities would protect them. There was no more need for mob violence. To a chorus of groans from the obviously pro-southern majority, he said that because Maryland was still a member of the Union, it was his duty to protect soldiers summoned to defend the nation's capital.

The crowd cheered him, however, when he revealed that he and the governor had telegraphed Lincoln to plead that no more soldiers pass through Baltimore. Having gotten across his main points, Brown ended by pandering to the sentiments he knew swayed most of his audience. He denied the right of secession, but he affirmed the right of revolution, to the angry delight of the crowd. Their response was unambiguous, as recorded in the notations of a journalist who scribbled down the mayor's words: "It is the height of madness or of folly," Brown cried, "for one portion of this country to attempt to subjugate the other. [Great cheering.] The South could never be coerced, never! *never!* NEVER! [Wild cheering, long continued.] If neither section will yield, then, in God's name, let them part in peace."[26]

After another speaker exhorted the gathering, the man they had all waited for rose to speak. With slow tenacity, Thomas Holliday Hicks had climbed the greasy pole of state politics, first as a Whig and then a Know-Nothing. Short of stature like Brown, the ruddy-complexioned governor had endured his share of troubles. Ill health, financial disappointment, and above all the wrenching loss of his children to premature death added lines of sadness to his face. Despite these blows, he maintained a stubborn attention to his public duties. As a mark of the respect he had gained in Maryland politics, he earned the affectionate nickname "Old Caesar."

Though of dogged character, on the great question of the day he had so far proved to be a vacillating unionist. Just two days before, he had reiterated an earlier plea to Washington for arms in case he needed to put down rebellion in his state. But when the prospect of confrontation arrived, he blanched. Like his fellow chief executives in the upper South, he clung to the goal of concerted action among those states to find some middle way, possibly even a middle confederacy.[27]

His timidity showed when he spoke that afternoon, though in fairness he had good reason to fear the crowd. He, like Brown, worried whether he could control the raging beast of anarchy that glared up at him with ten thousand angry eyes. Could some of them have written the death threats that had often crossed his desk in the past few months? Very likely.

Under enormous strain, Hicks was close to physical collapse. He spoke briefly and said he could add little to the mayor's comments other than to endorse them. He had always supported the Union. He regretted that it now seemed to be broken. To groans from his listeners, he said he hoped it could yet be reconstructed. He meekly concluded that he would bow to the will of the people. "If separate we must, in God's name let us separate in peace; for I would rather . . . this right arm should be separated from my body than raise it against a brother."[28]

That night, city officials still had received no word from Washington. Brown's delegation reached the capital too late to see Lincoln and had to wait until morning for an appointment. Public emotions remained at the boiling point. Brown and the police commissioners feared that further clashes between civilians and more soldiers on their way to Washington would lead to greater bloodshed. They believed they could avoid it only by keeping soldiers out of Baltimore. In the absence of any word from Lincoln, they began to think their only recourse was a highly provocative one: to burn the railroad bridges leading into the city. A breathing spell might calm their agitated citizens.

They were toying with an action that, if not treason, certainly bordered on the seditious. Lincoln would view it that way and later damn them for "unmistakable complicity" with the rebellion.[29] Whether they anticipated that response or thought at all about the rage their action might provoke in the North is uncertain. Even if they had known, they likely would have proceeded as they did. They believed the immediate threat of renewed carnage on their streets was the greater danger.

Before sending men to carry out the order, they sought Hicks's approval. Shaken by the town meeting, and disconcerted by the fearful whirligig of emotions that day, the governor did not return to the capital in Annapolis, thirty miles southeast of Baltimore, but opted to stay the night at a hotel in town. After checking in, however, he changed his mind and, still fearing for his life, took refuge in Brown's house.

It was midnight when the police chief, George Kane, called on Brown to report that more northern troops were on their way. Kane, Brown, and two others went to the governor's bedroom to tell him it was time to take extreme measures. They were exhausted, too, wrung out by the tumult and violence of the past twelve hours, but they believed their course was the least bad one to ensure the city's safety. Would Hicks consent to burn the bridges? He later denied it, but with great reluctance and some confusion, he agreed.[30]

It was about 1:00 a.m. when members of the city's fire and police departments and others from local militia companies streamed out of town and set fire to several bridges on each of the two rail lines that ran north and northeast. In one case, they found that alarmed inhabitants of the farmland along the railroad had anticipated them and were already burning one of the spans. By daybreak, the work was done, as the surprised engineer of the first passenger train from Philadelphia discovered early on Saturday morning.[31]

THE PRATT STREET RIOT influenced national affairs far less than the reaction of Baltimoreans to it. Burning the railroad bridges, and thereby cutting off not only Baltimore but also Washington from the North, alarmed the federal government far more than the attack on its soldiers. City officials may honestly have believed that preventing more troops from passing through was the only way to maintain peace. They were probably right. If they had been more supportive of the government, not burned the bridges, and allowed more northern regiments to come through the center of town, there likely would have been even greater bloodshed than on Pratt Street. And that outcome probably would have pushed Maryland over into secession. But by burning the bridges and gaining time to restore calm, they brought down on themselves the wrath of the North. They ensured that undoing what they had wrought would become the immediate goal of the Lincoln administration, something more pressing than dealing with the Confederacy. For the fate of the national capital hung in the balance after Baltimore acted on Friday night to insulate itself from the outside.[32]

If the rail lines from Pennsylvania to Washington had run to the west of town without going through the center of Baltimore, the isolation of the city would have been a lesser concern to Lincoln. But the fact that Baltimore lay astride the capital's link to the outside world changed the equation. The city at the head of the Chesapeake Bay would learn that it could not retreat into splendid seclusion without attracting the undivided attention of the federal government, the anger of the free states, and the hopes of the Confederacy. Whatever their expectations were for detaching themselves from the fray, Brown and his colleagues had dramatically invited confrontation. They only deferred the day of reckoning; they had not avoided it.

The high-water mark of the Confederacy—in retrospect usually noted as coming two years later at Gettysburg—actually came when the sentiments, if not the actual borders, of the southern republic, in the span of only a week, raced six hundred miles north from Charleston and lapped at the headwaters of the Chesapeake Bay. Fortune was on the side of the South, or so it seemed. The disparity between the sections in military-age population and industrial might would tell in the long run. But they counted for little in the weeks before either side could mobilize. What counted was energy and momentum. Both seemed to be with the Confederacy a week after the cannons spoke at Fort Sumter.

By Friday evening, telegraphed reports of the confrontation on Pratt Street reached Richmond. That word only inflated the exuberance of thousands in the Virginia capital as they set out on their delirious torchlight celebration of secession. Dozens of hastily improvised illuminated signs praised "the gallant Baltimoreans," whose fight with the soldiers electrified Virginians.[33]

On April 19, stunned officials in Washington received Lieutenant Jones's report about Harpers Ferry, with its news that, as at Fort Sumter a week before, no one had died from hostile action. But by then, as they read Jones's account, Americans were dying in the streets of Baltimore. Washington was cut off from outside help, not only by way of the B&O northwest through Harpers Ferry, but now also by the rail line northeast through Baltimore.

By nightfall, the news of what had happened raced northward. It sent thousands of distraught Philadelphians "raving and wildly gesticulating in the streets." The velocity of news began to overwhelm people. "Men never realize the rapidity with which a *revolution* moves," opined a New York writer, reeling from the effect. "Three months ago a person would have been regarded as a madman who had predicted the present state of affairs."[34]

In the past week, the news from Fort Sumter energized the Confederacy and the free states. It convulsed the upper South and forced it to face a fearful decision. Now violence in Baltimore brought the war to the very edge of the North and threatened the federal capital. Both sides clutched at the symbolism of the date, April 19, branded upon the memory of all Americans: "It reads like a rehearsal of the Past—another battle of Lexington—another immolation of life for the purposes of another war upon Freedom."[35]

On Friday night, even before the burning spans of the railroad trestles dropped hissing into the water, an anonymous Baltimore resident composed an open letter to the editor of the *Washington, D.C., Evening Star.* He wanted to give readers in the capital a sense of the violent confrontation he had witnessed that morning. It was his opinion that the Massachusetts soldiers acted entirely in self-defense. He said they fired only under extreme provocation. The writer laid the blame for the attack at the feet of "rabid secession-ists," whose leaders he listed by name. The night before, these men had held a meeting of their followers, "exhorting them to riot and bloodshed." No doubt his candor in naming names while disunion held the upper hand in Baltimore prompted him to withhold his own identity from his correspondent.[36]

Despite this clear assignment of blame, the author typified the ata-vistic response of many in the middle states caught between extremes. The Union was beginning to break apart. As it did, they began to look for safety closer to home, to an allegiance to state and local com-munity. They turned inward. "At all events," the letter writer con-cluded, "the fight to-day has effectually stopped any more troops passing through our city, as we intend to protect it against all com-ers, let them be from the North or South, and hold Maryland firm." He signed the letter, with far more hope than the contents expressed, simply as "Union."[37]

CHAPTER 12

ALONE

Washington, D.C., April 18 to 21

The White House is turned into barracks.

—John Hay, April 18[1]

"I remember nothing but fear." Those were the words Clara Barton chose to describe her unhappy childhood bruised by her parents' vexed marriage and the death of a deranged sister. Barton, a contentious Massachusetts native with an iron will, was one of the federal government's few female employees. After teaching school, she moved to Washington, where she carved out a position for herself as a copyist at the Patent Office. She joined the crowd of townspeople who gathered expectantly at the B&O station on Friday afternoon, April 19, after the telegraph had alerted them that a Baltimore mob had attacked the 6th Massachusetts Regiment en route to the capital. At 5:00 p.m., they heard a piercing whistle, and then around the bend in the tracks a solitary engine approached bearing a signal flag. The engineer reassured them that the soldiers were indeed in another train following not five minutes behind. When it arrived, people cheered and surged forward to hear the story.[2]

Barton offered to help bind up the wounds of the injured, some of whom she recognized as childhood friends from home. The army had no place to house them, much less a general hospital to treat the injured. They carried some men to the infirmary on E Street. Barton took others to her sister's house to nurse them, an act of compassion that launched her life's work and led to the founding of the American Red Cross. That achievement, however, lay in the future for the thirty-nine-year-old Barton. When she rushed to aid countrymen wounded in the defense of her adopted city, she could not know if the capital would long remain in the hands of the government.

ALTHOUGH WILLIAM SEWARD misjudged much in his failed effort to prevent war, his opinion on the state of Washington's preparedness was shrewder. "It must be remembered," a visiting foreigner recorded him saying, "that the bold bad men who were their enemies were equally unprepared for active measures of aggression." Events would bear out that assessment. But it offered cold comfort the week after Major Anderson surrendered, as Washingtonians nervously looked out at hostile southern territory on all sides of the lightly defended District of Columbia.[3]

The frisson that rippled across the country after April 12 gave a vicarious thrill to Americans reading about the fighting at a safe distance. Detachment from that turmoil, however, was not an option for residents of the District of Columbia. For months, the standoff at Charleston had been a far-off quarrel. Now, stunned, they realized that the fighting there might instantly leapfrog hundreds of miles to the doorstep of their city. Newspapers could not keep up with the demand for information. On the Sunday Anderson surrendered, Washington's churches were less well attended than usual because of the mania for getting the latest news in person at the newspaper and telegraph offices.[4]

The people of the North had worked themselves up into a frenzy of patriotic fervor about Fort Sumter, but within a week, sudden secession in Virginia and the burned bridges at Baltimore jerked their attention away from the Confederacy to the danger to Washington. "He is the true Pope who lives in the Vatican," wrote a New Yorker about the president and the capital, recognizing the power of symbol. "It must be defended at any cost."[5]

The aged, ailing hero of the Mexican War, Gen. Winfield Scott, presided over that defense. Swollen by gluttony and ambition, he had a huge head, unkempt gray muttonchops, and a wide frown wreathed in fleshy jowls. At seventy-five and too fat to ride a horse any longer, the vain, quarrelsome commanding general remained loyal to the national government, even as dozens of other southern officers resigned their commissions. Scott, a former presidential candidate and longtime political foe of Jefferson Davis, spurned an attempt by a delegation of fellow Virginians to suborn him. Southern newspapers vilified him. "With the red-hot pencil of infamy," spat one of them, "he has written upon his wrinkled brow, the terrible, damning word, 'Traitor.'"[6]

Lately, Scott had fallen out of favor because of his meddling in policy beyond the scope of purely military affairs. Because the president had listened to bolder voices about Fort Sumter, rumors of bad feelings between the general and his chief found their way into print. Lincoln accepted Scott's devotion, however, and the general bent his energies and still sharp intellect to the defenses of the nation's capital.

"I am . . . much embarrassed by the non arrival of troops," Scott confessed to the president even before the disastrous news from Harpers Ferry and Baltimore. He could count on little help from the weak and confused secretary of war, Simon Cameron. Under him, the War Department's ninety clerks presided over a maze of archaic regulations designed, it seemed, more to perpetuate routine than to respond to demands for action. They would be swept away by the imperatives of total war, but that would take time. For the moment, until reinforcements arrived, Scott relied on six companies of regular soldiers, a few marines at the navy yard, and the questionable local militia.[7]

Suffering from gout and cramp, the general could barely hold a pen to write his daily situation reports. In the one written the day fighting began at Fort Sumter, he listed for Lincoln the contingents of the nation's tiny, far-dispersed peacetime army that he had recalled to the capital. Until the regiments of volunteers from the states could be mustered into federal service, the whole army numbered fewer than twenty thousand professionals. Moreover, very few of them were in or near Washington. Even beyond the capital, they lacked much of an offensive capability. At no point in the country could the army assemble more than a few hundred men because their duties scattered them across half a continent, mainly along the western frontiers.

Scott anticipated receiving a few more of these regular troops in the coming days to supplement the anemic local forces at hand. After clearing up the misunderstanding about their terms of duty, more District of Columbia militia companies took the federal oath, including one unit composed entirely of artisans working on the Capitol. Within several days of the resignation of most of the secessionist National Rifles, that disloyal unit filled its vacancies with reliable volunteers, and it too reported for service.[8]

Scott told Lincoln that once he was satisfied that he could withstand attack, his next objectives would be to safeguard the rail lines north to Wilmington, Delaware, and to secure Fort Monroe, the army's major bastion in southeastern Virginia near the entrance of the Chesapeake Bay. For the time being, on April 16 Scott thought they were "a little a head of impending dangers."[9] Within three days of offering that cautious hope, he learned from Harpers Ferry and Baltimore how wrong he was.

Col. Charles Pomeroy Stone, Scott's chief subordinate in the defense of Washington, drafted a worst-case contingency plan. They would need it if rumors proved accurate and thousands of secessionists attacked from the surrounding Virginia and Maryland countryside. Stone was a decorated Mexican War veteran, with a fashionable Louis-Napoleon goatee and confident manner. Widely traveled, he was experienced in military construction and surveying. He would be the whipping boy for the Union disaster at the Battle of Ball's Bluff in October, but in April his star was ascending, and he applied his skill to Washington's defense.[10] He identified three strong points.

One would be the Capitol, where soldiers stored flour and firewood for a siege and began to build defensive barriers. A second would be City Hall, together with the nearby Post Office and Patent Office. The third would be the executive square, encompassing the White House and the War, Navy, State, and Treasury departments that clustered around it.

Scott feared that Stone's plan disbursed the few defenders too thinly. He therefore revised it by drawing up the order in which the three centers should be abandoned if pressed. First to go should be the Capitol. He thought it would survive even if given up because he believed it was fireproof, except, he noted, for the libraries of the Supreme Court and Congress. Second to go, City Hall. He decreed that the key redoubt should be the executive center of government, with the massive stone Treasury building as the final stronghold where Lincoln's administration would make its last stand.[11]

As preparations for defense accelerated, the appearance of the city changed. Each day, more sandbags and makeshift wooden barricades blocked the entrances to public buildings. The tramp of hobnailed army boots gave the streets an unaccustomed martial sound. "Soldiers are now met with at every turn and the drum and bugle are heard almost all the time," wrote a resident. Guards posted at the bridges across the river and on the main thoroughfares into the Maryland countryside added to the appearance of a city under siege. Scott ordered these pickets, the first line of defense, to resist any attack "till actually pushed by the bayonet" and then rally with the main body of defenders at the designated strong points in town.[12]

The government commandeered the output of flour mills in Georgetown, and long wagon trains carted it off under guard to more secure storage in public buildings. To improvise a waterborne defense, Scott requisitioned and armed several small steamers that normally plied the Potomac between the capital and the town of Alexandria, just downstream on the Virginia side.

At Trinity Church, a grand Gothic confection near the Capitol, the administration's political supporters gathered to give one another moral support and sing patriotic songs to the accompaniment of a

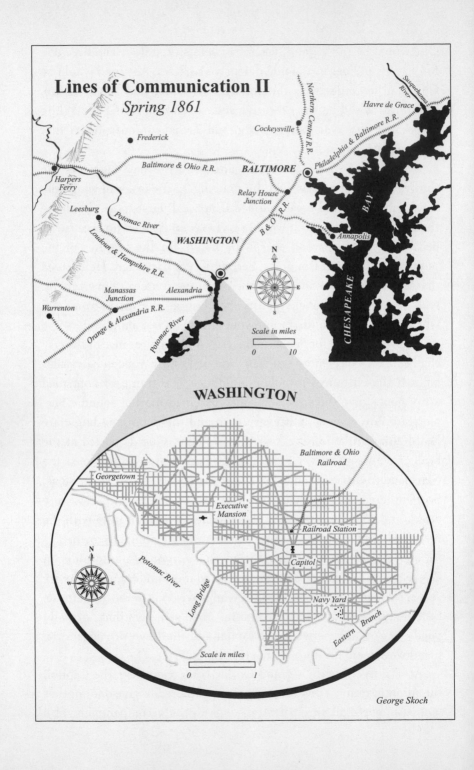

Lines of Communication II
Spring 1861

Frederick

Cockeysville

Northern Central R.R.

Havre de Grace

Susquehanna River

Philadelphia & Baltimore R.R.

Baltimore & Ohio R.R.

BALTIMORE

Harpers Ferry

Relay House Junction

Leesburg

Potomac River

B & O.R.R.

WASHINGTON

Loudoun & Hampshire R.R.

CHESAPEAKE BAY

Annapolis

Manassas Junction

Alexandria

Warrenton

Orange & Alexandria R.R.

Potomac River

N W E S

Scale in miles

0   10

WASHINGTON

Georgetown

Baltimore & Ohio Railroad

Executive Mansion

Railroad Station

Potomac River

N W E S

Capitol

Long Bridge

Navy Yard

Eastern Branch

Scale in miles

0   1

George Skoch

melodeon. They proposed a resolution, entitled "United We Stand," that in florid prose denounced the anarchy, perfidy, and treason of the South. To their way of thinking, secession threatened to make America "a reproach in the sight of the civilized world." The day after they learned about the Baltimore riot, older citizens met on Capitol Hill to organize a company of men exempt from militia service because of age. They called themselves the Silver Greys.[13]

By virtue of many residents' connections with the federal government, the District remained mostly loyal. Even so, a large number of southern sympathizers lived in town, and their presence worried the administration. Fear of what they might do troubled Horatio Taft, the Patent Office bureaucrat. "Treason is in our midst," he fretted. "One hardly knows whom to trust." In an effort to maintain public order, Mayor James Berret, who himself would later land briefly in jail for refusing to swear a loyalty oath, exhorted the populace to remain calm. He invoked police authority to suppress "harangues in public places" or anything else that might inflame passions "in the present unhappy condition of national affairs."[14]

When the Lincoln family had moved into the White House in March, the building filled up every morning with applicants for political appointment. They infested every room except the family's private quarters, and Mary Lincoln fumed at the insouciance of strangers presuming a right to intrude on her space. Now, if the rumors were true, the building was about to be besieged by more sinister forces. Because the evil-smelling Potomac mudflats came right up to the southern border of the park that surrounded the mansion, the upper windows afforded a view straight down the river and across to the Virginia shore as far as Alexandria. Occasionally, the president sat at a window and through a telescope propped on the sill spied on that disloyal town that now refused to recognize his government.[15]

Supporters of the administration organized two impromptu companies of irregulars. Cassius Clay of Kentucky, a fearless, brawling abolitionist, had come to Washington to accept appointment as American minister to Russia. Unable to leave for his post abroad, he formed

Clay's Battalion. Newly selected Kansas senator James Lane, an unkempt, sarcastic demagogue with "the sad, dim-eyed, bad-toothed face of a harlot" and a record of battling pro-slavery forces back home, formed another group.[16] Clay's Battalion, led by its captain armed like a pirate with three handguns and a bowie knife, lodged at the Willard Hotel and patrolled the surrounding streets. Before a proper complement of soldiers arrived to guard the White House, that duty fell to the band of political opportunists who constituted Lane's Frontier Guards and camped out in the East Room. Colorful, undisciplined, and outlandish in appearance, both groups were easy marks for ridicule, but the administration was grateful for whatever support it could garner.

Offers of help poured in. An African American resident, Jacob Dodson, promised he could raise a company of three hundred black Washingtonians to defend their city. Dorothea Dix, the celebrated social reformer and champion for humane treatment of the mentally ill, offered to send Washington a corps of experienced nurses.[17]

Allan Pinkerton promised his special sort of aid. A Scottish immigrant of hard features and driving ambition, he had made a name investigating mail fraud and spying on railroad employees. In February, he had warned Lincoln of an assassination plot on his journey to Washington and secretly escorted the president-elect through Maryland. Some thought the self-promoting Pinkerton had concocted the whole story. He now wired from Chicago that his detectives were ready to ferret out traitors and undertake dangerous secret assignments in defense of the capital. As an earnest of his capabilities, he included with his message an elaborate telegraph cipher for the president to use in sending coded cables.[18]

Lincoln probably did not take as much heart from a letter sent by Neal Dow, a Maine temperance zealot, later called the father of Prohibition. Despite his Quaker pacifism, he would soon don a blue Union general's uniform. Dow told the president that if rebels were about to overwhelm Washington, it would be best to burn the Capitol and the White House. He apparently did not share General Scott's confidence in the Capitol's fireproof qualities. In any event, given the city's location between the contending sections, Dow doubted its suitability as the U.S. capital. That being the case, he concluded, "the destruction of the public buildings there would not be a very great national calamity."[19]

Telegraph lines provided another source of threats to security. The impetus to control the flow of information first came, however, not from the government but from employees of the American Telegraph Company. Operators took it upon themselves to pass along to the president's office cables that they thought treasonous. Soon enough, official censorship, which all wartime governments invoke in the name of national defense, would constrict civil liberties. The night the battered 6th Massachusetts Regiment reached Washington, the army tentatively took over the lines leading north, to the anger of correspondents frantic to report the sensational news from Baltimore.[20]

The importance of intelligence and the swift pace of events prompted the administration to install a telegraph receiver in the White House for the first time. Lincoln's newfound access to the outside world, however, was short-lived. Though at least one of the eight telegraph lines running north from Washington through Baltimore functioned until Saturday night, April 20, the next day it fell silent. Now even electrical offers of help could not get through.

The government was not accustomed to quartering large numbers of troops and scrambled to find lodging for those who answered Lincoln's call. With Congress out of session and the new dome still under construction, the Capitol became a barrack for regiments of volunteers. The raw, unarmed militiamen from central Pennsylvania who braved the taunts of Baltimore rowdies on April 18 camped out that night in hungry splendor. They would have traded the marble halls and brocaded curtains for a square meal, not having eaten since boarding the train in Harrisburg that morning. To meet the need, the Commissary Department set up kitchen stoves in the basement and cooked bacon for them. The cushioned, damask-covered sofas and chairs filled rapidly with lounging soldiers who had never seen such opulence. After battling its way through Baltimore the next day, the 6th Massachusetts also took up quarters in the Capitol.[21]

The sounds of drilling filled the hallways of Tennessee marble with the echoing clatter of ramrods and rifle butts thumping on tiled floors. If they were unused to such luxurious surroundings, the soldiers settled in soon enough. They wrote their letters home from the desks of senators and made themselves at ease in the seat of government. One of them, Lyman Furber, a private with the 6th Massachusetts, bragged to his mother, "Remember that it was the sixth regiment that killed the first secessionist."[22]

Newly decorated legislative committee rooms filled with military baggage and gear. Soldiers hung their knapsacks and cartridge belts on gas chandeliers and the gilt brackets that held back silk curtains. Expensive Brussels carpets suffered under their boots, and rough boxes of commissary provisions piled up in rude heaps. Worse was to come. As more men crowded into the building, the callous destructiveness and indifference that was second nature to soldiers everywhere depressed Thomas Ustick Walter, the Capitol's architect. "The smell is awful," he lamented. "The building is like one grand water closet—every hole and corner is defiled."[23]

Because of construction on the dome, workers had already boxed up the statuary in the old rotunda and covered the paintings with wooden planking. To make the building defensible, soldiers fortified the porticos. They diverted cast-iron plates meant for the dome to serve as breastworks between the great marble columns. Piles of stone and barrels of cement augmented the barricade. As soldiers erected their defenses and drilled in the corridors, the Capitol's artisans continued at their tasks. A visitor with a melodramatic imagination marveled at the contrast between the soldier preparing for battle and the workman who "lingers to enrich with his skill the parapet and dome that the morrow may see leveled to their foundations."[24]

More soldiers bivouacked at the Treasury, a giant colonnaded marble building that the army found especially suitable for defense. Engineers fashioned removable wooden barricades for the lower story and piled up sandbags on the steps. The preparations sparked fears among neighbors ready to believe any rumor about sabotage. Reports of metallic sounds coming from the Treasury at night prompted alarm that incendiaries were trying to undermine the building and blow it up. The source of the noise turned out to be artisans working late drilling holes in the doorjambs for iron security bars.[25]

Calmer Washingtonians tried to brush aside such hysterics. With the city cut off from the outside world, however, the diminished ability to sift truth from rumor gave an edge to alarmist newspaper accounts of affairs beyond the District. Garbled reports of railroad bridges burning north of Baltimore proved true enough, though it was untrue that rebels had scuttled the iron steamer used to connect the rail lines on opposite banks of the Susquehanna River. Stories from and about Baltimore filled the papers. One declared that "bad temper and bad whiskey appear to rule the day" and temporarily defeated that city's presumed unionist sentiment.[26] But the Washington writer who thus sneered at his Maryland neighbors could not be so certain his city's future was any brighter.

THE FEAR OF BETRAYAL from within took on heightened intensity for Washingtonians who conjured up an army of enemies lurking just across the Potomac beyond the tree line of secessionist Virginia. Jumpy residents looked askance at their neighbors. Ever since the cotton states formed the Confederacy, the loyalty of bureaucrats from the South was suspect. That feeling grew exponentially in the weeks that followed. On Monday, April 22, several hundred government clerks resigned en masse. Their action cut both ways: the administration lost experienced employees but rid itself of disloyal ones.

More worrying was the steady stream of southern army and naval officers who gave up their commissions to avoid fighting against their native states. For weeks, a new kind of notice appeared in northern newspapers, at first sporadically and then in a steady stream. These tiny announcements of the departure of southern officers for home bore witness on an individual level to the cost of breaking up the Union, a quickening hemorrhage of talent and experience.

When Secretary Gideon Welles took over the Navy Department, he found "great demoralization and defection." By the third week of April, it was clear to a northern writer that they could place "not the

slightest dependence" on the loyalty of any southern officer, army
or navy. He was nearly right: in the end, fully 85 percent of southern
West Point graduates returned home. In all, the call of native soil
compelled more than a quarter of all army officers, both West Point
graduates and others, to leave the service and join the Confederacy.[27]

These dry aggregate figures mask the anguish of individual decisions. For some, the choice was relatively easy; for others, it formed
a lifelong scar. The self-justifications varied. Lt. Lunsford Lomax,
who had commanded the cavalry escort at Lincoln's inauguration,
said he would remain in the army as long as he conscientiously could.
But once it became, in his eyes, a conflict between the sections, he
had to go south. He admitted it was "suicidal" but concluded, "I must
go with my own people." He would end the war as a Confederate
major general.[28]

Another distressed southerner was Franklin Buchanan, the griz-
zled, balding, sour-featured superintendent of the Washington Navy
Yard. A highly opinionated Marylander and strict disciplinarian celebrated for his stamina, he commanded loyalty by personal example.
He made no secret of his southern sympathies, but he still invited
President Lincoln to his daughter's wedding at the navy yard in early
April. When Buchanan believed Maryland was about to secede, he
resigned his commission. He stepped down as superintendent on
April 23, while Washington was still cut off from the North. On
leaving, he addressed the workers at the yard, who cried and cheered
him as he exhorted them with loaded words: "Be loyal to the Government whilst in its service."[29]

When Maryland failed to secede, however, Buchanan regretted
his haste and asked the navy secretary to reinstate him. "I am ready
for service," he pleaded pitifully. He hoped to receive a posting on
some foreign station where he would not have to fight fellow southerners. Welles cut short his reverie of returning to the service he had
loved for nearly half a century. "By direction of the President," the
secretary wrote with brutal finality, "your name has been stricken
from the rolls of the Navy."[30] Buchanan went south.

The most famous example lived in the mansion on Arlington

Heights, just across the river, commanding a clear view up the Mall to the Capitol. Robert E. Lee had married the daughter of George Washington's adopted son. That direct connection with the father of the nation gave added weight to Lee's capacious sense of duty. A protégé of General Scott, he had returned home in March from a posting in Texas to accept a new commission, signed by Lincoln, as colonel of the 1st Cavalry.

He scorned the "selfish and dictatorial bearing" of the Deep South for undermining the Union. There could be "no greater calamity" than dissolution of the country.[31] Yet like most Americans, he acknowledged the right of revolution even as he denied the legality of secession. Troubled by Virginia's radical drift, on April 18 he accepted an invitation to meet with Francis P. Blair Sr., father of the strident Republican postmaster general. With Lincoln's blessing, Blair offered Lee command of the army. This was three days after the proclamation calling for volunteers to suppress the rebellion. Lee declined and called on a sorrowful General Scott the same day to reiterate his position.

As Lee returned over the Long Bridge across the Potomac to Arlington for the last time, he passed the augmented patrol of cavalry pickets and artillerymen guarding the approaches to the capital. In the early hours of April 20, while burning bridges lit up the darkness north of Baltimore, he composed a resignation letter to Scott. In one terse sentence, he gave up the career he had made the devotion of his life. He anguished over the decision, but he could not bring himself to fight Virginia. It was his personal tragedy and the lot of hundreds of other officers that their sense of nationalism paled in comparison with a deeper allegiance to state.

If the southerners going home were conflicted, their loss had a depressing effect on those who remained. Lincoln took the resignations hard. When the president learned about a particularly dismaying case of a defector who had just professed his undying commitment to the Union, his secretary observed, "This canker of secession has wonderfully demoralized the Army."[32] Momentarily, it infected the commander in chief.

———

WORD OF THE city's isolation prompted an exodus of apprehensive civilians over the weekend. Some people took the uncertain train service that still ran as far north as Baltimore in the belief that even in the hands of a secessionist mob, the Maryland metropolis would be safer than Washington. Others piled their belongings into wagons or trudged out of town on foot to a hoped-for refuge with relatives in the countryside. Hired vehicles commanded premium prices. An ominous report came into the city from across the river in Virginia. Notices in Fairfax County warned residents of northern background that they must take an oath of allegiance to the state or leave their homes within fifteen days. Such threats—whether from zealous individuals like those in Fairfax or those sanctioned by governments—opened an era of intimidation and fear all along the border between free and slave states. It would produce a sad crosscurrent of refugees and outcasts, stigmatized by their neighbors and fellow Americans for their place of birth, their politics, and their suspected capacity for treason.

A rumor that one of the banks in the District of Columbia was about to close its doors led to a run on all the financial houses. Trying to avert panic, the press denied the story but admitted that the multitude of frightened people leaving town was the cause. The natural desire to take gold and silver rather than paper currency produced a temporary shortage of specie. Moneylenders kept on discounting paper notes issued by Washington banks.

Baron Gerolt, Prussia's diplomatic representative, put up a large sign in German script lettering to identify his legation and, he hoped, keep it from harm if secessionists captured the city. As the days of isolation passed, the streets took on a more forlorn appearance, with more and more shuttered shops. The hotels emptied of strangers. "Property is valueless, business is dead," lamented a resident.[33]

Some aspects of daily life went on despite the exodus and the siege mentality. Funerals in Washington churches necessarily continued to be held, but so too did weddings. Merchants continued to advertise bravely in hopes of attracting custom. The city government tried to keep up a semblance of normal operations and even scheduled a demonstration of a prototype for automatically watering dusty Pennsylvania Avenue through a perforated pipe.

The public was encouraged to buy George Eliot's new novel, *Silas Marner*. Newspapers touted a dramatization of *Oliver Twist*. They recommended the antics of Joe Jefferson, whose first theatrical role as a child had been to play a blackface character named Jim Crow, as the best way to pass the time. Casting about for happy stories amid the gloom, they were reduced to heaping praise on a Georgetown resident for continuing the construction of his new brick house despite the threat of war. The *Evening Star* even tried to make light of local secessionist sentiment. When one of the militia companies, the Potomac Light Infantry, disbanded in Georgetown, the paper reported that a member offered the self-mocking toast "Invincible in peace; invisible in war."[34] As long as the city remained cut off from reinforcements, however, the strained geniality of the press convinced few readers. They knew to keep an ear cocked for the sound of rebel musketry, which they expected at any moment.

As THE DAYS of isolation and fear stretched on, the tension became almost intolerable. Every morning brought a new rumor, but they all offered the same grim outcome. Virginians were prepared to attack from across the Potomac; secessionists were plotting to burn the city; Jefferson Davis himself was riding at the head of a Confederate army to capture Washington. Worse than no rail transport was no news. NO TRAINS—NO TELEGRAPH—NO ANYTHING, lamented the headline of a frustrated *Evening Star*.[35]

It proved too much for Henry Born, who lived on Pennsylvania Avenue three blocks from the White House. A Parisian immigrant who had anglicized his name, Born was shaken by the prospect of civil strife. He had witnessed firsthand the class warfare of the "June Days" of 1848 in Paris. In the working-class districts, people had built improvised barricades across narrow residential streets and broad thoroughfares, like those General Scott's few soldiers now hastily constructed at public buildings in Washington. French workers fought pitched battles with their countrymen in uniform. Ten thousand Parisians were killed or wounded. The thought of seeing the same horror reenacted in the capital of his adopted country pushed Born over the edge, and he snapped. His friends took him to the infirmary to be treated for insanity.[36]

CHAPTER 13

BROAD STRIPES AND
BRIGHT STARS

April 18 to 21

We are living a month of common life every day.

—George Templeton Strong, April 18[1]

In *Uncle Tom's Cabin,* Eliza flees from bondage in Kentucky across ice floes in the Ohio River. The tension that real runaways experienced making the escape from slavery to the free states could hardly have been less nerve-racking. If they reached the river towns of Ohio and Indiana, they could not rest easy. The river was an artery of commerce for Americans living on both banks, in slave and in free territory. For people in lower Ohio and Indiana, most of them originally from the South, the simmering national crisis was a distant irritant in spring 1861, far removed from daily problems. When they thought about it at all, they likely were swayed by a thick web of commercial and filial bonds with the South, which led them generally to favor compromise and reconciliation.

The guns firing on Fort Sumter, therefore, stunned them at first. Some clung for the moment to old partisan verities. "Lincoln, with the lie of peace upon his lips," had inaugurated civil war, snarled a Democratic newspaper in eastern Ohio. That sentiment proved short-lived. Patriotic indignation quickly trumped all other feelings, and the cry for Union drowned out dissenting voices. "Our city looks like the 4th of July," crowed a delighted Cincinnati editor after Lincoln's call for volunteers.[2]

As soon as people made that instinctive, reflexive decision to support the government, however, paranoia reared its head. An irrational dread of attack from the South overtook reason. Slave territory lay just across the river. When Virginia seceded, the fear that Kentucky would follow its example struck terror in the minds of Ohio's people. The governor pleaded with Washington for artillery for defense, not realizing that the federal capital could hardly defend itself. Gov. Oliver P. Morton of Indiana expressed similar concerns as he received a stream of delegations pleading for arms. "Our river towns are full of alarm," he cabled Secretary of War Cameron.[3] It was not just the federal capital that feared invasion.

THE FEARS OF PEOPLE in the Ohio Valley reflected distress across the free states, even those that did not share a border with slavery. With the surrender at Fort Sumter, northern eyes focused on Virginia, Maryland, and Washington and waited anxiously for the next telegraphic bombshell. One disaster in the border states overtook another, and each one heightened anxiety in the North. By the time some cities could hold the large solidarity rallies they planned right after hearing about Fort Sumter, much more bad news had arrived. Anger at Virginia's secession, rage at Baltimore, and fears for Washington compounded the apprehension. "Maryland should feel the power of the General Government," blustered a Pennsylvanian.[4] If they refused a passage through the state, vowed a New Yorker, "we will carve one for ourselves."[5]

Democrats were not to be outdone in their fervor for the war effort, even those who still mistrusted Lincoln. The shock of Fort Sumter and the humiliation of the national flag there outraged the North. Now, a week later, the perception of betrayal in Richmond and Baltimore heightened that emotion. The whole swath of the upper South from the Chesapeake to the Mississippi, including Kentucky and Missouri, seemed about to reject the Union. In many eyes, that prospect was a result of the actions of misguided Americans following the bad examples of Virginia and Maryland. For the moment, the wrath of the North focused especially on them as it had targeted South Carolina the week before. The rough-hewn Kansas buccaneer James Lane, camping out at the White House with his motley band of volunteers, seethed at the effrontery of the South. "They did a good thing stoning our men at Baltimore and shooting away the flag at Sumter," he admitted. "It has set the great North howling for blood, and they'll have it."[6]

The reception of a few U.S. Army regulars traveling from western Minnesota toward Washington manifested the mood in the upper Midwest. Two companies of artillery, numbering only seventy-five men, with five officers and a surgeon, made up this modest force hurriedly ordered to the nation's capital. Ordinarily, their transit would have attracted little notice. But at every rural train station along their route through Wisconsin and Illinois, whole communities greeted them. Every time the engine stopped for water and wood, and even when it did not stop at all, people gathered from miles around. Flags and bunting decorated the stations. Farmers abandoned spring plowing to come and cheer the soldiers on. At larger towns, brass bands played at their passage. When the train reached Chicago, an estimated ten thousand people turned out.[7]

These two companies of regulars were but a vanguard of the volunteer regiments of midwestern farmers and clerks soon to follow. The president's proclamation called forth a massive recruiting drive in Chicago and other towns. Reading the reports pouring in about companies forming in nearly every community in the state, a Republican editor contrasted the mania for enlistment with the tepid response during the Mexican War. Unlike then, he rejoiced, people "are touched as with a live coal from off the altar of their country."[8] In four days' time, they filled the six-regiment quota for Illinois.

Massachusetts was the first state to send fully equipped regiments south in response to Lincoln's call. Like other large cities of the region, Boston was a mass of flags. Even William Lloyd Garrison's

Liberator, which had derided the Constitution as a pact with slavery, showed an unaccustomed patriotism, gushing about the red, white, and blue "displayed with a prodigality never before witnessed even on the Fourth of July." A violent storm soaked people to the skin but could not keep them from gathering wherever troops assembled the day after Lincoln's proclamation. Within hours of the summons from Governor Andrew, militia companies from outlying towns began streaming into Boston to rendezvous at Faneuil Hall. Cheering crowds waving small American flags mobbed the railway stations bringing in the soldiers, though bad weather prevented a muster on the Common. Telegraph companies kept their lines open for militiamen to communicate free of charge with their families back home until their units were ready to leave Boston.[9]

The news that the 5th Massachusetts would leave on the afternoon of April 22 drew an immense crowd to the State House to see them off, perhaps largely because of the fate of the 6th in Baltimore. After the calamity there on Pratt Street, the *Boston Daily Advertiser*, like newspapers across the North, printed a map showing the rail network linking northern cities with Baltimore and Washington. It was the first of many graphic sketches that would acquaint newspaper readers with the geography of their country as they had never known it before.

In Philadelphia, the city's proximity to Baltimore imparted a near hysterical quality to the display of emotion. Dense crowds thronged the downtown. Mass public agitation continued throughout the week of electrifying news that followed Fort Sumter. Rumors sent mobs racing through the streets, to threaten an allegedly pro-secession newspaper office with burning, to smash a purported Confederate recruiting shop, to beat up southern sympathizers. One victim barely escaped lynching, and another was saved only when the police intervened. Uniformed officers struggled to keep order. The mayor canceled a mass Union meeting at Independence Square for fear a riot against suspected Confederates would ensue. A headline summarized the prevailing sentiment: OBNOXIOUS PERSONS AND PLACES IN PERIL. Distraught Pennsylvanians credited a fanciful account of a suspicious schooner that had sailed up the river to Chester, near the Delaware line, and traded shots with militiamen onshore.[10]

Philadelphians' numerous southern connections, by virtue of commerce and kinship, fed the suspicion of traitors in their midst. Observing the reaction, a young doctor's wife worried about what such suspicions would mean for her family. Sarah Butler Wister was the oldest daughter of the unhappy marriage of Fanny Kemble, a renowned English actress and abolitionist, and Pierce Butler, owner of vast slave plantations in Georgia. Though she shared her mother's politics, Wister did not let her father's Confederate sympathies alienate her from him. Going into town, she described the sea of flags, the streets "filled with a crowd of idle, eager, hurrying, lounging, talking, listening people, men & women, old & young, rich & poor." They gathered at the telegraph offices to read the latest messages pasted up on bulletin boards outside. Wister interpreted the theft of the paper from her doorstep, twice, as a sign of the mania for news.[11]

After a week's theatrics, people began to channel their energies into more productive efforts, but the rage at their near neighbors down the rail line in Baltimore burned white hot. In place of trying to uncover nonexistent Confederate spies, Philadelphians focused their energies on militia recruitment and other preparations for war. Wealthy citizens offered to outfit companies of soldiers. Women began making uniforms and banners. Schoolchildren took up collections to support the troops. It was the same across the free states.

New York, the largest northern city, put on the most spectacular demonstrations of patriotism, beginning with the reaction to Fort Sumter. "Broadway is a cloud of stars and stripes," read one account. "Business is abandoned and every man is a soldier." A youth who enlisted the day of the president's proclamation wrote in exaltation over the flood of volunteers that "the feeling runs mountains high." With the passage through town of the first Massachusetts volunteers going to Washington, the departure of its own regiments, and the arrival of the *Baltic*, the city was filled with excitement. "Every gun fired at Fort Sumter has found an echo here," boasted the *New York Times*.[12]

The grandest display of nationalistic ardor came on Saturday, April 20, with a monster rally that turned Union Square into "a red, white, and blue wonder."[13] Without exaggeration, the press proclaimed the event the largest gathering of humanity ever witnessed on the continent. The organizers anticipated such a huge crowd that they provided for multiple stands for speakers on different sides of the square. That arrangement gave a chance for more citizens to hear the oratory, though still only a fraction of those in the square. A few hundred privileged owners of tickets printed on green-colored paper gained admittance to the main stand at the base of the statue of George Washington. "Flags from almost every building. The city seems to have gone suddenly wild and crazy," marveled a diarist.[14] To cheers from the crowd below, the people lining the housetops and windows around the square sang "The Star-Spangled Banner." The latest news that morning gave added urgency to the gathering: in lurid detail, newspapers began printing accounts of the bloodshed in Baltimore and the seizure of Harpers Ferry.

As existing militia units filled their quotas, new regiments formed to keep up with the surge of volunteers. The most colorful was the regiment of Zouaves recruited exclusively from the ranks of New York firefighters by Col. Elmer Ellsworth. A headstrong young Chicagoan, he made a name for himself by creating crack militia units modeled on French Algerian troops, known for their intricate drills and gaudy, baggy uniforms of red, gray, and blue. After working in Lincoln's Springfield law office, Ellsworth followed the president-elect to Washington and was lobbying to set up a national militia bureau when the fighting began. Because of the federal capital's anemic defenses, Ellsworth rushed to New York and began recruiting the Fire Zouaves as reinforcements three days after Lincoln's proclamation. Filled with impulsive, martial élan, Ellsworth typified the patriotic spirit of April 1861.[15]

New York's business community stepped forward to pledge capital for the war effort. The city's merchant princes created the Union Defense Committee to coordinate local expenditures for the conflict. War with the Confederacy threatened their livelihood. The South's issuance of letters of marque and reprisal, licensing privateers to attack northern shipping, hit the commercial classes in their pocket-books. "Jefferson Davis might as well have thrown a lighted match into a powder magazine," growled the *New York Times*.[16]

It was not just economic self-interest, however, that annealed them to the Union. The insult to national honor that the assault on Fort Sumter represented in the eyes of northerners who had no love for Lincoln aroused a storm of patriotic outrage. A discreet southern observer witnessed the power of that emotion on the streets of Man-hattan, and it filled him with anger and not a little fear for his cause. "The North has at a bound," he charged, "jumped from abolitionism into a military despotism." Another wrote, "The universal burst of feeling against the South . . . contains a most malignant and persis-tent element and hellish hatred."[17]

Out on the Plains, different fears animated people when they heard about the clashes in the East. As the army withdrew its small units stationed on the frontier in order to defend Washington, offi-cers worried about Indian unrest. By the end of the month, such fears were no longer fictive. Bands of Cheyenne and Sioux took advantage of the soldiers' withdrawal, according to one report, and destroyed a stagecoach mail station in the Platte Valley. The frontier demanded strong measures "to keep the Indians in check."[18] Despite this special local concern, the newer states on the Plains eventually would send their regiments to swell northern armies. Like the longer-settled free states farther east, they viewed attack on the symbol of national unity as an offense of high treason to be put down with all the force necessary.

FROM A DISTANCE, the mass meetings that agitated both the Confed-erate States and the North were indistinguishable. Military bands, cheering crowds, and waving banners clogged the streets of towns large and small. Of course, none of the anguish over the week's catastrophes that afflicted northerners marred Confederate celebra-tions. For the moment, no setback dimmed their joy. In Mobile, com-mission merchants salivated over the prospects for increased trade with Europe that independence would bring, unfettered by subordination to northern capital. The news from Virginia sent people into ecstatic public demonstrations. At an immense meeting, a band played "Carry Me Back to Old Virginia," and an effigy of Lincoln being ridden out of town on a rail provoked great merriment. In New Orleans, the largest city and port in the Confederacy, the same news about the Old Dominion sparked immense demonstrations. They fired a hundred-gun salute and festooned the city with the new Confederate banner with its three broad stripes—red, white, red—and blue union of seven stars.[19] Now events and not just speculation added to the number of those stars.

Secessionists, delirious with victory for their long-suffering cause, let their wildest dreams take flight. In the future, foreign commerce would shun the North for southern ports, rhapsodized a Virginian. New York was finished, exulted the editor of the *Richmond Examiner*, perhaps even believing his hyperbolic words would come true. "A gilded corpse lies on the shores of Manhattan."[20]

Some Confederates were pleased that Lincoln, despite their taunts that he was a coward, had actually provoked conflict. By his actions, he would drive the border slave states into their arms. It angered others, who hoped for peaceful separation from the Union. Now they would have to fight for their independence after all. In the same breath, they could exult that they had broken their chains of bondage to the North and rail at Lincoln for his aggression. But they would need all that nationalistic energy, for it was clear by late April that a contest of arms at an insignificant coastal fort, and the reaction to it, had called forth a powerful, opposing patriotism in the loyal states. What still remained to be determined was which states in the middle would hold fast to that loyalty and which would choose a competing allegiance.

Barnwell Rhett had been one of the original fire-eaters who educated southern opinion to despise the North and crave an independent slave republic. Easily offended, he demanded to know if there had ever been "a more causeless, wicked and detestable war" than the one Lincoln now proposed to wage. "It has scarcely its parallel for ingratitude, perfidy and folly in the annals of the world. It is hideously unique."[21]

Another similarity between the excitement in North and South was the loss of the freedoms both sides purported to defend, most pointedly freedom of expression in all its forms. Freedom of speech and press suffered greatly that week in all parts of the fragmenting country as the ugly suppression of dissent manifested itself. It had long been impractical for an abolitionist voice to be heard in most of the South. With the guns of Fort Sumter, the same intolerance for secessionist views blanketed the North. In the first weeks of patriotic enthusiasm and hysteria, every northern city of any size experienced the intimidation of citizens rightly or wrongly suspected of harboring southern sympathies.

The *Chicago Tribune* piously objected to violence against individuals and pleaded for the North to shun the southern practice of muffling unwelcome opinions: "Let us have no mobs—no violence—no limitation of the right of free discussion." It was a cynical and mendacious stance, for three days later the same paper demanded that anyone holding secessionist views keep silent: "Treason must be dumb." Not to be outdone, a southern editor demanded that anyone with unpatriotic opinions "should be made to disappear at once."[22]

ACROSS THE NORTH and the Confederacy, and the anguished states in between, the news from Charleston, Richmond, and Baltimore galvanized Americans as never before. It took Lincoln's proclamation to inflame the great swath of territory represented by the hesitating upper South. By the time the telegraph had spread the news from Baltimore, with its implied threat to the federal capital, the whole country was aroused. The dizzying succession of explosions was hard to take in. Events tumbled over one another too quickly for people to digest their impact.

Two days after Lincoln's call for volunteers, Davis authorized southern vessels to prey on northern shipping. Three days after that, Lincoln instituted a blockade of the southern coast. For the moment, the two presidents were just hurling bits of paper at each other. Fitting out privateers would take time, enforcing a blockade even longer. In the meantime, all eyes turned to the shocking events along the border, where Virginia and Maryland civilians clashed with uniformed representatives of the national government.

In every town of any size, militia units drilled and citizens raised new companies of volunteers. They were unarmed, untutored volunteers, fired with patriotic fervor but lacking in martial training. Former army officers were in great demand. One of them, a thirty-eight-year-old veteran of the Mexican War with sad eyes and poor prospects, helped drill a company formed in Galena, Illinois, on the day after Lincoln's proclamation. Three days later, Ulysses S. Grant wrote his pro-southern father-in-law that "every true patriot [should] be for maintaining the integrity of the glorious old *Stars & Stripes*, the Constitution and the Union." Grant had resigned his army commission in 1854 and struggled with alcohol and business failure since then. In Galena, the spiral of downward mobility ceased. With thousands of other Americans on both sides, he now saw his purpose clearly. There were, he wrote with quiet, burning conviction, "but two parties now, Traitors & Patriots."[23]

CHAPTER 14

SUNDAY REST

Gosport Navy Yard, April 21

*At 4:20 [a.m.] sent up a rocket, and the ships, buildings, etc.,
were fired.*

—Log of USS *Pawnee*, April 21[1]

On Sunday, April 21, Richmond's churches filled with worshippers. In the space of a single week, their world had turned upside down. If those seeking spiritual calm and reassurance that morning found it, the effect proved momentary. At noon, just as services concluded, the bell in the redbrick guard tower on Capitol Square shattered the weekend repose, clanging to summon militia companies to duty. According to a cabled warning, the steamer *Pawnee*, one of the newest ships in the U.S. Navy, would soon round the bend in the James River just below town and attack Richmond.

The past week's excitement had worn out people's emotions. First came anxiety over the secret deliberations of the convention, then the word that it had passed the ordinance of secession, and then the explosive news from Harpers Ferry and Baltimore. Now, with this Sunday morning alarm, the prospect of war even closer to home, so abstract before, became frighteningly real. A young visitor who had just arrived said it plunged the city into "a terrible state of excitement."[2]

All the volunteer companies that could be mustered hurried down to the riverfront east of town. Thousands of civilians poured into the streets and followed, many ludicrously armed with shotguns and pistols. Soon a multitude of men, women, and children crowded the hillsides near Rocketts Landing, straining to see into the distance. All day long, telegraph operators downriver sent the same message to the governor: The *Pawnee* was expected but "not yet in sight." As the hours slipped by, some of the artillery companies decided to pass the time with a little gunnery practice before the sun set. The sound of cannon fire terrified residents back in town who feared the worst.[3]

The *Pawnee* never appeared. As the authorities later discovered, the alarm came from what one observer called a "tell-lie-gram," a misleading cable sent by an excitable operator keen to pass along the latest rumors.[4] Looking back later, Richmonders remembered what they indulgently called "*Pawnee* Sunday" as an episode in the days of innocence, before they came to know what war really meant. But if Richmond that Sunday resembled a comic opera, with its people teeming over the riverfront bluffs to confront a make-believe threat, the same could not be said about the state's principal seaport on that brilliant, sunny day.

THE *PAWNEE* was indeed in Virginia waters that weekend. But its captain never considered steaming up the James and shelling Richmond for the simple reason that the ship's draft was too deep to navigate the river that far upstream. In any event, the *Pawnee* had other orders. It led a desperate rescue mission to the navy yard near Norfolk seventy-five miles southeast of Richmond, and the result was the greatest disaster to befall the U.S. Navy before the twentieth century.

Hampton Roads, a large expanse of tidal water where the James River widens as it flows into the mouth of the Chesapeake Bay, was home to two of the most important military sites on the mid-Atlantic coast. Fort Monroe lay on the north shore of Hampton Roads, on a sandy spit at the entrance to the bay. A low, massive, irregular, star-shaped bastion of stone and concrete surrounded by a moat and—unlike Sumter—defended by a reinforced garrison, it commanded the waterfront with large-caliber artillery. A few miles across the water to the south was the port of Norfolk and, nearby, separated by the narrow estuary of the Elizabeth River, the Gosport Navy Yard and the adjoining village of Portsmouth.

A visitor that spring remarked on the dozens of oyster boats that dotted the harbor every day and the "ancient and fishlike smell" of the ramshackle seaport. It was no wonder, because the area had not yet recovered from the great pestilence of 1855, the "death storm," a yellow fever epidemic that felled one in seven residents. But if Norfolk had a forlorn aspect, the yard itself boasted the best shipbuilding and repair facilities in the country: modern machine and boiler shops, sail lofts, foundries, three large ship houses, an ordnance laboratory, thousands of naval cannons, many of the latest design, and the finest granite-lined dry dock in the nation, capable of servicing any ship in the U.S. Navy.[5]

The ships at Gosport, mostly sailing vessels, ranged from the giant *Pennsylvania,* immobilized as a receiving ship, a kind of floating warehouse, down to the brig *Dolphin.* Their states of readiness covered a wide range as well. Most were "in ordinary"—that is, out of commission and in storage. But the sloops of war *Plymouth* and *Germantown,* both of twenty guns, lacked only crews to be battle ready. The most valuable ship, the powerful fifty-gun steam frigate *Merrimack,* required some work on its propulsion system as well as a crew, but then it too would be fit for action.[6]

The navy's concern for Gosport had grown earlier in the year with the worsening secession crisis, but miscues, bad information, and faithless officers undermined efforts to avert disaster. The burden came to rest on the shoulders of Secretary Gideon Welles as soon as he took office in March. Nearly sixty, a leading antislavery advocate and prominent moderate Republican, he was a logical choice for the Navy Department because earlier he had been its first civilian bureau chief. This bewhiskered, acerbic former shipbuilder inherited a dispirited service with forty-five vessels, many of them unfit for duty. Worse, more than half of his officers either had resigned, or were planning to quit, or were about to be dismissed on suspicion of disloyalty.[7]

As worries about Fort Sumter consumed the administration in late March, Welles could not convince the president of the need to safeguard Gosport. Lincoln feared that any obvious measures taken to defend the yard or send reinforcements would irritate the Virginians and embolden the secessionist element there. There were few vessels to spare, anyway. Treaty obligations kept some U.S. ships tied to their station off the west coast of Africa to suppress the international slave trade. With so many of the navy's few ships on foreign duty, planning for the Sumter expedition committed most of the rest.

Happily for Welles, in late March the flagship of the home squadron, the *Cumberland,* had just returned from Veracruz, Mexico. A succession of gales and contrary winds turned the journey into a twenty-seven-day ordeal that compelled Commodore G. J. Pendergrast to seek repairs for his sailing vessel. The requirements of his ship thus coincided with the greater needs of the service, because his guns would help furnish a defense for Gosport while he refitted.

In early April, Welles still worried that the sprawling navy yard, full of armaments but with none arrayed for defense like those at nearby Fort Monroe, might not be able to resist assault. On April 10, two days before the attack on Fort Sumter, he wrote the commandant at Gosport to warn him against "unlawful attempts" to seize his ships, especially the *Merrimack.* He told Capt. Charles McCauley it might be wise to send his seaworthy vessels out into Hampton Roads under the protection of Fort Monroe's guns. McCauley should make these changes, though, without raising alarm. Not content to leave the matter as a suggestion, the next day Welles issued a flurry of orders dispatching an engineer to make emergency repairs on the *Merrimack,* an officer to take command, and enough sailors from the New York Navy Yard to man the ship.[8]

The warning was well founded. Henry Wise's conspirators had had their eyes on the navy yard even before they surreptitiously ordered Shenandoah Valley militia companies to capture Harpers Ferry. The day before the Virginia convention voted to secede, a Norfolk telegraph operator promised his supervisor in Richmond he would keep the line open for orders to insurgents gathering to assault Gosport. For days, secessionists had been pressuring John Letcher to act. "Our people are intensely excited & are anxious to take the Navy Yard," one of them cabled the governor. Just put someone in charge, he pleaded, highly agitated, and the rebels would act.[9]

For the past week, naval officers worried that secessionists would try to sink derelict hulks in the Elizabeth River to block the narrow passage leading from the yard out into Hampton Roads. On April 18, Washington learned from a revenue cutter that hostile Virginians had indeed begun blocking the channel. The same day, a steamer crowded with militiamen forced a U.S. Navy lighthouse inspector to surrender his ship at gunpoint.[10]

Since his teens, Benjamin Franklin Isherwood had tinkered with machinery and boilers. As a civilian employed by the navy, he made some of the earliest mathematically documented studies of steam power. Just a month before, Isherwood had become engineer in chief of the U.S. Navy, and it was he whom Welles sent to Gosport for the most important assignment of his career, to rescue the *Merrimack*.

He found the engines in deplorable shape. But with an astonishing effort, working his steamfitters around the clock, he managed within three days to put the warship in good enough shape to move under its own power. With the boilers fired up on the morning of April 18, Isherwood made ready to cast off. When he called on McCauley to give the order, however, to his great surprise and disgust, the commandant refused. He proved irresolute in everything but his decision to thwart Isherwood. The engineer had done his duty, but McCauley's obstruction in the face of an imminent threat confounded the engineer's achievement.[11]

The actions of one weak officer doomed one of the navy's most powerful ships. McCauley would shortly top that baleful decision with one even worse. Welles later damned the man with sour praise, branding him "faithful but feeble and incompetent."[12] The day after McCauley refused to allow the *Merrimack* to put to sea, Isherwood and the others sent for that purpose reported back to the secretary of the navy. Alarmed, Welles brought them immediately into a cabinet meeting to dramatize his concern. Lincoln needed all the forces available to protect Washington, but he consented to Welles's risky plan for a second mission to Gosport.

For this expedition, they sent a ship then at Washington, the twin-screw steamer *Pawnee*, under Commodore Hiram Paulding, supplemented with sailors to be transported in civilian vessels from northern ports. A fifty-year veteran of the navy—Paulding had joined as a teenage midshipman and was a hero of the Battle of Lake Champlain during the War of 1812—he had witnessed the transition from the age of sail to steam power. Balding, with tufts of white hair sticking out either side of his head, he had a flinty gaze that suggested his unbending character. He was beyond the mandatory retirement age, but he came back into service as one of the few trustworthy senior officers available to the new administration.

Welles ordered Paulding to take charge of the yard from McCauley and to bring out the *Merrimack* and any other vessel that could be rigged for sailing on short notice. At the same time, the navy secretary burned up the telegraph wires with orders to Philadelphia, New York, and Baltimore chartering boats and dispatching sailors to assist the *Pawnee*. They would be too late. When the president of the Baltimore Steam Packet Company replied to Welles's request for a boat to carry naval recruits to Norfolk, he refused: it was the unfortunate day Pratt Street became a household name across the country.[13]

By then, the upper South had erupted in protest against Lincoln's proclamation, and Virginia's convention announced its vote for secession. Welles realized that it might no longer be possible to save the ships at Gosport. In that case, they must be destroyed to prevent their falling into unfriendly hands. Therefore, the second mission took on board at the Washington Navy Yard a cargo of forty ominous barrels of gunpowder, eleven tanks of turpentine, and other combustible materials.[14]

Making good time, the *Pawnee* steamed down the Potomac and Chesapeake Bay. On Saturday afternoon, it stopped first at Fort Monroe, where a regiment of Massachusetts volunteers, hungry but eager, had just disembarked that morning. The men cheered heartily when a second regiment from their state also arrived by ship later in the day, swelling the number of defenders to well over a thousand. There would be no repeat of Fort Sumter. The garrison had cut off all contact with civilians in the neighboring town of Hampton and prepared for a siege by prudently repositioning their guns and mortars to cover assault from the landward approaches.[15] The officers therefore agreed they could temporarily spare the 3rd Massachusetts Regiment for the expedition across Hampton Roads to the navy yard. This decision added more than three hundred soldiers to the hundred marines aboard the *Pawnee.*

The captain ordered his crew to battle stations. They loaded the ship's guns and ran them out for action, tampions removed, as they steamed the few miles across the broad water to the Elizabeth River, which led to the navy yard. They spotted several vessels newly sunk in the channel to obstruct navigation, but so far that effort was inept and posed no threat to their passage. As they approached their destination, the first signs were encouraging. When the ship pulled alongside the wharf at the yard, sailors on the receiving ship *Pennsylvania* sent up three cheers. So did the crew of the flagship *Cumberland.* A histrionic Norfolk secessionist heard them, too, and cabled Richmond for action: "I now hear the black Republican cheers at the Navy Yard," he cried.[16]

The robust welcome proved to be terribly misleading. All but one of the ships capable of being sailed or towed out of harm's way had, in fact, been scuttled. Weak and timorous, completely unnerved by the prospect of attack and the defection of his southern-born officers, McCauley concluded he had no choice but to open the seacocks and flood the ships at anchorage. Only the *Cumberland* remained intact for escape. Its captain, Commodore Pendergrast, had unaccountably not opposed McCauley's suicidal orders. Paulding's men immediately went to each vessel to see if they could reverse the damage, but it was too late. They were sinking fast.

The task of the navy's would-be rescue mission now turned to demolition, with the help of the Massachusetts soldiers and sailors from Pendergrast's ship. One party made a frustrating, ultimately futile effort to destroy the big naval guns stored at the yard, of which there was a disconcertingly large number. The cannons had been recently manufactured, and the high quality of their metal defeated the sailors' attempts to break off the trunnions or disable the guns other than by a temporary spiking.

Other parties took explosives and combustible material to the storehouses, barracks, ship houses, shops, and the luckless ships themselves and prepared for a coordinated demolition. Two officers, one each from the army and navy, directed a party of forty soldiers in laying charges to blow up the massive dry dock. As each party completed its tasks, the men returned to the *Pawnee* and the *Cumberland*. After midnight, only a handful of sailors remained ashore, awaiting orders to light the fuses and fires.

At the last minute, the young son of Commodore McCauley appeared, in tears, with word that his father, befuddled and disoriented, refused to abandon his post. Sailors ultimately persuaded McCauley that immolating himself with the navy yard would serve no purpose, and he reluctantly boarded the *Cumberland*.[17]

Before dawn, the *Pawnee* got up steam and took the *Cumberland* in tow. At 4:20 a.m., a signal rocket arced over the navy yard, trailing a shower of yellow sparks. At that sign, the men left onshore fired the buildings and ships. Within minutes, a sheet of flame engulfed the yard. The *Pawnee*'s captain ordered the crew to beat to quarters. With their marines on deck, under arms, sailors opened the magazines and stood by the ship's guns. They knew the secessionists could hear and see their work of demolition for the past several hours and fully expected to be attacked as they steamed up the narrow Elizabeth River past the flanking towns of Norfolk and Portsmouth. The Virginians were rumored to have positioned artillery covering the waterfront, though none had been visible the day before.[18]

No one molested the *Pawnee* or the *Cumberland*. As they edged slowly out into the stream, the burning buildings at the navy yard backlit the doomed ships left behind. Flames raced along the tarred rigging and spars of the anchored vessels and outlined them in gold against the predawn darkness. Now, rowing like madmen, sailors in longboats carrying their shipmates who had set the fires intercepted the two larger ships and were taken in tow. Though their enemies had sunk even more hulks in the channel since the previous day, the *Pawnee* and *Cumberland* easily passed by the obstructions as the sun rose over the flat tidal marshland to the east. Without further incident, the navy's little expedition, bearing a scant few refugees from one of the world's greatest maritime facilities, sailed across the wide stretch of Hampton Roads to the safety of Fort Monroe.[19]

As at Harpers Ferry, the fate of the Gosport Navy Yard arose from misunderstanding and a colossal failure of military intelligence on both sides. There were not thousands of well-armed insurrectionaries about to assault the yard, as McCauley had feared. William Taliaferro, sent by the Virginia government to take charge of state forces in Norfolk and Portsmouth, knew that very well. A Tidewater lawyer and veteran of the Mexican War, he was the competent but cautious major general of the state's militia. He had been in command at Harpers Ferry when they hanged John Brown.

When he arrived on the scene, Taliaferro was appalled to find only about six hundred militiamen from Norfolk and Portsmouth. Most of them lacked arms. On their own initiative, locals had ineffectively sunk boats in the channel to the navy yard and removed marker buoys. But in their eagerness to attack the U.S. Navy, they discounted the firepower arrayed against them. Just before Taliaferro arrived, a near hysterical insurrectionary cabled the governor, "For gods sake put some body in command. Norfolk will be taken." Some of the overeager secessionists urged Taliaferro to attack at once, but the circumspect general declined. The sailors at the yard, especially when augmented by the force of marines and soldiers on the *Pawnee*, plus the broadsides of the *Cumberland*, were more than a match for anything the rebels could throw at them any time soon.[20]

There would have been ample opportunity for the navy to save all of the ships and much of the equipment at Gosport. Certainly there was no immediate need to destroy any seaworthy vessel. Paulding, however, could not know the weakness of Taliaferro's command. He had no reason to doubt they would erect artillery batteries and continue to obstruct the channel until they eventually succeeded. In any case, once the fainthearted commandant of the yard had scuttled his ships, prudence demanded an orderly withdrawal, but a rapid one.

Despite the pyrotechnics at Gosport, just as at Harpers Ferry, the destruction proved much less extensive than either the U.S. government or the Virginians expected. The Confederates called it "the most abominable vandalism" but could not conceal their glee. Taliaferro's state militia volunteers clambered over the smoking ruins on Sunday morning to assess the damage. Ten ships had burned to the waterline or sunk, but all could be raised and refitted. Some sail lofts and two large ship houses went up in smoke, but many buildings emerged unscathed by the flames. Thousands of rounds of shot and shell survived, and even those thrown into the water could be salvaged. More than a thousand cannons would see service under the Confederate flag. Incredibly, thousands of barrels of scarce powder managed to escape destruction. Most important of all, the explosives set to demolish the giant granite dry dock inexplicably failed to do the job. The Confederates had inherited a formidable treasure of shipbuilding equipment, military stores, and repairable capital ships.[21]

Once again, another great military asset of the United States government had fallen into the hands of the rebellion. Once again, it happened without loss of life. For the Confederates, it seemed as though nothing could stop their advance northward through the upper South. The rapid course of their success vindicated those calling for boldness. It was a time for men of action. Henry Wise was on the scene, in his element, firing off telegrams to the governor urging him on. After sending militia to Norfolk and Harpers Ferry, he urged an attack on Washington without delay. A week after the Gosport fire, John Janney wearily speculated that Wise was "engaged in breaking and burning things at Norfolk."[22]

Within this larger drama, a smaller one bizarrely juxtaposed chivalric notions of warfare against the stronger atavistic hatreds welling up in the populace. An army captain, H. G. Wright, and a navy commander, John Rodgers, had led the party of men assigned to destroy the dry dock. With only a short time available to them, they hastily rigged an explosive charge from a ton of gunpowder that they had carried from the *Pawnee*. To ensure the charge exploded, they connected four slow-burning fuses to it. Rodgers and Wright sent their work party back to the boats while they waited for the signal rocket. By the time it appeared overhead and they lit the fuses, the portion of the yard closest to the wharf was a mass of flames. The boats had to leave without the two officers.

Driven back from the water's edge by the flames, they eventually found their way to the river and pushed off in a rowboat. Their luck failed them when Virginia militiamen spotted them and began firing at them. Seeing they would have to pass within musket shot of the shore, they surrendered. The commander of the Virginia militia treated them kindly and put them up at the Atlantic Hotel for the rest of the day. Sent to Richmond, they were treated as guests of Governor Letcher, who personally escorted them from the executive mansion to the train station. Because some Richmonders threatened to harm the prisoners, the governor detailed two militia officers to protect them from harassment and escort them to Washington. With exquisite politesse, both Rodgers and Wright wrote letters to Letcher thanking him for his kindnesses during their "very hospitable detention." They could not have imagined the fetid prisoner-of-war camps that both sides would erect in the coming struggle.[23]

Lincoln's government momentarily took heart when the *Pawnee* steamed unmolested up the Potomac two days later. At first, Washingtonians thought it might be bringing the long promised regiments of volunteers from the North. But word quickly spread that the ship had come from Gosport, and with bad news, not massive reinforcements. For the capital, still cut off by rail, the *Pawnee* brought a few more sailors and marines to strengthen the weak defenses. But the knowledge that the largest naval base was in hostile hands increased the despondency in Lincoln's cabinet as they listened firsthand to the account of sailors fresh from the debacle at Gosport.

The shocking news reached Washington as it worried about its own safety. With the North enraged over the perfidy of Baltimore and the risk that the capital might fall, word of catastrophe at Gosport received less attention than it otherwise would have. By itself, it would have been bad enough news. As it was, the loss took its place in the litany of disasters that the North had to absorb in a week's time. For the Confederates, it confirmed the hostility of the federal government and also the seemingly irresistible tide of their cause, but they too focused on Baltimore and Washington.

LONG AFTER THE DRAMA at Gosport, Americans would reflect on the irony of the *Merrimack*'s fate. Up to the last moment before McCauley undermined Isherwood's heroic feat of repairing the engines, the navy could have moved the vessel out of harm's way. If that had happened, the Confederates would have had no burned hulk to raise and refit as the *Virginia*, the ironclad that briefly terrorized shipping in Hampton Roads a year later—including the hapless *Cumberland*, which it sank. Without the *Virginia* to delay the Union's Peninsula Campaign, the outcome of it and also of the larger conflict would have been different, perhaps dramatically so.

In addition to the *Merrimack*'s fate, another poignancy attended the destruction at Gosport. One of the after-action memoranda filed with the Navy Department contained an ironic symbolism that apparently went over the head of the author. Among the ships at Gosport was the ancient frigate *United States*, not seaworthy at all, out of commission, but still bearing a proud name and tradition. Over a long career stretching back to 1797, it had fought French privateers and then the Royal Navy. In the 1840s, it sailed the Pacific and then suppressed the slave trade off the west coast of Africa. In their frantic triage of destruction in the predawn hours of April 21, sailors concluded that the *United States* was "in so decayed a condition," so useless and rotten at its moorings in the stinking tidal muck, that it was not worth the waste of turpentine needed to burn it.[24] The officer making that report, intent on laying out the details of the Gosport fiasco in dispassionate prose, failed to note the connection between the parlous state of his country that spring and that of its sad naval namesake.

CHAPTER 15

WILD EXCITEMENT

Baltimore, April 20 to 21

Send no troops here. We will endeavor to prevent all blood-shed.

—George William Brown, April 19[1]

In 1858, the Baltimore & Ohio Railroad chose John Work Garrett as its president. He lived by his middle name. Shunning a paternalistic view of labor relations, he tightened control over his workers, set up a company police force, and ruthlessly suppressed strikes. By dint of willpower and financial acumen, the thirty-eight-year-old businessman revived the distressed line and turned it into a prosperous sinew tying the East to the Midwest. But the location of his railroad astride the border between the upper South and the free states placed it in extreme peril. A premonition came in his second year as president, when one of his employees flashed the first telegraphed warning directly to Garrett that John Brown was at Harpers Ferry.[2]

Now, in April 1861, the railroad took on critical importance as the means of bringing iron-shod salvation to the nation's capital. But in a single weekend, Washington was cut off at one end by the burned trestles north of Baltimore and taken hostage at the other by militiamen at Harpers Ferry. Frantic telegrams from up and down the line flooded Garrett's office at Baltimore's Camden Street station. From that vantage point, the harried businessman had already seen first-hand on the day of the Pratt Street Riot the turmoil that threatened the B&O.

A large, vigorous, barrel-chested man, Garrett for once found he could not exert his personal dynamism to resolve a problem. He was wedged between opposing forces hostile even to the notion of recon-ciliation. The day before the riot, a message from the mayor of tiny Charles Town, Virginia, warned Garrett he must not transport troops or munitions from the Midwest to Washington. If he did, Virginians would blow up the bridge at Harpers Ferry. The next day, southern sympathizers in western Maryland demanded that he fire any Repub-licans working for him. "If they are not removed," they threatened, "your *Road will be made one continuous ruin.*"[3]

The day after excited Baltimoreans burned the bridges, a telegram reached Garrett's office from the B&O agent in Wheeling. It quoted at great length a passenger who had just arrived from the east. He had left Washington the afternoon before. On reaching the B&O's Relay House Junction outside Baltimore, he met rattled eyewitnesses to the violence on Pratt Street. From the junction, his train rumbled westward through Maryland, uncertain which flag would be flying at the next station.

At Harpers Ferry, Virginia soldiers, cocky and suspicious, flagged down the locomotive. As it juddered to a dead stop and vented steam along the banks of the Potomac, field artillery was clearly visible, placed to enfilade the carriages. The militiamen threatened to fire if they found any United States agents or soldiers on board. Satisfied after searching, they let the train proceed. At Martinsburg, it encoun-tered more cheering for the Confederacy. At another town, people said they would not fight against the old flag unless Maryland for-mally seceded. At Cumberland, they cheered for the Union. Finally, the train reached Wheeling, where strong Union feelings predomi-nated.[4] The dizzying change in sentiments the train encountered as it threaded its way through pro- and antisecessionist districts of western Maryland and Virginia vividly brought home to Garrett the dangers faced by his company and his nation.

On the same weekend that fire engulfed the Gosport Navy Yard, an even greater conflagration threatened the city at the other end of the Chesapeake Bay. "Send no troops here," Mayor Brown implored Lincoln. Railroad executives in Philadelphia cabled Secretary of War Cameron for instruction when they received the same plaintive request from Governor Hicks. Cameron bluntly denied the governor's right to stop troops and ordered the railroad men to do their duty: "Send them on prepared to fight their way through, if necessary," he demanded in reply. Burning the bridges may have thwarted the passage of reinforcements for the moment, but it only put off a confrontation at the cost of raising doubts about the loyalty of Maryland and enraging the North against the little state caught in the middle.[5]

With daylight on Saturday morning, Baltimoreans could see all around them tangible evidence of the overnight revolution in sentiment. A large Confederate flag floated in the breeze over the headquarters of the States Rights Club on Fayette Street. It was echoed in innumerable miniature Confederate flags defiantly pinned to the lapels of residents on the day after the riot. After the events of the previous morning, few people were surprised to see so many symbols of the southern cause. More astonishing was the complete disappearance of American flags. It was as though the banner that had inspired Francis Scott Key's paean to the nation, written in Baltimore Harbor, had never existed. A few blocks away from the States Rights Club, the Minute Men, a Union political organization, took down the Stars and Stripes. To cheers from a crowd that gathered, in its place they ran up the centuries-old black, orange, red, and white device of Lord Baltimore, the Maryland state flag.[6]

For the people of Baltimore, in the hour of their distress, local and state loyalty trumped alliance to the nation. It could not have been otherwise, for them or for any community similarly traumatized. The Constitution and the Union were revered, but they were ethereal abstractions when set against the flesh-and-blood realities of families, neighbors, and livelihoods. Every sign pointed to a decisive shift that could lead only in one direction. "There never was such a

sudden conversion of a whole people from right to wrong," despaired
a unionist. "Mark my words," predicted another the day after the
riot, "Maryland will formally secede before ten days. She has virtually done so already."[7]

Armed men roamed the streets, looking for weapons. There was a
frantic search "for arms, muskets, pistols, Bowie knives, pitchforks,
clubs and every other instrument of attack or defense." Mayor
Brown recalled that weekend as "a time like that predicted in Scripture . . . when he who had no sword would sell his garment to buy
one." Stores and individuals suspected of Union sentiments became
objects of abuse. Mobs singled out German immigrant social clubs
and shops. They attacked the *Sinai*, an abolitionist paper that had
branded slavery "the cancer of the Union." The editor, Rabbi David
Einhorn, fled the city. "Anxiety alarm and rage have taken possession of the town," lamented former congressman John Pendleton
Kennedy.[8]

Governor Hicks left Baltimore for the state capital at Annapolis,
thirty miles southeast of the city, but he kept in touch with Mayor
Brown by telegram. In the wake of the riot, the bridge burning, and
the general disorder in Maryland's largest city, on Saturday Hicks
dispatched another message to Cameron. It sent a shudder through
the administration. The governor confessed that he and Brown had
failed to preserve order. He admitted that insurrectionary forces held
the upper hand. "They had arms; they had the principal part of the
organized military forces with them," he conceded. In consequence,
he amended his earlier positive response to Lincoln's request for four
regiments of Maryland volunteers: "I therefore think it prudent to
decline (for the present)."[9]

On Saturday, the mayor finally received a reply to the plea he had
sent the previous day urging Lincoln not to send more troops through
Baltimore. The delegation he dispatched to Washington on Friday
night had arrived too late to see the president but arranged for an
interview first thing the next morning. Lincoln acknowledged the
volatility that prevailed in Baltimore. He could see as well as his military advisers that they depended on the rail line through that city,

especially now that they could not count on the B&O to the west. In his reply, he thanked Brown and Hicks for attempting to keep the peace. In the future, he said, "troops *must* be brought here, but I make no point of bringing them *through* Baltimore." He told them General Scott agreed that he could march soldiers around the city to avoid another clash unless civilians sought to foment one. In that case, he would hold Maryland officials responsible.[10]

Brown was enormously relieved. He wrote back assuring the president he would do his utmost to prevent anyone from interfering with soldiers in transit, if they would only keep out of town and not "provoke the uncontrollable feeling" of Baltimoreans. It would have been more prudent if he had also expressed gratitude that Lincoln granted his request. Perhaps his anxiety over events overcame his best instincts, for Brown's message concluded undiplomatically with what amounted to scolding the president and warning him not to incite a recurrence of what he euphemistically called "the melancholy occurrences of yesterday."[11]

Lincoln made his concession, but as soon as he communicated that decision to Brown and Hicks on Saturday morning, he sent a telegram asking them to come to Washington immediately for a face-to-face meeting. Hicks did not receive the message, having left Baltimore for Annapolis. In the confusion, the request did not reach Brown until early the following morning.[12]

In the meantime, unrest and alarm rippled through Baltimore all day long on Saturday, April 20. Everyone knew that burning the bridges directly challenged the federal government. By evening, the delayed but reassuring response from Lincoln to Brown's request mollified some people, but probably a majority did not believe it. It was just one more piece of questionable intelligence amid a flood of rumors, mostly ominous if not outright alarming. Why should they believe this one scrap of unverified good news? The events of Friday convinced many Baltimoreans, at least that weekend, that Lincoln meant to oppress them.

As early as Saturday afternoon, artists began sketching the scene of the fighting along Pratt Street.[13] The North's weekly illustrated magazines provided a mass market for images of the violence, and the boost in sales would go to the first to record the details. But the placid image of sketchers at work along the waterfront belied the circumstances. Pratt Street itself might have returned to normal, but the enemy was at the gates of the city, if reports reaching Baltimore that weekend could be credited. Most people refused to accept that Lincoln had called for volunteers only to defend the national capital, not to attack Baltimore. After the events of Friday, all a majority could imagine was a growing threat of assault on their community by outsiders.

Armed men from the surrounding counties poured into town. By afternoon, a large number of miscellaneous bands, some in uniform and others not, had reported for duty to the mayor. Brown thanked these rural volunteers for their help but told them to return home. With the whole city seemingly in arms and with Washington now consenting not to send more troops through Baltimore, he did not believe he needed more citizen soldiers. To help tempers subside further, he ordered the bars closed on Saturday evening.

That weekend, the small garrison of U.S. troops at Fort McHenry, commanding the entrance to the inner harbor, kept the Stars and Stripes flying where it had inspired Francis Scott Key half a century before. That they did so became a cause for alarm. As the knowledge of what had happened on Friday sank in, Baltimoreans worried that the fort would train its cannons on the town and bombard it. With its large-caliber artillery pieces, Fort McHenry had the means to inflict horrific damage on the city it was built to protect. But the garrison had no such intention. On the contrary, the army captain in command there wrote to the War Department about his own fears, a mirror image of those of the townspeople, and no less far-fetched. He said he expected to be attacked any minute by Baltimore forces, but he thought he could withstand the assault.[14]

On the luminous morning of Sunday, April 21, with the rooftops of their city shining in the sunlight, Baltimoreans thronged the streets in search of the latest news. The excitement of the past two days abated a little, in part because more people heard that Lincoln had agreed to the mayor's request not to send troops through town. For the moment, people realized that the burned bridges achieved the same result, even if the president had resisted. The effect was to lessen tensions. On Sunday morning, residents traded gossip about Fort McHenry and wondered if it was true that northern regiments, frustrated by the blocked rail lines, had sailed down the Chesapeake Bay to Annapolis below Baltimore. The latter rumor was in fact the truth, though no one knew whether it meant the soldiers would try to go on from there to Washington or would turn and assault Baltimore from the south.

Then startling word arrived from the other end of the Chesapeake Bay: the navy had scuttled its ships and left Gosport in flames just a few hours before. People had little time to react to this bombshell when a greater excitement closer to home led to one of the most turbulent days in the city's history. Troops were coming from Pennsylvania and had already reached Cockeysville, seventeen miles north of town. The first report said two thousand men, but soon rumors inflated the figure five times over. Whatever the number cited, "instantly the street was in an uproar." Church bells picked up the alarm sounded by the town clock and broke up religious services in progress. "The tocsin of war was sounded," cried a newspaper editorial the next day, "not metaphorically but literally." The populace teemed into the streets. Before the disruption, at the Universalist church congregants heard their minister preach on a verse from the book of Joel that inverted the better-known figure of speech: "Beat your ploughshares into swords, and your pruning hooks into spears."[15]

The police commissioners, convinced that the news from Cockeysville was authentic, ordered militia companies to assemble at their armories and await further orders. About four thousand men not yet members of a company enrolled on the spot. They came from all classes, "merchants, mechanics, professional men, gentlemen of leisure and loafers."[16] As each company formed, it marched to the old City Hall to receive an issue of firearms, many of them antiquated weapons from a condemnation sale the year before at the Harpers Ferry armory. Unarmed men broke into gun shops and looted the picked-over weapons not purchased in the buying frenzy of the day before.

General George Steuart, who had graduated next to last in his West Point class and campaigned against Indians and Mormons, commanded the state militia. The handsome, sleepy-eyed Steuart, who would resign his commission to enter Confederate service a week later, established his headquarters on St. Paul Street, where messengers hurried in and out with the latest intelligence about the approaching Pennsylvanians. Steuart sent a cavalry troop north to reconnoiter. Thousands of people crowded into the square near the old City Hall to learn what was happening. The riot on Friday had involved a limited number of civilians, and the mass meeting that afternoon a few thousand more, but in the excitement of Sunday, virtually the whole city of more than two hundred thousand filled the streets, agitated and angry, like the Gadarene swine rushing headlong toward destruction.

While the militia and newly mustered volunteers awaited orders, their impatience got the better of them. According to one rumor, a second body of northern troops was marching on the city from a different direction from that of the Pennsylvanians at Cockeysville. "All the addenda of horrors that the fertile imagination could depict" addled the fidgeting and eager volunteers, who became increasingly agitated as the hours passed.[17] When no order to march came down from city leaders, some men decided to take matters into their own hands. They set out toward Cockeysville to confront the enemy and exact revenge for the victims of Pratt Street.

While these impetuous citizens enacted their own version of what Virginians were doing in Richmond that same hour on "*Pawnee* Sunday," negotiations between Baltimore's leaders and the federal government continued. Lincoln's request for a personal meeting, sent on Saturday, did not reach Mayor Brown until 3:00 a.m. Sunday. As soon as he received the message, though, the mayor responded that he would come "immediately. Hope to see you at once."[18] With three colleagues, he arranged for a special train and reached the capital in late morning.

At the White House, Brown faced an awkward task. He had to explain why his city's leadership thought burning the railroad bridges necessary to preserve order, when it threw a potentially fatal obstacle in the path of defending the nation's capital. After long discussion, Brown believed the president recognized his good faith. In fact, Lincoln had little option other than seeking some accommodation with the mayor until the national government had the strength to deal more forcefully with Baltimore's threatening actions. Lincoln repeated that it was absolutely necessary to concentrate troops in Washington to protect it from attack. That meant finding some way through Maryland. Because the government feared that Virginians had erected artillery batteries to contest the Potomac River below Washington, resupply by water seemed unwise.

Two routes remained. Northern soldiers could march overland to the west of Baltimore, or they could sail to Annapolis and take a small rail spur from there to Washington. Brown agreed to keep civilians from leaving Baltimore and attacking soldiers in transit either way. Lincoln reiterated his promise of Saturday to send no more through the city unless Marylanders obstructed them on one of these alternate routes.

The mayor and his colleagues left the president, buoyed by their accomplishment. But they realized that the anger in Baltimore toward the national government was still beyond their control. Just as Brown's train was about to leave for home, the mayor received an urgent telegram from John Garrett, the B&O president, about the furor just provoked by word of the Pennsylvania troops at Cockeysville. "Intense excitement prevails," Garrett warned. "Churches have been dismissed and the people are arming *en masse*."[19]

Brown hurried back to the president and showed him the cable. Surprised at this news, Lincoln summoned Scott and Cameron. He told them that he had not known about the troops at Cockeysville. To show good faith, he ordered them to return to Pennsylvania. Scott agreed, and Cameron issued the order. Brown returned to Baltimore, if not in triumph, then at least with a sense of keeping the city from certain explosion.

If he had known the situation at Cockeysville, the mayor would not have felt so relieved. The officers in charge of the Pennsylvanians may have been part-time militia volunteers, not professionals, but they were resourceful. They had brought enough lumber and other materials with them to make temporary repairs on the sabotaged railroad bridges. They intended to force their way into Baltimore, and they did not at first believe the order from Washington to retreat. They mistrusted the sporadic telegraphic contact with the capital and expected to receive a countermanding order by the next morning.[20] Only because they eventually accepted the original command as valid was the confrontation with the Baltimore militiamen defused.

A decision taken by a few individuals, on their own and without direction from above, could easily have produced a dramatically different outcome and profoundly influenced the course of events. Maryland might have gone over completely to secession if the Pennsylvania officers had been more assertive and pushed on provocatively into Baltimore before being ordered to return home.

Tensions subsided when news of the president's order for the Pennsylvanians to withdraw filtered into Baltimore on Sunday evening. That result did nothing for Lincoln's problem, though. By agreeing to Brown's request, the president kept Maryland from exploding and seceding—for the moment. But his urgent need for soldiers in the District of Columbia grew with the perceived threat of attack from Virginia. He could not have taken solace from the words of Pennsylvania's U.S. senator David Wilmot, one of the founders of the Republican Party. Wilmot found himself stuck in Baltimore just as word came in that the railroad bridges were burning. He wrote a desperate letter to General Scott. Without vigorous action by the government, he pleaded, "we will have to give up the capital."[21]

In Baltimore itself, unionists who had recently been the majority cowered in fear. A mass of angry men crowded the streets, arrayed in a multiplicity of militia uniforms and armed with every weapon that came to hand. They heralded the imminent possibility of greater violence. No more clashes occurred like those on Pratt Street, but for several days the frequent accidental discharge of guns carried by careless volunteers frayed brittle nerves and sent a steady stream of wounded to the doctors. "The only law prevailing here is mob law," wrote a minister to a colleague in Washington. "I cannot write any more. I know not what to write; surrounded by a mob, all I can do is to hope and trust in God."[22]

On Sunday night, the Baltimore police cut all the telegraph lines to the north. An enterprising vendor set up a pony express to bring in his regular supply of northern newspapers, but whatever he managed to bring into town invariably contained stale news. Intelligence two or three days out of date was no use at all to people battered by repeated alarms on an hourly basis. Cut off from the most current news, Baltimoreans believed each new and improbable rumor of attack. Jefferson Davis was even said to be riding personally at the head of a hundred thousand men toward the north.

The Protestant Episcopal bishop of Maryland exhorted his clergy to use in all services a new prayer beseeching God to "assuage the tumults by which this people are rent and torn." Fearing a lack of food, city police seized a German ship bound for Liverpool loaded with corn, lard, and wheat. The state seethed with hostility toward the federal government. Confederate recruiting in Baltimore boosted southern hopes for Maryland's secession. The prospect of northern regiments disembarking at the state capital below Baltimore, the alternate route that Brown and Lincoln had discussed, kept the crisis at fever pitch.[23]

Baltimore's actions infuriated the North. The president of the Pennsylvania Central Railroad demanded that Maryland be taught a lesson. The administration must strike "terror into the malcontents," he insisted. The government would have preferred to deal forcibly with Baltimore but could not do so before assuring the defense of the capital. Weak as he was, Cameron vowed to redeem the humiliation of withdrawing the Pennsylvanians from Cockeysville, calling it "one of the most painful acts I have witnessed."[24]

He had good reason to be chagrined and to worry. With Virginia militiamen astride the B&O at Harpers Ferry and hostile civilians blocking access to Baltimore, Washington remained cut off from the outside by train. Worse, the secessionists now had a rail connection that skirted the capital and could reinforce Baltimore directly from Virginia. Indeed, they began sending the Marylanders some of the confiscated arms from Harpers Ferry. If they had pursued that objective with more vigor, they might have changed the outcome in both Baltimore and Washington. Militia commanders in the former city moved to safeguard the B&O for their own uses and deny it to Washington. They may have believed they were only insulating their city from outside threat, but they must have known it put them at odds with Lincoln. Mayor Brown's neutrality was anything but that. It would be a race to see which side could take the initiative, either to besiege or to relieve the national capital.[25]

JABEZ PRATT was a native of Boston but embraced political views much like those that predominated among his colleagues in the business community of his adoptive city on the Chesapeake Bay. That is to say, once the secession crisis reached a boil, he favored letting the lower South leave the Union peacefully to avoid conflict at all costs. Once Baltimore crowds collided with troops from his home state, Pratt became outraged over what he called Lincoln's attempt to subjugate Maryland. His brother, John Pratt, still lived in Boston. On hearing about the riot, he telegraphed Jabez to offer his family shelter if they chose to flee the chaos. The day after Americans spilled one another's blood in the streets of Baltimore, Jabez wrote back to thank John but declined. He denounced Lincoln and vowed that "by God in heaven, we are determined to die in the work" of opposing more northern troops.[26]

In the days that followed, the brothers, both in their forties and neither of them ideologues, flung angry missives back and forth. The deterioration in their personal ties tracked the erosion of national unity. Jabez armed himself on April 20 and stood ready to defend his home during the "wild excitement," as the *Baltimore American* described that weekend.[27]

John replied that Marylanders had better let the northern volunteers pass, for it would be a shame "to apply the torch to [Baltimore]

and widen the streets with artillery."[28] Closer to the scene of violence than John, and shaken by it, Jabez was in no humor to let such
banter pass unchallenged. Robert Davis, the merchant bystander
whose death in the riots so inflamed the business community, had
been a close friend. Jabez angrily wished that "Massachusetts and
South Carolina [would] swallow each other up" and leave the border
slave states in peace.[29] When John allowed one of Jabez's messages to
be printed in a newspaper—from which it was reprinted by others,
including the abolitionist *Liberator*—his brother denounced this
"private treason."[30] Jabez later regretted using such intemperate language with his brother, but the heat of the moment got the better of
his judgment, as it did for so many of his countrymen that month.

CHAPTER 16

COUNTLESS RUMORS

April 21 to 25

And I heard a great voice out of the temple saying to the seven angels, Go your ways, and pour out the vials of the wrath of God upon the earth.

—Revelation 16:1

In Athens, Ohio, near the wide river border with northwestern Virginia, a newspaper editor brooded over the unnerving catalog of conflicts and natural disasters threatening mankind that spring. Poland looked set to revolt against its Russian overlord. Famine gripped India. Floods devastated Holland. Nationalists plotted the unification of Italy. South American republics were at daggers drawn. Spain and France meddled dangerously in Mexico. Now, at home, the festering tumor of sectional hatred had finally burst.

To the editor's mind, all signs pointed to Judgment Day. He could not resist invoking the incandescent Revelation of the blind seer John of Patmos, who wrote from his island exile with fevered words of prophecy about the wrath to come. "The world is convulsed," the *Athens Messenger* concluded, "as it probably never has been since the creation, with wars and rumors of war, by famine and desolation. . . . It would seem that the vials of the Revelations were opened, and that discord and blood were rained down upon our generation."[1] The fears expressed in that small town in Ohio resonated powerfully with the Washington editor who reprinted this account in the days when his city was cut off from the North and rumors of assault by ravening hordes of secessionists threatened an apocalypse in the federal capital.

FOR THE LINCOLN GOVERNMENT, it seemed that the unfolding string of calamities would never end. After the debacle at Fort Sumter, a daily avalanche of punishing blows reduced supporters of the administration to impotent rage and disbelief at the turn of events. On April 17, Virginia seceded. Word reached Washington the next day on the lips of unionist delegates who fled Richmond after the vote. On that same day, the arms works at Harpers Ferry fell to insurgent militiamen. News reached the federal capital the following morning. On that day, the nineteenth, Washington learned of deadly riots in Baltimore from the mouths of harried soldiers who fought their way through. On the twentieth, the burned bridges north of Baltimore cut off access from that direction. Word came on the evening of the twenty-first that the great navy yard at Gosport had gone up in flames before dawn. The editor of the *Washington Daily National Intelligencer* beseeched Virginia "to take up the godlike office of mediator." Too late.[2]

Private individuals, some well-meaning and others presumptuous meddlers, clamored for Lincoln's ear to give advice, admonition, and warning. A large delegation from the Baltimore YMCA—including Jabez Pratt, the transplanted Massachusetts merchant ready to shoot federal troops marching through his adopted city—sought an audience at the White House. The president's secretary privately sneered at these "whining traitors." Lincoln ignored their impertinent advice that he recognize Confederate independence to avoid further bloodshed. He lectured them on their indifference to what he believed was an imminent threat to the city from Virginia. He told them that although he had no wish to invade the South, "I must have troops to defend this Capital. . . . Our men are not moles, and can't dig under the earth; they are not birds, and can't fly through the air."[3]

Lincoln showed restraint despite his irritation at fence-sitting Marylanders who, to his thinking, wanted peace at any price, even the price of the Union. Despite the threats that beset his government, he promised to find a way around rather than through Baltimore. "Go home," he rebuked them, "and tell your people that if they will not attack us, we will not attack them, but if they do attack us, we will return it, and that severely."[4]

Attorney General Edward Bates was beside himself. A frowning sixty-four-year-old Missouri lawyer with the manners of an older generation, without flair or dynamism, he resented the more strong-willed, younger members of Lincoln's inner circle. But in the crisis, the stolid Bates rose to the occasion and recommended bold action. The events at Harpers Ferry and Gosport outraged him. He was even more angered by the government's seeming inability to react to the secessionists. He brusquely admonished his cabinet colleagues that both Maryland and Virginia, "by violence and terror," were undermining the nation. "They think and in fact find it perfectly safe to defy the Government, And why? Because we hurt nobody; we frighten nobody; and do our utmost to offend nobody."[5]

As ANXIETY ENVELOPED the federal capital, exhilaration blossomed across the growing Confederacy. Virginia's secession and Maryland's violent response to passing soldiers brightened radicals with the hope that all of the border states would join the southern cause and deliver Washington into their hands. Lincoln and his supporters, they crowed, "will be hemmed in by slaveholding States, which will girdle them with walls of steel."[6]

Southern sympathizers and spies reported on the state of mind of Washingtonians, on details of the city's defenses, and on the latest rumors in a flood of letters and telegrams sent south, many of them urging attack. Associate Justice John Campbell, still smarting from his failed diplomacy as Seward's go-between, sent encouraging words to Jefferson Davis from the isolated capital. To lose Washington would devastate the North, he wrote before resigning from the

Court; "their pride and their fanaticism would be sadly depressed."
He believed the fulcrum for deciding the issue was Baltimore, "for
there is the place of danger. . . . There is a perfect storm there."[7]

The Confederate government had to decide how to respond to the
opportunities opened up by the dramatic turn of events in Virginia
and Maryland. Even the fire-breathing *Charleston Mercury* cautioned
against a precipitate attack on Washington. Better to abandon it after
the victory of southern arms and leave it a magnificent ruin, "a strik-
ing monument to future ages of the folly and wickedness" of the
North. That was wishful thinking on a grand scale. Davis did not
have the luxury of indulging in speculation. Thinking more practi-
cally about the present, he preferred not to appear the aggressor.
Though it would be good to take Washington, it would be best if
Virginia or Maryland state troops, and not Confederate ones, did the
deed.[8]

The truth of the matter was that events were moving too swiftly,
and on a local level, for the Confederates at Montgomery to affect
the outcome in the border states. During the two weeks after Fort
Sumter, an hourly barrage of telegraphic intelligence flew back and
forth, while on the ground in Virginia and Maryland, civilians took
matters into their own hands.

Southern hopes for Maryland and Washington crested the last
week of April. On the twentieth, a Virginian wrote the Confederate
secretary of war, "One dash and Lincoln is taken, the country saved,
and the leader who does it will be immortalized." By the twenty-
second, the man he had in mind, Jefferson Davis, had become more
optimistic about their prospects. He sent Virginia's governor an epi-
grammatic injunction: "Sustain Baltimore, if practicable. We re-
enforce you." The secessionist press became distraught about seizing
Washington to aid their allies in Baltimore. "It can be done," urged
the *Richmond Dispatch*, "but now is the time to do it." With Harpers Ferry in their hands and the B&O at their mercy, the Virginians
did, in fact, order a thousand of the arms captured at the arsenal to be
sent to the Baltimore insurgents. By then, however, though the out-

come was not yet obvious, northern regiments streaming around, and not through, Baltimore had taken the initiative.[9]

BENJAMIN FRANKLIN BUTLER was a flamboyant Massachusetts attorney with a reputation for flashy courtroom tricks. He rarely flinched from poking a stick in the eye of convention. He rose from a humble background, married an actress, and got himself elected to the state legislature. In 1860, he quixotically supported Jefferson Davis for the Democratic presidential nomination. He wielded great influence in the state militia and convinced Gov. John Andrew to buy soldiers' overcoats from his textile mill. The smell of corruption would grow much stronger in the military career about to unfold for the balding attorney whose jowls and hooded eyes suggested something other than probity.[10]

Andrew commissioned Butler a brigadier general in charge of the Massachusetts regiments dispatched to Washington in answer to Lincoln's call. Before leaving home, he addressed a cheering throng of Bostonians at the State House, telling his men, "You are the advance guard of freedom and constitutional liberty." Someone asked if he had heard the news just in that Virginians had captured Harpers Ferry. Unimpressed, Butler shrugged and replied, "Seventeen Yankees took it once," a reference to John Brown.[11]

Butler reached Philadelphia late on the evening of April 19 with the 8th Massachusetts Regiment, where he learned that the 6th, which had gone a day earlier, had come to grief on Pratt Street. When word arrived the next morning that Marylanders had burned the railroad bridges, Butler had to find an alternate route to the capital.

Two railroad executives proposed a solution. Because there was no bridge across the Susquehanna River on the line from Philadelphia to Baltimore, trains had to board a large steamer that ferried them across the river to continue on their journey. The solution for Butler's men was to board the ferry and, instead of crossing the Susquehanna, go down the river to the Chesapeake Bay and on to the Maryland capital at Annapolis. From there, a small rail spur connected to the main B&O track between Washington and Baltimore.

This detour would allow them to circumvent the latter city entirely.[12]

Butler discussed the Annapolis option and other possibilities with Pennsylvania officials and Col. Marshall Lefferts of the 7th New York Regiment, which reached Philadelphia the day after Butler's men. A slim, mustachioed, self-made engineer and pioneer in telegraph construction, Lefferts seemed an incongruous choice to head the 7th, the prestige regiment of the Empire City, manned by the sons of high society. Perhaps it was the similarities in background that led these two proud commanders to take a dislike to each other. That antipathy opened the first chapter in a testy dispute between their regiments that would be picked at and debated by veterans long afterward.

In the end, considering their choices, including a dubious overland route, Butler decided to put his men on the ferry at the Susquehanna River and head for Annapolis. Lefferts chose to await further authorization from Secretary of War Cameron and later chartered a steamship directly from Philadelphia.[13]

The tiny Maryland capital on the bay's western shore became the unwelcome focus of attention as a result of Baltimore's act of self-isolation. Annapolis was located thirty miles southeast of the metropolis in a rural, slaveholding part of the state that overwhelmingly sympathized with the South. The Maryland General Assembly, when in session, met in a statehouse dominated by a bulbous wooden dome that dated from colonial times. With the legislature out of town, Governor Hicks represented authority on the weekend of the Pratt Street Riot. He had left Baltimore and returned to the capital but could not escape the crisis. Indeed, its next installment appeared unbidden on his doorstep in the form of Ben Butler.

Without incident, the 8th Massachusetts traveled down the rail line from Philadelphia to the north bank of the Susquehanna, a few miles inside the Maryland border. There it boarded the railroad's large ferry, appropriately named *Maryland*. In mild weather under a waxing, gibbous moon, it steamed uneventfully down the Chesapeake, the soldiers sleeping like dead men on the deck, despite the constant thrumming of the engine. The moon had set and cast them into darkness by the time they neared Annapolis. After waiting for the sun to rise, the *Maryland* pulled alongside the black masts of the school ship at the U.S. Naval Academy wharf early on Sunday morning, April 21.[14]

Dissension roiled the academy that spring. The superintendent, George Blake, warned Secretary of the Navy Welles that Annapolis was indefensible against assault. All he had to rely on were his students, "many of whom are little boys, and some of whom are citizens of the seceded States." He did not trust the telegraph line, convinced that disunionists in town read everything he transmitted. If threatened with attack, Blake said, he planned to evacuate the academy on board the school ship, the venerable *Constitution*, "Old Ironsides." Blake was wise to make contingency plans, for news of the Baltimore riots shocked public opinion in the Maryland capital. The few previously staunch supporters of the Union in Annapolis now cried for immediate secession. Perhaps unconscious of the symbolism, Welles ordered Blake to do his duty in a cable that carried a double meaning: "Defend the *Constitution* at all hazards. If it can not be done, destroy her."[15]

Blake was unnerved by the defections of his southern officers and midshipmen and relieved to learn that the *Maryland* carried northern volunteers. He had been expecting Baltimore rowdies, drunk with disunion fervor. A few hundred yards inland, a contrary emotion troubled Governor Hicks. He sent a message addressed to "the Commander of the Volunteer Troops on board the steamer" because he did not yet know Butler's identity. Because of the anxiety among the populace, he pleaded, "I think that you should take your men elsewhere."[16]

This was not the welcome Butler had hoped for, but he did not want to provoke a violent response. His reply to Hicks mixed irritation and restraint. After all, it was the burning of the Baltimore bridges, sanctioned by Hicks, that had forced the Massachusetts soldiers to come through Annapolis. Butler underscored his objection to Hicks's characterization of his men: *They are not Northern troops; they are a part of the whole militia of the United States, obeying the call of the President."* He argued that there was no cause for alarm and refrained from ordering his soldiers to disembark until the next day when the steamer with Colonel Lefferts and his regiment arrived.[17]

On April 22, Butler met Hicks on the grounds of the Naval Academy, where the Massachusetts and New York regiments made their temporary headquarters. The governor repeated his opposition to their presence. He protested the landing of troops, refused to let them buy provisions in town, and predicted that all of Maryland stood ready to take up arms against them.[18] The two men parted in ill humor, with nothing resolved.

Hicks now sorely tested Lincoln's trust. He even had the temerity to suggest that the British ambassador be asked to mediate the issues "between the contending parties of our country."[19] Looking over his shoulder at Maryland's rising disunionist faction, which continued to send him death threats, and firing messages at Washington and at the Naval Academy, Hicks tried to bend Lincoln and Butler to his will. In vain.

In his conversations with other Maryland officials, Butler assured them he had not come there to subdue their state but was passing through to defend "the Capital of our common country." Officers of the New York regiment also met with local people and tried to allay their fears. The New Yorkers said they were surprised at Maryland's reaction. They had expected no opposition. They appealed to the good relations they had earlier formed at joint exercises with southern militia regiments and ended with a genteel warning that was tinged with a chivalric innocence that would not survive the first battle. If compelled to face their old friends in the Baltimore or Richmond regiments in war, they said, "we shall return their first volley by presenting arms; but on the second fire we shall be compelled to defend ourselves."[20]

Butler told the governor his soldiers had commandeered the rail spur from Annapolis to the main Washington–Baltimore line and were repairing the tracks torn up by saboteurs. Sensing that he had enough men to repel any likely attack, Butler dismissed Hicks's objections. He sarcastically assured the governor that just as soon as he fixed the line, he would leave for Washington "and not be under the painful necessity of encumbering your beautiful City."[21]

The citizenry, though fiercely pro-southern, ignored Hicks and sold wagons, horses, and provisions to the soldiers at exorbitant prices. One Confederate sympathizer in Annapolis wrote her cousin that the populace was safe "provided we behave ourselves, and don't attempt to 'play Baltimore' upon them."[22]

While he sparred with Hicks, Butler renewed his feud with Lefferts. As Lefferts's senior in rank, Butler proposed that the 7th New York came under his command and that both regiments immediately set out together for Washington. Lefferts demurred. After consulting his officers, he told Butler they would wait for further reinforcements before leaving Annapolis. The New Yorkers also thought it would take less time if they marched overland instead of repairing the rail spur. Objecting, Butler later claimed that he shamed them, saying they were "fit only to march down Broadway in gala dress."[23] Although he probably embroidered his comments in retrospect, Butler did convince the officers of the 7th to change their minds and agree to his plan of march. The two regiments patched up their disagreement for the moment and set out together for Washington.

Before leaving Annapolis, Butler sparked a controversy with his own governor as well as Maryland's. It happened, paradoxically, because of his effort to mollify Hicks. The day after his regiment landed, Butler heard rumors of a revolt planned by slaves in the surrounding countryside. He told Hicks that his men were armed only against those who disturbed the peace. He therefore vowed that the soldiers stood "ready to co-operate with your excellency in suppressing . . . any insurrection against the laws of Maryland."[24]

No slave uprising occurred, and the offer might have passed unnoticed had Butler been from any other state than Massachusetts. Governor Andrew chastised his general for deviating from his duty. It should not have been Butler's task, the governor scolded, to defend Maryland against a slave revolt when that state was itself in rebellion. In his defense, Butler argued that he had "promised to put down a white mob" in Baltimore if necessary and could not understand why he should not have opposed a black one.[25]

When they had put an engine in working order, the soldiers began their cautious progress from Annapolis through contested territory toward the main rail line between Washington and Baltimore. They sawed off the tops of two cattle cars to create open carriages pushed ahead of the locomotive. The first mounted a howitzer loaded with grapeshot. It was slow going. Not far out of town, the soldiers could see Marylanders destroying track up ahead and sent skirmishers on foot to chase them away. The gunners in the lead carriage, however, never had an opportunity to open fire.[26]

A greater challenge faced them where the Annapolis spur connected with the Washington–Baltimore line. This was a point only a couple of miles south of the Relay House Junction, where the main branch of the B&O running to the west also connected to the Washington–Baltimore line (see map on page 140). City officials in Baltimore sent a large militia force to occupy the Relay House Junction and defend it against all opposition. Thus Butler's soldiers and these militiamen occupied respective rail junctions only a few miles from each other. A clash between pickets from these forces could have provoked the first large-scale violence between opposing bands of uniformed men in the border region. But such a confrontation did not take place. Once again, flukes of timing, geography, and decision making spared Maryland a showdown that could have precipitated the state's secession.[27]

With this stroke of luck, and despite all his bluster and feuding with colleagues, the rude, conceited Massachusetts commander got the job done. A more timid citizen soldier might have waited at Annapolis, fearful of what lay down the rail line, leaving Washington cut off even longer, with unpredictable results. Another commander, more rash than Butler, might have considered every sullen Marylander in the state capital an enemy, shot some of them as exemplary punishment, and thereby provoked a violent reaction. Butler's dogged course, which avoided either extreme, served Lincoln well.

Geography also played a part. If there had been no rail line from

Annapolis to Washington, Butler might have chosen to fight his way through on foot. What that might have done to inflame Maryland opinion is impossible to know. But there is more than a hint in the reaction to the garbled news about Butler that came into Baltimore. People learned, correctly enough, that he had reached Annapolis, but they also briefly believed rumors that Hicks was opposing him by force. This distorted intelligence stoked the anger that overflowed in Baltimore on the wild Sunday of April 21.[28] Actual bloodshed between the Massachusetts men and the Maryland militia might have tipped the scales in Baltimore in favor of disunion in the whole state. The cascading effect of such a decision on Washington would have altered the bigger picture dramatically, and not in Lincoln's favor.

The crisis for the Union passed, however, in part because secessionists in Baltimore had no coherent leadership and the soldiers en route to Washington did. Bypassing Baltimore proved to be a masterstroke that relieved the federal capital while leaving the metropolis at the head of the Chesapeake Bay to stew in isolation for a few more days.[29]

The divergent paths taken by Maryland and Virginia profoundly influenced the larger course of events. By the time Butler reached Annapolis, Virginia had already made its decision, but Maryland's hung in the balance. Now it seemed likely that the combination of self-isolation by Baltimore and bold action by northern regiments had averted another border state's secession. But no one could yet know for certain.

At noon on April 25, after an agonizing delay that was "the parent of countless rumors," a train arrived in Washington with Marshall Lefferts's 7th New York Regiment.[30] With Butler's 8th Massachusetts, they had finally reached the Washington–Baltimore line that morning, hungry and sleep deprived but elated at their accomplishment. Butler's regiment remained to secure the junction, and the New Yorkers continued on to the capital. No secessionist irregulars attacked them on the way, though they could see men on horseback standing away from the rail line, watching their progress.

Immediately after stepping off the train, the men of the 7th New York marched behind their band down Pennsylvania Avenue toward the White House. It was not their first time. They had often visited other cities to drum up interest in forming volunteer militia units, and the year before they had come to the District of Columbia. On that occasion, as a token of thanks, the city government presented the visitors with a stand of regimental colors, and the soldiers proudly carried those same flags as they marched through the relieved capital.[31]

Residents flooded the streets and windows along the way, "shouting as if mad, while handkerchiefs were waved, bells rung." Secretary of State Seward rode in his carriage to meet the regiment at the depot, and then he, Lincoln, and Cameron came out on the portico at the White House to review the troops.[32]

"We breathe a little free[r] now," wrote Horatio Taft at the Patent Office, after he admired the soldiers on Pennsylvania Avenue. The dismal cloud that had hung over the government began to lift. Now, instead of fearing that it would lack enough men to defend the capital, the War Department could worry about more mundane troubles, like having too many troops to provision and quarter. The acting surgeon general fretted that with approaching warm weather, the thousands of soldiers pouring into Washington, unless given healthy campsites, would invite a rash of deadly epidemics. With confidence that his capital would now be secure, Lincoln could turn to the greater crisis beyond the District of Columbia.[33]

The northern capital would never again be so gravely at risk, but the volatility of the political landscape remained, and the course of most of the border states was still in flux. Virginia had seceded, but North Carolina had not, nor had the slave states on the far side of the Appalachian Mountains. The *National Intelligencer* lamented on the day before the 7th New York marched down Pennsylvania Avenue that the country was facing the just deserts of years of sectional discord: "Vituperation and abuse, North and South, founded on nothing but misapprehension and ignorance, have produced their legitimate fruits, which, like Dead Sea apples, are already proving ashes to the taste."[34]

RIDING IN THE CAB of the first train into Washington was a young railroad official, a short, nimble Scottish immigrant bursting with both idealism and hard-nosed determination to elbow his way to fortune. A few years before, as a telegraph operator he had pioneered the recording of messages by ear, listening to the sound of the clicking key rather than waiting for the paper tape produced by the receiver. This talent brought him to the attention of Thomas A. Scott, the ambitious head of the Pennsylvania Railroad's western division. On his appointment as assistant secretary of war for transportation, Scott brought his protégé with him. So it was that as the locomotive chugged toward Washington, pulling the cars of soldiers slowly over problematic track, twenty-five-year-old Andrew Carnegie rode in front with the engineer and fireman.

He had arrived in Philadelphia on April 20 with a small band of handpicked railroad men. They reached Annapolis by water and then supervised Butler's soldiers as they coaxed a disabled engine back to life. When his train neared the District of Columbia, the sharp-eyed Carnegie spotted a problem up ahead with the telegraph line that ran along the right-of-way. Saboteurs had not cut the wire but had pulled it down and pinned it to the ground. Grounding the line was just as good as cutting, because it disabled the electrical signal. Carnegie stopped the train and jumped down to release the wire. As he pulled up the restraining stakes, the line snapped back into place and slashed him across the face. Undeterred, he jumped back into the cab. With blood streaming down his cheek, he waved for the engineer to proceed.

By the end of the war, he would be wealthy enough to quit the railroading business and devote his Midas touch entirely to investments, vilified and praised, rich beyond measure. But Carnegie's mammoth fortune and philanthropy lay on the far side of the titanic war for the Union that now was about to unfold. Long afterward, those postwar accomplishments could not outshine in his own memory the drama of being, as he exaggerated, the first man wounded in defense of the capital.[35]

CHAPTER 17

DISMEMBERING THE NATION

Late April to Early May

Americans, unspeakable horrors stare us in the face.

—Joliet (Illinois) *Signal*, April 23[1]

ontrary to Gustavus Fox's hope and expectation, the steamer *Baltic* served not to relieve the garrison at Fort Sumter, but to evacuate it. It was the outcome the ebullient sailor most wanted to forestall. On April 17, sailing up the coast from South Carolina toward New York, he scratched out a note in pencil to Montgomery Blair, his wife's brother-in-law and Lincoln's acerbic postmaster general. Blair had championed the plan to aid the beleaguered fort, and Fox wanted to spell out for him exactly what had happened.

After the adrenaline high of sailing toward Charleston and danger, and then the frustration of being no help at all to Major Anderson, Fox had three days of relative calm at sea before facing a tumultuous hero's welcome in New York. Contemplation did not make him serene. He poured out his scorn for the secretary of state, accusing Seward, but not naming him, of thwarting the mission. "As for our expedition," he seethed, "somebody's influence has made it ridiculous."[2]

Fox was naturally hot to justify his actions, but events now tumbled over one another with alarming speed. Within days, if not hours, of the time he wrote, Virginia seceded, Baltimore erupted in violence, Harpers Ferry and the Gosport Navy Yard went up in flames, and the Confederates threatened to grab all of the border states and maybe the nation's capital, too. It was no surprise that Blair, replying to Fox the day after northern troops broke the isolation of Washington, had no time to discuss the drama in Charleston Harbor. It was fast receding into the past. "Indeed," he concluded hurriedly, "events of such magnitude are crowding on us that Sumpter and Anderson are not thought of for the moment."[3]

AT THE BEGINNING of the month, probably a majority of Americans believed their leaders would stitch together a compromise, just as they had done so many times before. National politics intruded only sporadically into the lives of ordinary people, who went about the hard labor of spring planting and keeping the country's workshops humming. Putting bread on the family table was the paramount concern of most Americans in April 1861, not matters of high policy or constitutional dispute. When politicians intimately involved with the secession quarrel professed hope for a peaceful resolution, there seemed little reason for the average citizen to fret.

The explosion at Fort Sumter and Lincoln's forceful reaction to it, however, called forth a groundswell of patriotic emotion on all sides. In most places, all that people could do was demonstrate outrage or joy, wave the flag of their choice, and denounce their opponents. But what happened in Virginia and Maryland during the week after Anderson's surrender influenced history more fatefully than all the agitated demagoguery in the rest of the country put together. Events there altered the political and military landscape in ways unimaginable at the beginning of the month. For a brief time, the balance could easily have tipped in another direction.

A misleading hiatus followed the violence of mid-April. It was certainly not a period of calm; effusive patriotic displays and martial preparations accelerated almost everywhere. Still, there was a note of false grace as the North exhaled in relief once Washington was reinforced. The storm of disasters that had beset the federal government immediately after Fort Sumter abated for the time being. The movement toward secession in the upper South continued to gather steam, but the absence of bloodshed for the moment allowed hope that a way could still be found to stop the rift from widening. Peacemakers on all sides cited the dread of full-scale war as incentive to prevent further violence—though in late April they could hardly begin to imagine the scope or horror of the conflict they warned against.

Private efforts to reach a settlement abounded. Some, like the Baltimore YMCA delegation to the White House, espoused narrow goals. The YMCA men focused on keeping northern soldiers out of their city to prevent further rioting. Others, like Tennessee unionist W. R. Hurley, sought a grander objective. The editor of the *Nashville Democrat,* Hurley denounced "cotton traitors" and urged supporters of the Union to stand firm. He realized he represented a minority in his state and took the long train ride to Washington to lobby for restraint on all sides. On his way there through Virginia, he posted a letter to the governor. Whether from palsy or the swaying of the train, the erratic penmanship of his letter mimicked the agitation that rattled him. Hurley told John Letcher that Tennessee was divided, and he implored the Virginia convention—even after it endorsed secession—to plan for a concerted, armed neutrality of the border states.[4]

The mirage of upper South solidarity still glimmered for many Americans caught between the Confederacy and the North. A week after Pratt Street, John Pendleton Kennedy, the unionist former congressman from Baltimore, proposed his own scheme to avert war. Like Hurley, he looked to those in the middle and urged "that the President should invite the Border States to confer on terms of settlement."[5]

This dream that salvation lay in the hands of the upper South appealed to many in the North as well. And if not a meeting of those in-between states, then some grand convention of all the states. A Philadelphian urged Virginia's governor to take the lead and all would hail him "as a rainbow in the deluge."[6] Many northerners, like unionists of the border, "hope[d] against hope," as a Wisconsin paper declared, that a Union-saving compromise could be had.[7] In Joliet, Illinois, the *Signal* denounced extremists of both sections and vowed that the people of the United States loathed "malignant fanaticism" and the war that it threatened to provoke. The people "will yet make known" that they yearned for compromise and peace.[8]

One by one, however, the previously loyal slave states were compelled to choose sides. If all eight of them had seceded, the Confederacy likely would have been too strong to be defeated. If none had left, it would have been too weak to last long. The tragedy for the country was that the upper South split roughly down the middle. It was the outcome most likely to prolong the conflict, and it was strongly influenced by what happened in Virginia and Maryland, with the divergent paths they chose.[9]

Virginia led the way in the second wave of disunion. Then the other states of the upper South made their decisions, some to secede, others to stay. The addition of the most populous slave state to their cause tempted even the most cautious Confederates to anticipate victory. "Will Lincoln's stomach for war carry him on against this demonstration?" one of them asked doubtfully. "We shall see." The Confederate vice president, Alexander Stephens, hurried to Richmond to negotiate. The convention ratified a treaty with the Confederacy, even before the electorate had its chance to vote on the ordinance of secession. The state moved to a war footing, urged on by the radical press. Showing its racist assumptions, it proclaimed that Virginians were not neutrals: "They are Southern people and not border people. . . . They are not hybrids, they are not mulattoes." On April 27, still nearly a month before the people voted, Virginia invited Jefferson Davis to move his capital to Richmond.[10]

After the convention endorsed secession and many Virginians who once scorned it rallied to the southern cause, bitter resentments remained in the minds of others. They would abide by the decision of their state, but with the greatest reluctance. Alcinda Janney, furious with both Lincoln and the Confederacy, bewailed the revolution in her nation's affairs. "'The Flag, the Flag—the stars & stripes' I feel that it is as much mine as theirs," she cried.[11] Even after the ordinance passed, her husband stayed on in Richmond out of a profound sense of duty to the convention over which he had presided. At the end of April, Alcinda beseeched him, "Dearest one *come away* you have labored in vain. . . . *Come home.* Shake the very dirt of that city from your shoes but cry against their iniquity to the last . . . *come home* there is nothing more you can do."[12]

The Old Dominion was about to pay a dreadful price for its actions. Unionist delegates from the northwestern part of the state went home to caucus with their constituents. A Wheeling newspaper summarized their long-standing grievances in a single, rancorous sentence: "We can look to Richmond for taxes and treason, but for little else." A traveler through the western counties saw the growing resistance to rebellion and wondered if Virginia, after railing against force by Lincoln, "will attempt to coerce her own citizens." Lincoln's attorney general, Edward Bates, predicted that when Virginia "dismembers the nation she will herself be dismembered."[13]

Aggrieved for decades at domination by the eastern part of the state, westerners seized their chance. They argued that they were the only loyal Virginians, the iniquitous easterners having embraced the whore of secession. The newspaper in tiny Wellsburg, far up in the northern panhandle, almost to Pittsburgh, added an engraving of the Stars and Stripes below the paper's name and the words "Nailed to the Mast." The result would not be a neat division of the state. There could be none without leaving thousands of partisans on the wrong side of the divide. Though northwestern Virginia was fixed solidly in the unionist camp, many mountain counties with strong opinion on both sides would find themselves hotly fought over. A brand-new state, West Virginia, would be distilled in the alembic of war. Henry Wise called it "the bastard child of a political rape."[14]

Three other states in the upper South followed Virginia's lead. With Lincoln's proclamation, everything shifted, even in Tennessee and North Carolina, which had weaker secessionist sentiment than the Old Dominion. Nashville unionists, like their colleagues across the region, remained confident into the middle of April. But like them, when news of the proclamation arrived on April 15, they denounced Lincoln and screamed betrayal. On April 20, both the Union and Southern Rights parties gathered for a giant meeting in Nashville to proclaim their solidarity against war from the North. As a sympathetic account breathlessly reported, "There the mountains were on fire."[15]

Unionists who converted to the southern cause tried to rationalize their about-face with a constitutional distinction. Tennesseans did not assert a right to secession, they argued. Instead, they acted "like freemen ought always to act, upon the inherent right of revolution."[16] Gov. Isham Harris called the legislature into special session. It arrogated to itself the rights of a convention called by the electorate. On May 6, it passed a declaration of independence and submitted it to the voters for pro forma approval. The next day, a riot in Knoxville left one man dead, prefiguring the strife that would afflict Union-leaning east Tennessee for the next four years.

After sneering at the secession of the lower South and especially at South Carolina's "insufferable arrogance," North Carolinians joined hands across factions in the wake of the president's proclamation. Those who two months before had rejected calling a state convention now excoriated Lincoln, the "Arch Fiend Satan." One who had opposed secession up to that point conceded that "resistance is now on every man's lips and throbs in every bosom." Antisecession editor William Holden declared that the proclamation, with a stroke of forked lightning that rent the southern sky, "made the North wholly North and the South wholly South."[17]

The surge of anger at Washington may have carried North Carolina out of the Union even without Virginia's action, but the decision of its northern neighbor sealed its fate. On May 1, the legislature set in motion the mechanism for formal secession. Through quiet efforts behind the scenes, John Adams Gilmer, the congressman from Greensboro, had labored more than anyone to safeguard his region against disunion. A week after Lincoln's proclamation, he wrote a sorrowing letter to Seward. In despair, Gilmer blamed the president for doing what the fire-eaters had hoped. "As matters now stand there is a United North against a United South, and both marching to the field of blood."[18]

In Arkansas, a regional divide pitted the north and west, which opposed secession, against the south and east, where pro-Confederate planters dominated. Unionists held a slight majority in the convention that met in early March and defeated an ordinance of secession. The delegates adjourned with a promise to hold a referendum on the issue later in the summer. After Virginia acted, however, Arkansas's convention reassembled. Gov. Henry M. Rector delayed responding to Lincoln's request for troops for a week, but when he did, he denounced the president's effort "to subjugate the Southern States." On May 6 at Little Rock, the convention voted overwhelmingly to leave the Union.[19]

The tide of southern patriotism in Virginia, Tennessee, North Carolina, and Arkansas swept the opposition before it. In each of these states, though, large unionist minorities remained, cowed but unconverted.

The uppermost tier of southern states was even more conflicted. Powerful secession interests in Missouri denounced the Lincoln administration "with words of peace on its tongue, but with the sword of hatred in its heart."[20] Advocates of Union and states' rights set up opposing militias. In a camp outside St. Louis, pro-southern militiamen organized with the support of the governor. When a larger pro-Union force surrounded them, though, they surrendered peacefully on May 10. But when the prisoners were escorted back through town, a crowd gathered, and a riot far larger than the one in Baltimore broke out. Nearly thirty people died in the shooting, more the following day. The pro-southern governor signed an accord to keep the peace with the local commander of federal forces in Missouri, but the state's political leadership was divided. In the coming months, a civil war within Missouri would pit guerrilla bands against one another and threaten to wrench the state out of the Union.

Before Fort Sumter, the opposing sides jockeyed for position in slaveholding Kentucky. Gov. Beriah Magoffin fiercely denounced

Lincoln's proclamation. The state's elder statesman, John Crittenden, implored his fellow Kentuckians to spurn both sides. Crittenden, whose eponymous Senate committee had failed to find a compromise, called on his state to mediate the national crisis and endorsed neutrality for Kentucky.

A special session of the legislature met on May 6. Unionists and states' rights supporters agreed to a position of armed neutrality. Though it was enormously popular, neutrality was no more a legal right of a state than secession. Already, voices in the North denounced it as just "another name for treason covered by cowardice." Still, George Prentice's *Louisville Journal* called for an "*armed mediation* between the combatants in this unnatural strife.*" Kentuckians embraced this policy to avoid choosing sides as long as possible. It would last much of the summer, long enough for unionists to gain the upper hand. But ultimately it could not keep the war from Kentucky's borders or Kentucky's people from harm.[21]

Neutrality appealed to Maryland, too, though its location made such a position possible for far less time than in Kentucky. Recognizing secession in the lower South, the predominant Maryland opinion in late April argued for acquiescence rather than war to restore the broken past. "Let them depart in peace" was the typical formula. For their own safety, they clung to hope for the proposed border state conference. Unionist delegates to the Virginia convention had proposed that idea, and it possessed an amazing vitality even after the violence of late April. The *Baltimore American* refrained from advocating either Confederacy or Union and instead urged the legislature to appoint delegates to the border state meeting. To many Marylanders, a middle confederacy between North and South seemed the least bad outcome.[22]

Lincoln treated Maryland gingerly. He knew its pacification, either by suasion or force, was key to maintaining control over his capital. He toyed with the idea of arresting members of the General Assembly to forestall secession but decided instead to let them make the first move. As a precaution, Winfield Scott gave Benjamin Butler authority for whatever measures he deemed necessary if the legislature acted to take up arms against the United States. Delay paid off. Governor Hicks convened the legislature in western Maryland at Frederick instead of at Annapolis, a hotbed of secession. His refusal to recall the legislators earlier was a testimony to the residual strength of his unionism, however wavering. Earlier, they might well have endorsed secession. When the legislature finally met, momentum had shifted, and the lawmakers voted decisively against disunion.[23]

Lincoln faced the classic dilemma of democratic leadership in times of national emergency, a dilemma that every wartime president of the republic to follow him would confront. He believed he had to curtail some civil liberties in order to preserve the greater good. Whether he was justified in the extent to which he trod on Americans' rights is still debated. On April 27, he suspended the writ of habeas corpus along the vital rail line between Washington and Philadelphia. His action allowed army commanders to hold without trial any civilian suspected of disloyalty. Roger Taney, the aged chief justice from Maryland who had sworn Lincoln into office, denounced his act as illegal. Lincoln ignored Taney. He would accept the constitutional consequences later. For the present, he needed to control the railroads through Taney's home state.

In his message to Congress on July 4, Lincoln encapsulated the hard choices he made with a single rhetorical question: "Are all the laws, *but one*, to go unexecuted," he asked, referring to the dilemma over habeas corpus, "and the government itself go to pieces, lest that one be violated?" He was beginning to show the backbone that even his supporters doubted he possessed during the weeks of drift. Seward thought, perhaps melodramatically, that these bold and constitutionally suspect actions in late April nearly "brought them all to the scaffold."[24]

The isolation of Baltimore gradually allowed elected civic authorities to reassert control. In the absence of strong leadership among the secessionist movement there, radicals failed to take the initiative in the confusing aftermath of the riots. They never confronted Benjamin Butler's forces head-on and allowed him to consolidate his control over Annapolis and the rail lines.

Under the cover of a violent electrical storm on May 13, Butler moved in force to occupy Baltimore. By then, passions had subsided. Residents did not protest, as they had done on Pratt Street a month before, but greeted Butler's men with stony silence. The economic distress resulting from the city's isolation reminded business leaders where the source of their prosperity lay. It was not as much with their friends in the South as with the more proximate and robust economy of the Northeast and the border hinterlands drawn into Baltimore's commercial orbit by the B&O.[25]

Among the great unintended consequences of the secessionists' campaign was the effect of disunion on African Americans in the South, even before they began to use the chaos of war to flee from bondage and help the Union cause. Nervous whites feared disloyalty from their slaves as the nation tore itself apart. Alarmists charged that the North, "whose saint is Brown," had sent its spies to foment a servile insurrection.[26] But the widespread rumors that slaves were planning uprisings sprang more from the fears of owners than from actual plots. Even so, those fears ensured that whites would become more vigilant to keep control over enslaved people.

The week after secession, a frantic telegrapher on the rail line through southern Virginia articulated those fears. He begged for a shipment of revolvers because his operators were stationed at lonely outposts "where the Negroes are numerous and white persons few."[27] White southerners had to get used to restrictions on their own freedom, too, as a member of the Virginia convention mused without irony three days after the passage of secession. "Even now," marveled unionist Robert Conrad, anyone leaving Richmond had to have a pass, "exactly such as we give to negroes."[28]

As the examples of Conrad and the telegrapher illustrate, though the free and enslaved African Americans of the upper South were not the primary actors in the tumult of April, they figured prominently in the calculations of those who were. For it was how to order relations among the races that lay behind all the high-flown arguments about constitutional rights. And it was a mark of the limitations of white southerners' imaginations that they could not envision a South without slavery. But then, in April 1861, neither could most people in the North.

ON APRIL 29, Jefferson Davis sent a long message to the Confederate Congress restating the justification for secession. He concluded with his famous protest that the South wanted only peace, not war: "All we ask is to be let alone." His wish was irretrievably at odds with Lincoln's determination to preserve the Union whole. Passions were aroused throughout the country; blood had been spilled. A stubborn unionist later recalled that "the whole Southern country presented the appearance of one vast lunatic asylum." Confederates laid the same charge against the North.[29]

Each side was astonished at the force of the other's angry resolve. Many northerners believed that southerners who did not own slaves would never rally to the Confederate cause. Many southerners believed the downtrodden laborers and immigrants in the North would never fight for the Republican cause. To their shock, both expectations were confounded. To upper South unionists, Lincoln's decision to confront the Confederates over Fort Sumter was insanely reckless. He put the Union in jeopardy, just as Davis risked all over the same issue. They thought they could hold the line against secession even after Major Anderson surrendered, but Lincoln's call for volunteers compelled them to make the choice they feared, and they cursed him for it.[30]

The burst of patriotism evident across America after Fort Sumter buoyed people's emotions with the promise of communal solidarity, but it also evoked more sinister feelings. Decades of mounting sectional alienation had spawned a loathsome progeny, as each side vilified its opponents. "[Southern] traitors and ingrates have sneered their last at the *Puritans*," snarled the *Chicago Tribune*. "They have called us psalm-singing cowards the last time for *one* century." Not to be outdone, the *Richmond Examiner* spat its venom back at "mean, hungry, avaricious, lying, cheating, hypocritical, cunning, cowardly

Yankee[s]." Almost overnight, many people discovered that their fellow Americans were mortal enemies, subhuman vermin fit only to be cast into eternal flames.[31]

While each side marked time until uniformed armies could train and take the field, the slurry of invective they hurled at each other testified to the newfound hatred Americans felt for one another. Virginia's secession—"a piece of low-bred, stupid, villainous treachery"— called forth special outrage and denunciation in the North. Each side was willing to believe the most pusillanimous behavior of the other. No sooner did word reach Boston of the Pratt Street Riot than stories circulated that the mob had mutilated the bodies of fallen Massachusetts soldiers. If northerners came out to cheer the volunteers headed to defend Washington, some southerners thought, well, that was just "what might be expected of those sewers into which the whole world has poured its superfluous filth and scum."[32]

Political leaders on all sides received hate-filled correspondence. Virginia's governor, unionist John Letcher, who had borne the vicious taunts of secessionists for months but then led his state into the Confederacy, received a cascade of insults from strangers. "The game of brag is now played out," one man wrote him with chilling glee. "We have our foot now fairly in, and the greatest misfortune that can now befall us, is to *have you cave in.* Now my dear Traitor we want a few heads." In a similar vein, a Wisconsin correspondent promised Letcher that northern soldiers would hang Henry Wise on the same gallows as John Brown and threatened that "your body may yet dangle from the same gibbet." Two venomous Mississippians itching for blood wrote Lincoln they would pay $1 million "for your miserable traitorous head."[33]

IT WAS AS RECENT as 1844 that Samuel Morse had set up his new telegraph apparatus in Roger Taney's Supreme Court chambers and tapped out the first official message on the experimental line from Washington to Baltimore. He let a friend's daughter pick the text of that first telegram. She chose a biblical passage that would be taught to schoolchildren from that day forward: "What hath God wrought!"

In less than two decades, Morse's magical wires had crisscrossed the nation. In this spring of supreme discord in 1861, they united the country in instantaneous knowledge of tumultuous events. But what had the people wrought?

Sometimes through their elected leaders and sometimes through unplanned mass action, many of them were striving to rip the nation apart. Still, even as April ended, knowing about Fort Sumter and Pratt Street, Harpers Ferry and Gosport, many Americans prayed that they could avert a general civil war. This was a special hope along the upper South border. Even after Virginia, North Carolina, Tennessee, and Arkansas seceded but Maryland, Delaware, Kentucky, and Missouri wavered, residents of those states hoped the fighting could be contained, even if completely peaceful separation was no longer possible. Maybe some other outcome not yet dreamed of might still result. Such sentiments were obscured by the more bellicose and dominant emotions of the North and the South, but the more pacific hopes along the border persisted long and died hard.

By May, no one could discern the future any more than before. Prospects for the republic, however, looked grimmer than at any time since its birth. Recruitment of volunteers and mass political meetings accelerated the taking of sides, shoving would-be peacemakers to the margins. John Moncure Daniel mocked them as hissing "fangless serpents" who could no longer thwart the glorious march toward southern independence.[34] In the North and in the Confederate States, the eruption of patriotic spirit silenced nonconformity. The rasping bellow of intolerance shouted down dissent and cast a veneer of unity over public opinion, when in fact divergent, though muted, sentiments persisted.

There were some desultory exchanges of cannon fire between Union ships and southern shore batteries but no ground battles in late April or even May. Northern soldiers did not set foot on Virginia soil until the day after the state's referendum approved the ordinance of secession on May 23. The gathering forces on both sides were still only armed mobs.

For the moment, angry words and flag-bedecked public gatherings allowed Americans to vent the pent-up hostility they felt toward their fellow citizens. For many, the failure of compromise brought an overwhelming sense of relief. Talking was at an end. The long-festering sectional dispute would be put to a brutal and clear-cut test of arms. Or so they thought. In that time of exuberance, before the toll of war killed the naive welcoming of it, a cathartic release of tension purged the land. "Civil war is actually upon us," mused Ohio senator John Sherman, "& strange to say it brings a feeling of relief—the suspense is over." Historians have likened the joyous demonstrations of patriotic northerners and southerners to the later spontaneous mass expressions of national fervor in 1914 in London, Berlin, St. Petersburg, and Paris.[35]

It was easier for people in the Deep South and in the free states to rally around their respective causes. It took longer for the upper South, torn internally in different directions, to reach that point. But once the time came to choose, many of the wavering unionists there made the decision for the South. For them, it was motivated not so much by support of the Confederacy as by defense of their local communities against the perception that Lincoln meant them harm. Unlike secessionist radicals, they made the atavistic decision for families and friends, not for abstract constitutional principles of states' rights or defense of slavery. When confronted with the rending of society, they believed they had no other choice.

The community solidarity so evident that spring masked continuing divisions, especially in the upper South. Some there greeted Lincoln's proclamation as a blinding light on the road to Damascus and became fervent Confederates. Some would have done so anyway and seized upon the proclamation as a convenient excuse. Others donned gray uniforms more sorrowfully in solidarity with their communities. Thousands who had no truck with disunion and spurned the blandishments of fire-eaters before April now ensured that half of the upper South would join the Confederacy. "Men who had no heart for secession," observed an east Tennessee unionist, "did have heart for their neighbors and kindred."[36] And so they marched toward the field of blood, as John Gilmer lamented, a darkling plain they had never seen before.

ON MAY 27, after American blood had flowed in Baltimore, St. Louis, and Knoxville, after four more states had seceded, and after national troops tentatively crossed the Potomac to Virginia soil, a forlorn body of men convened in Frankfort, the capital of uncertain Kentucky. They represented the culmination, fulfillment, and failure of the great desideratum of upper South unionists.

Since the secession crisis began, the chimera of regional consultation had lulled unionists of the border into thinking they could control events. They fancied themselves pragmatists, unlike the hotheads in the cotton states or the fanatical abolitionists of the North. If only they could work together, they could win over fair-minded northerners and reach another grand compromise worthy of those of bygone generations. But a not unsympathetic northern journalist observed that the in-between states could no longer remain detached from the fray: "They will be dragged into the vortex of strife in spite of all resistance and will be compelled into active participation."[37]

At the last moment before the Virginia convention voted to secede, unionists had appealed once more for consultation with their neighbors. The resolution proposed by Robert Scott called for such a meeting at Frankfort. Scott and his fellow vacillating unionists still believed, and not without reason, that concerted action made more sense than piecemeal secession. They still hoped that a powerful bloc of upper South states could deter the North from putting down the Confederate rebellion.

Even after the failure of Scott's resolution, proponents of the idea did not let the vision die, which explains why those delegates gathered in Frankfort on the proposed date. On May 27, a dozen emissaries came from Kentucky, four from Missouri, and a single, irregularly chosen one from Tennessee. That was all. Virginia, the originator of the idea, sent none. None came from Arkansas, North Carolina, Delaware, or Maryland. Fittingly, the convention chose as its president

the grand old man of failed national compromise, former senator
John Crittenden. His calming eloquence had so far helped steer Kentucky away from war during the days immediately after Lincoln
called for volunteers.[38]

The same day the Frankfort meeting convened, Jefferson Davis
was braving the cinders spewed by the South's wood-burning loco-
motives to make his triumphal progress through the enlarged Confederacy to his new capital at Richmond. He was thronged at stations
along the way by delirious well-wishers who were drunk with patriotic excess, and he was smothered in garlands of flowers presented
by happy young girls. In Washington, defending the capital and
building an army absorbed Lincoln's waking hours. But he took the
time to mourn his young friend, "brave and early-fallen" Elmer
Ellsworth, the first soldier to die when government troops crossed
the Potomac into rebellious Virginia.[39]

There was little for the pitiful rump congress in Frankfort to do
but deplore the poor attendance and beseech Congress to find a compromise. If that effort should fail, Congress should then call a grand
convention of all the states.[40] The North and the South, both feverishly arming for the coming struggle, ignored the Frankfort meeting,
and it adjourned in failure. With it expired the self-delusion of unionists in the upper South. There were barely enough mourners to carry
the coffin of border state cooperation to its grave.

EPILOGUE

Spring 1865

He maketh wars to cease unto the end of the earth; he break-
eth the bow, and cutteth the spear in sunder; he burneth the
chariot in the fire.

—Psalm 46:9

The story did not have to turn out the way it did. Today, we have
trouble imagining a different course of events, because we know
the results, good and bad: devastating civil war, slavery's death, the
modern United States of America. But Americans in spring 1861
could not know what the future held, any more than we can know
what lies ahead for us. For many conflicted souls in the upper South,
an uncharted middle way between extremes still beckoned in April.
It behooves us to understand them in their own time, to imagine,
with them, a different outcome.

These conservatives of the border may not seem entirely attrac-
tive to modern sensibilities, but that is not a fair test. It is undeniable
that the Union they wanted to preserve, as much as the nation their
Confederate foes envisioned, rested upon slavery. They could not
conceive of a South where black southerners were not fastened by
their color to lifelong bondage. That was their failing, and it blinded
most northerners, too. Despite that limitation, they deserve some
respect for their quest for peace and their determined, if ultimately

futile, stand against the turbulent states' rights zealots who smashed the Union and gladly risked the horrors of civil war in order to build a pure, more perfect slave republic.

Ultimately, the dream of upper South unionists for joint action among the border states failed, and failed utterly. But the hope for that cooperation most certainly affected the course of the war they were not able to prevent. Seemingly impotent in the face of secessionist passion and northern resolve, they still influenced the outcome as the Union fragmented. In the end, all the states along the border were forced to choose, and in some of them, notably in Missouri, eastern Tennessee, and western Virginia, society descended into internal civil wars paralleling the larger one.

Only in retrospect, however, can the chronology of that spring be portrayed as an ineluctable march toward the inevitable national tragedy. It was not foreordained. During March and April, before large-scale fighting erupted, the decisions of individuals could have diverted the nation's trajectory in a different direction at numerous points. Some of the might-have-beens are familiar. Most starkly put, what would have happened if Lincoln had shown restraint over Fort Sumter? Or if Davis had let him resupply the garrison there and maintain the status quo? Or if Lincoln had delayed or limited his proclamation calling for troops? But there were other pivotal moments as well. At a whole host of lesser-known turning points that spring, mostly in Virginia and Maryland, events could have taken an equally and dramatically different course.

If Henry Wise had not been at the Virginia convention to rally the dispirited secessionist minority in March, the assembly might have adjourned earlier. The largest slave state would then have faced the issue of disunion in a different context, without a sitting convention. If, on the other hand, upper South unionists had capitulated instantly over Fort Sumter, a larger and stronger Confederacy might have emerged more quickly. If the proposed coup by radicals against the Virginia convention had taken place, it might have provoked a unionist backlash. If Robert Scott's alternative to the ordinance of secession had passed, Virginia might have led the way toward a convention of the border states. A middle way between the Confederacy and the North might have opened up for the conflicted upper South unionists.

If Baltimoreans had not burned the bridges north of town after the Pratt Street Riot, greater bloodshed might have occurred when the next northern regiments came through. Secession would then have been more likely for Maryland, and the fate of Washington, D.C., would have altered dramatically. The same would have been true with different choices by Gov. Thomas Hicks and Gen. Benjamin Butler at numerous points during the following week. Irreconcilable differences between the Deep South Confederacy and the North may have made war in some form unavoidable by spring 1861. But the various might-have-beens in Virginia and Maryland suggest that there could have been different shapes to the fragmentation of the Union and different, perhaps more attenuated, narratives to the war that followed.

The human cost of the war that did result beggars description. Six hundred thousand soldiers died in a nation of thirty-one million. Countless widows and orphans faced a bitter future. For a generation, legions of veterans bearing empty sleeves, or hobbling down the street on prosthetic legs, were a common sight. Lincoln said it well: "[The war] has carried mourning to almost every home, until it can be almost said that the 'heavens are hung in black.'"[1] One of the best historians of the conflict summed it up more brutally and without poetry: "Slavery was dead; secession was dead; and six hundred thousand men were dead. That was the basic balance sheet of the sectional conflict."[2]

The events of spring 1861 yielded the ultimate failure of the American political system—resort to arms, not compromise. Of all the manifold tragedies of that tragic era, there was this: White southerners rallied to defend hearth and home against what they perceived as an alien aggressor. Northerners rallied to defend Union, Constitution, and the rule of law against what they saw as assault by radical revolutionaries. Both saw a threat to their way of life. Both suffered as a consequence.

In the wake of that confrontation, Americans of African ancestry found their way to freedom, however imperfect. The United States of America that emerged at the other end of the fratricide was vastly different from the one that divided against itself. But those two momentous outcomes, however desirable, are different stories. Focusing on them distracts us from appreciating the perspective of Americans, especially in the upper South, as they looked into the clouded, uncertain, and not yet determined future in spring 1861.

IN THE END, the war that seemed to have no end did finally end. In spring 1865, with the South laid waste beyond anyone's imagining four years before, the Confederate government fled its capital, its tattered armies in headlong retreat. Little more than a day after Jefferson Davis abandoned Richmond, Abraham Lincoln sat in his rival's chair. He reached the city the day after the great evacuation fire. As he walked up from the riverfront, through streets choked with smoldering ashes, throngs of former slaves cheered him.

Mechanics Hall no longer echoed with ghostly voices from the Virginia convention, having collapsed in a shower of sparks the day before. Jefferson's Capitol survived, a desolate neoclassical temple surveying ruination at its feet. A snow squall of official papers and worthless Confederate banknotes fluttered in the breeze. In his proclamation of April 15, 1861, Lincoln had specifically shunned the destruction of southern property, implying slaves as well as material possessions. Before the war was over, though, the ruin of Confederate property and the end of slavery became fixed policy. The fruits of that policy, and of the wild gamble made by secessionists bent on splitting the country, were manifest in the free men and women who greeted Lincoln as he walked through the gutted landscape.

With the war winding down, the government prepared a grand ceremony on the fourth anniversary of Fort Sumter's surrender. On the appointed day, April 14, Major, now General, Robert Anderson returned to the scene, grayer and thinner than before, pallid yet erect. Sumter was hardly recognizable, battered into a pile of rubble by the blockading fleet. Like the day in 1861, it was warm and sunny.

A great gathering of notables swelled the ranks of the onlookers. Anderson had hoped for a short ceremony, but the War Department decreed a grand salute, the hundred guns that he had been denied in 1861. On hand was the Reverend Henry Ward Beecher, who gave a long, pompous, patriotic oration. After his own more moving and much briefer comments that simply invoked God's blessings for the return of peace, Anderson raised the same flag that he had taken down and carried away under his arm at the beginning of the war.[3]

On the day after Anderson's bittersweet reunion with Fort Sumter, Robert E. Lee returned to Richmond for the first time after Appomattox. He reached the city from the south, where an unobstructed view revealed terraced ranks of streets rising from the waterfront toward the Capitol. Everything below it lay in ashes. Tottering brick chimneys dotted the landscape. As Lee's horse crossed the pontoon bridge across the river, white Richmonders came out to greet him, silently waving their hats and hands, a sad pantomime among the ruins.

It was the same day Lincoln died, four years to the day after issuing his proclamation calling for volunteers to put down rebellion. One of the conspirators nearly killed Secretary of State Seward at the same time Booth shot Lincoln. For the rest of his life, Seward would bear the scars of the would-be assassin's knife. That he was there to be attacked was testimony to his changed relationship with the president. For after his failed attempt to dominate Lincoln in the weeks before Fort Sumter, Seward became his most loyal cabinet officer.

The death of the president contorted Washington in a paroxysm of grief and paranoia unlike any since it feared invasion in spring 1861. The war had transformed the city. To be sure, for decades to come, it would remain a southern town, not a world metropolis. But the vast wartime growth in federal power that presaged America's ascent onto the international stage could be seen across the landscape, not least in the completed new dome of the Capitol.

Old Gen. Winfield Scott had not lasted long. Lincoln turned to younger commanders, though it took him more than one false start to find his man. It would not be Ben Butler, despite his role in relieving the capital. Butler acquired the sobriquet "Spoons" because diehard Confederates accused him of stealing their flatware and "Beast" for his unchivalrous treatment of southern women. He was a disastrous battlefield commander, did more for the black soldiers under his command than any other general, and long afterward tiresomely refought disputes with those who crossed him, like the 7th New York at Annapolis. After being disappointed by too many of Butler's colleagues, Lincoln settled on the former army captain who had drilled clumsy volunteers in Galena, Illinois, in April 1861.

By staying in the Union, Maryland was not laid waste like its larger neighbor to the south, though it saw its share of war. The bloodiest day in American history took place in western Maryland at Antietam. Gov. Thomas Hicks, after walking a perilous tightrope in 1861, guided his divided state on the course of fidelity to the Union. Suspected of disloyalty, Baltimore's mayor George Brown spent several months in federal prison. He later reclaimed a leading role in the civic affairs of his city, which, despite its southern affections, profited greatly during the war.

Virginia, in contrast, became the main battlefield in the East and suffered terribly. Most of its leaders during the secession crisis faded from view after fighting began. John Baldwin reluctantly donned a gray uniform and served in the Confederate Congress. John Janney, the president of the convention, sat out the war at his home in Loudoun County in northern Virginia. It became the blood-soaked Rhineland of America, just as he had sorrowfully predicted. John Letcher finished his term as war governor, but he too retired home in time to watch the Shenandoah Valley ravaged by contending armies.

Henry Wise survived. His melodramatic moment in the convention on April 17, 1861, had been the high point. Fleeting glory. The governor who had looked John Brown in the eye, seen something of a kindred spirit, and still hanged him played no small part—at more than one point—in bringing war to the upper South. He served four years as a Confederate brigadier, irascible, erratic, competent, mistrusted by his superiors. Present with the remnant of his brigade at

Appomattox, he was a pitiful sight—a stooped, sickly, bespectacled figure, his spindly legs bound in gray blankets. He remained defiant, though crushed by defeat. Picturesque and eccentric as ever, Wise was "the quintessential Virginian, widely loved and deeply hated."[4]

Toward the end of the war, he petitioned the Confederate government to arm slaves and even emancipate them if that was what it would take to attain southern independence. Those original secessionists who had doubted Wise's soundness on slavery before the war were right after all. Later, he told anyone who would listen that slavery had been a curse. That was not an uncommon rationalization made by defeated Confederates unwilling to look their loss in the face or admit they gambled and lost everything for slavery and states' rights. But more unusually, with no act of self-deception, he also spoke often, obsessively, of John Brown's courage, even his greatness.[5]

After the surrender, Wise made his way back to his farm in Princess Anne County, on Virginia's Atlantic coast. There he found an extraordinary sight. Northern women with the American Missionary Association had set up a school in the run-down, ransacked main house. They would not let him come in, but he was able to determine that in that school on his property, newly freed black Virginians were learning how to read and write. And they did so at the instruction of a daughter of John Brown.[6]

ACKNOWLEDGMENTS

I n the course of writing my last book, about the fall of Richmond at the end of the Civil War, I sometimes found myself wondering about the proximate events that triggered the conflict. The present book is the result of my curiosity about how passions finally ignited long-running sectional hostility and how, almost overnight—at least that is the way it seemed to many people at the time—Americans turned violently against one another in the space of a few weeks in 1861.

At this distance in time, those passions seem a cold, ancient history. Then, however, they caused a nation to tear itself apart. "The poetry in history," observed English historian G. M. Trevelyan, "lies in the quasi-miraculous fact that once on this earth, on this familiar spot of ground walked other men and women as actual as we are today, thinking their thoughts, swayed by their own passions, but now all gone, vanishing after another, gone as utterly as we ourselves shall be, gone like ghosts at cock-crow." If *Cry Havoc!* can in a small way capture the moment as lived so intensely by Americans in the terrifying spring of 1861, it will have served some purpose. For me, the most tragic people were those caught in the middle, especially in the upper South states that had remained nominally loyal even after Lincoln's inauguration.

Readers should know that I have used the terms *upper South, border South,* and *upper South slave states* interchangeably. Some experts will dissent, but I have preferred to follow the perceptions of the time. Not knowing the future, people before the war did not distinguish between those upper South states that eventually joined the Confederacy and those that stayed with the Union. Similarly, in retrospect, we call those southerners who professed loyalty to the nation at the start of 1861 but who reluctantly sided with the Confederacy "conditional unionists." But before the ground was cut from beneath their feet, they saw nothing conditional about their devotion to the country.

I learned from writing *Richmond Burning* how immense the sources are for studying the American Civil War. The work for this book only reinforced that understanding. My debt to the librarians and archivists at the institutions cited in the bibliography is therefore a great one. I am especially indebted to my colleagues at the Virginia Historical Society, in particular Angie Boyer, Jon Bremer, Charles F. Bryan Jr., Toni Carter, Ann C. de Witt, Graham T. Dozier, Greg Hansard, Tom Illmensee, Margaret Kidd, Paul A. Levengood, John McClure, Frances S. Pollard, Paulette Schwarting, E. Lee Shepard, Greg Stoner, David Ward, and Tyler Young. Other authors who have helped through their advice, their writings, and their suggestions of sources include Paul Anderson, Edward L. Ayers, William C. Davis, Ervin L. Jordan Jr., William Marvel, Randall Miller, Elizabeth Brown Pryor, James I. Robertson Jr., Brent Tarter, James Srodes, and H. Alexander Wise Jr. No one who writes on this great conflict begins with a blank slate, and I am in the debt of so many others who have trod this familiar ground before me.

I thank my agent, P. J. Mark, for his advice throughout, from book proposal to publication. In things both large and small, my editor at Viking, Wendy Wolf, demonstrated her wisdom about the craft of writing, as she did for my last book. I have her to thank once more, and also her colleagues Cliff Corcoran, Bruce Giffords, and Sona Vogel. Also, once more my work has benefited from the illumination of George Skoch's splendid maps and Martin White's superb index.

Special thanks go to friends who gave their valuable time to read the manuscript and whose comments both enhanced the text and saved me from errors: Terry Alford, Stephen V. Ash, Charles F. Bryan Jr., John M. Coski, Daniel W. Crofts, Gary W. Gallagher, Dale Sorenson, and Richard Ugland. I am especially indebted to Dan, the dean of all the historians who have examined the upper South unionists and wondered how their course could have been different. My wife, Judy, made it all possible through her constant support and the occasional timely admonition to keep the writing in proportion to the rest of life. The faults that remain are mine.

The ways in which our society has changed since 1861 are legion. One in particular that has gone unnoticed until recently is the passing of the age of the citizen soldier. Now, time increasingly thins the ranks of World War II veterans and begins to take its toll on the generation that followed. With the advent of a smaller, professional military, moreover, fewer take their places. As a result, fewer civilians are acquainted with fellow Americans who bear arms. For many, the armed services have imperceptibly, unconsciously become a profession set apart, whose members' life experience is distinct and distant from that of their fellow countrymen. The debt of the latter to the former—today's heirs of the citizen soldiers of 1861—is a great one, for we now live in another time of war. I dedicate *Cry Havoc!* to all the men and women who wear the uniform of the republic and who, in their own day, defend the nation with their lives.

—Nelson D. Lankford
Richmond, Virginia
Ash Wednesday 2006

ABBREVIATIONS

The following abbreviations are used in the notes and bibliography.

AL-LC   Abraham Lincoln papers, American Memory project, Library of Congress

ANB   *American National Biography*

Basler   Roy P. Basler et al., eds., *The Collected Works of Abraham Lincoln*

CWH   *Civil War History*

DAB   *Dictionary of American Biography*

Dumond   Dwight Lowell Dumond, ed., *Southern Editorials on Secession*

JAH   *Journal of American History*

JSH   *Journal of Southern History*

LC Library of Congress, Washington, D.C.

LVA Library of Virginia, Richmond, Virginia

MHM *Maryland Historical Magazine*

MHS Maryland Historical Society, Baltimore, Maryland

Mearns David C. Mearns, ed., *The Lincoln Papers: The Story of the Collection with Selections to July 4, 1861*

NA National Archives, Washington, D.C.

OR United States War Department, *The War of the Rebellion: A Compilation of the Official Records of the Union and Confederate Armies*

ORN United States Naval War Records Office, *Official Records of the Union and Confederate Navies in the War of the Rebellion*

Perkins Howard Cecil Perkins, ed., *Northern Editorials on Secession*

Reese George H. Reese, ed., *Proceedings of the Virginia State Convention of 1861*

UVA Alderman Library, University of Virginia, Charlottesville, Virginia

VC *Virginia Cavalcade*

VHS Virginia Historical Society, Richmond, Virginia

VMHB *Virginia Magazine of History and Biography*

NOTES

All dates are in 1861 unless another year is specified. Complete publication data for works cited appears in the bibliography.

Prologue

1. For Brown, see Reynolds, *John Brown, Abolitionist,* and Oates, *To Purge This Land with Blood;* for the aftermath and legacy, see Peterson, *John Brown.*
2. Frederick Douglass, *The Life and Times of Frederick Douglass,* p. 324.
3. *Shepherdstown Register,* Oct. 29, 1859; Abrahamson, *Men of Secession and Civil War,* p. 8 (quotation).
4. This characterization of Brown's mental state is indebted to Bertram Wyatt-Brown, "A Volcano Beneath a Mountain of Snow," in Finkelman, ed., *His Soul Goes Marching On.*
5. Quoted in Peterson, *John Brown,* p. 3.
6. Michael B. Chesson, "Henry Alexander Wise," *ANB;* Simpson, *A Good Southerner,* pp. 204–5.

7. Quoted in Peterson, *John Brown*, p. 2.

8. Quoted in Simpson, *A Good Southerner*, p. 204.

9. Quoted in Peterson, *John Brown*, p. 21.

10. Reynolds, *John Brown, Abolitionist*, pp. 393–95; Hearn, *Six Years of Hell*, p. 41.

11. T. H. Hicks to J. M. Cole, Oct. 28, 1859, *MHM* 6 (1911): 277.

12. Quoted in Peterson, *John Brown*, p. 23.

13. Quoted ibid., p. 17.

14. Quoted in Blue, *No Taint of Compromise*, p. 86.

15. Emerson borrowed the image, with an alliterative change of phrase, from Kentucky abolitionist Mattie Griffith. Reynolds, *John Brown, Abolitionist*, pp. 367–68; Abrahamson, *Men of Secession and Civil War*, p. 8; Peterson, *John Brown*, p. 23.

1. FAITHFULLY EXECUTE

1. Inaugural address, Mar. 4, Basler, 4:271.

2. White, *Lincoln's Greatest Speech*, p. 35; Leech, *Reveille in Washington*, p. 45; Allen, *History of the United States Capitol*, pp. 253–55.

3. *Washington, D.C., Evening Star*, Mar. 4; *Richmond Dispatch*, Mar. 6; Leech, *Reveille in Washington*, pp. 43–45.

4. *New York Times*, Mar. 5.

5. Leech, *Reveille in Washington*, p. 44; Klein, *Days of Defiance*, p. 314; *New York Times*, Mar. 5; *Washington, D.C., National Intelligencer* (triweekly), Mar. 5; White, *The Eloquent President*, p. 77.

6. William W. Freehling, "The Divided South, Democracy's Limitations, and the Causes of the Peculiarly North American Civil War," p. 170, and David W. Blight, "They Knew What Time It Was: African-Americans and the Coming of the Civil War," p. 76, both in Boritt, ed., *Why the Civil War Came*.

7. Cooper, *Jefferson Davis, American*, p. 325; Davis, *Look Away!*, pp. 50–51.

8. Abrahamson, *Men of Secession and Civil War*, p. 108.

9. Cooper, *Jefferson Davis, American*, pp. 323, 330 (quotations).

10. Leech, *Reveille in Washington*, p. 24; Klein, *Days of Defiance*, p. 176 (first quotation), p. 224 (second quotation).

11. Abrahamson, *Men of Secession and Civil War*, pp. 122–26; McPherson, *Battle Cry of Freedom*, p. 251 (quotation).

12. William W. Freehling, "The Divided South, Democracy's Limitations, and the Causes of the Peculiarly North American Civil War," p. 167, in Boritt, ed., *Why the Civil War Came*; Ayers, *In the Presence of Mine Enemies*, p. 72 (quotation).

13. Gunderson, "William C. Rives," p. 467 (first quotation); Furgurson, *Freedom Rising*, p. 38 (second quotation).

14. *Richmond Dispatch*, Mar. 9.

15. Speech at Pittsburgh, Feb. 15, Basler, 4:211 (quotation); Gienapp, *Abraham Lincoln*, p. 74; Crofts, *Reluctant Confederates*, pp. 215–16.

16. Quoted in Sowle, "Trials of a Virginia Unionist," p. 18.

17. Potter, *Impending Crisis*, p. 554.

18. Quoted in Crofts, *Reluctant Confederates*, p. 252.

19. Leech, *Reveille in Washington*, p. 5.

20. Ibid., pp. 1–13; Green, *Washington*, 1:201–36.

21. Quoted in Elliott, *Winfield Scott*, pp. 691–92.

22. Donald, *Lincoln*, pp. 283–84; *Richmond Dispatch*, Mar. 6 (quotation).

23. White, *The Eloquent President*, pp. 94–95; Basler, 4:263 (quotation).

24. Abrahamson, *Men of Secession and Civil War*, pp. 128–29; Marvel, *Mr. Lincoln Goes to War*, Foreword; Basler, 4:266 (quotation).

25. Long and Long, eds., *The Civil War Day by Day*, p. 31 (first quotation); Basler, 4:268 (second quotation).

26. Basler, 4:271.

27. Ibid., 4:261; Matthew 10:34 (King James Version).

28. Basler, 4:271.

29. *Philadelphia Press*, Mar. 5; *New York Times*, Mar. 5; Klein, *Days of Defiance*, p. 315 (quotation); Sandra F. VanBurkleo and Bonnie Speck, "Roger Brooke Taney," *ANB*.

30. Leech, *Reveille in Washington*, p. 45.

2. WAIT AND SEE

1. Russell, *My Diary*, p. 107.

2. Walther, *Fire-Eaters*, p. 188; King, *Louis T. Wigfall*, pp. 3–4, 20–21;

Eric H. Walther, "Louis Trezevant Wigfall," *ANB;* Wigfall to Francis Pickens, Mar. 4, *OR,* ser. 1, vol. 1, p. 261.

3. This paragraph and the next draw on Standage, *Victorian Internet,* and Blondheim, *News over the Wires.*

4. *New Orleans Picayune,* Mar. 6.

5. *Charleston Mercury,* Mar. 5.

6. Entry for Mar. 5, Nevins and Thomas, eds., *Strong Diary,* 3:106 (first quotation); Barton, *The Life of Clara Barton,* 2:105 (second quotation).

7. *Indianapolis Daily Journal,* Mar. 5, Perkins, 2:618 (first quotation); *Chicago Tribune,* Mar. 5 (second quotation).

8. *Jersey City American Standard,* Mar. 5, Perkins, 2:625 (first quotation); *New York Journal of Commerce,* Mar. 5, ibid., 2:631 (second quotation); *Columbus Daily Capital City Fact,* Mar. 5, ibid., 2:634 (third quotation).

9. *Peoria Daily Democratic Union,* Mar. 7, ibid., 2:642–43.

10. *Wellsburg Herald,* Mar. 15 (first quotation); *Richmond Examiner,* Mar. 5 (second quotation); *Richmond Dispatch,* Mar. 5 (third quotation); John T. Thornton, Mar. 6, Reese, 1:427 (fourth quotation).

11. Robert Y. Conrad to Elizabeth Whiting (Powell) Conrad, Mar. 6, Conrad Papers, VHS (first quotation); William C. Wickham to Scott, Mar. 11, Mearns, 2:482 (second quotation); *Richmond Whig,* Mar. 6.

12. *North Carolina Standard,* Mar. 9, Dumond, p. 479.

13. *Baltimore American,* Mar. 6.

14. Crofts, *Reluctant Confederates,* pp. 256–57.

15. Link, *Roots of Secession,* p. 215.

16. From *Richmond Whig,* quoted in *Baltimore American,* Mar. 6.

17. Freehling, *The South vs. the South,* p. 41; Crofts, *Reluctant Confederates,* pp. 257–59.

18. Quoted in Dew, *Apostles of Disunion,* p. 33.

19. Quoted ibid., p. 67.

20. *Baltimore American,* Mar. 6.

21. Sowle, "Trials of a Virginia Unionist," p. 13 (first quotation); *Richmond Examiner,* Mar. 23 (second quotation).

22. *Richmond Dispatch,* Mar. 9.

3 . *Toujours la Politesse*

1. Quoted in Swanberg, *First Blood,* p. 134.
2. Quoted in Patrick G. Williams, "Joseph Holt," *ANB.*
3. Joseph Holt and Winfield Scott to Lincoln, Mar. 5, 1861, AL-LC.
4. Quoted in Donald, *Lincoln,* p. 285.
5. Russell, *My Diary,* pp. 33 (quotation), 34, 51.
6. Entry for Mar. 9, Beale, ed., *Diary of Edward Bates,* p. 177; Lincoln to Scott, Mar. 9, Basler, 4:279.
7. Russell, *My Diary,* p. 43 (first quotation); Jean H. Baker, "Montgomery Blair," *ANB;* Blair to Lincoln, Mar. 15, AL-LC (second quotation).
8. Ari Hoogenboom, "Gustavus Vasa Fox," *ANB.*
9. Hoogenboom, "Gustavus Fox," pp. 383–85.
10. Lincoln to cabinet officers, Mar. 15, Basler, 4:284–85.
11. Donald, *Lincoln,* pp. 286–87; entry for Mar. 16, Beale, ed., *Diary of Edward Bates,* p. 179.
12. Davis, *Look Away!,* p. 85; Abrahamson, *Men of Secession and Civil War,* p. 111; Davis, *Deep Waters of the Proud,* p. 82; Rable, *Confederate Republic,* pp. 68–70.
13. Cooper, *Jefferson Davis, American,* p. 337.
14. Davis to Lincoln, Feb. 27, *OR,* ser. 1, vol. 51, pt. 2, p. 8.
15. Crofts, *Reluctant Confederates,* p. 217; Russell, *My Diary,* p. 34.
16. This summary of Seward's position is drawn from Daniel Crofts, "William Henry Seward," *ANB; The Liberator,* Mar. 22 (quotation).
17. Crofts, *Reluctant Confederates,* p. 276.
18. Bancroft, *Life of Seward,* 2:108–13.
19. Saunders, *John Archibald Campbell,* p. 41.
20. Ibid., p. 147.
21. Ibid., pp. 135, 148.
22. Johnson, "Fort Sumter and Confederate Diplomacy," p. 450; John Forsyth to L. P. Walker, Mar. 14, *OR,* ser. 4, vol. 1, p. 165 (quotation).
23. Quoted in Klein, *Days of Defiance,* p. 349.
24. Russell, *My Diary,* p. 40.
25. Entry for Mar. 12, Horatio Nelson Taft diary, LC.

26. Quoted in Crofts, *Reluctant Confederates*, p. 293.
27. The following passage on John Gilmer is based on Crofts, *Reluctant Confederates*, and Crofts, "A Reluctant Unionist."
28. Quoted in Crofts, "A Reluctant Unionist," p. 246.

4. CONTRIVANCES OF DELAY

1. Crofts, *Reluctant Confederates*, pp. 26, 264.
2. Quoted in Link, *Roots of Secession*, p. 232.
3. John Janney to Alcinda "Alice" Janney, Mar. 12, transcription, box 2, Janney Papers, UVA.
4. *Richmond Examiner*, Mar. 5.
5. Jos. Segar to Cameron, Mar. 26, *OR*, ser. 1, vol. 51, pt. i, p. 318.
6. Osborne, *Jubal*, pp. 4, 10, 23.
7. Jubal A. Early, Mar. 6, Reese, 1:428–29.
8. Osborne, *Jubal*, pp. 42–44; Jubal A. Early and John Goode, Mar. 6, Reese, 1:428–38.
9. Quoted in Crofts, *Reluctant Confederates*, pp. 261–62.
10. Shanks, *Secession Movement in Virginia*, pp. 179–81.
11. Quoted in Link, *Roots of Secession*, p. 228.
12. Ibid., p. 16.
13. Simpson, *A Good Southerner*, pp. 244–45.
14. Link, *Roots of Secession*, p. 236.
15. Ibid., p. 237 (quotation); Crofts, *Reluctant Confederates*, p. 162.
16. Crofts, *Reluctant Confederates*, pp. 28–29; Ayers, *In the Presence of Mine Enemies*, p. 103.
17. John Baldwin, Mar. 21 and 22, Reese, 2:139–40 (first quotation), 2:173 (second quotation).
18. Crofts, *Reluctant Confederates*, p. 286.
19. Quoted in Freehling, "The Editorial Revolution, Virginia, and the Coming of the Civil War," p. 70.
20. *Richmond Examiner*, Mar. 7 (first quotation); Link, *Roots of Secession*, p. 233 (second quotation); *Richmond Examiner*, Mar. 5 (third quotation).
21. *Richmond Examiner*, Mar. 15.
22. Ibid., Mar. 19 (quotations); Bridges, *Pen of Fire*, p. 168.

23. Carmichael, *The Last Generation*, pp. 12, 122, 135, 146.

24. *Richmond Examiner*, Mar. 14, 15 (quotation).

25. Quoted in Crofts, *Reluctant Confederates*, p. 282.

26. Public letter from Douglas to *Petersburg Express*, Jan. 31, quoted in Crofts, *Reluctant Confederates*, p. 139.

27. Wells, *Stephen Douglas*, pp. 279–81.

28. *The Liberator*, Mar. 22 (quotation); Freehling, "The Editorial Revolution, Virginia, and the Coming of the Civil War," pp. 66–72; *Richmond Examiner*, Mar. 25.

29. Quoted in *Washington, D.C., Daily National Intelligencer*, Mar. 27.

5. COLLISION COURSE

1. *Philadelphia Daily Evening Bulletin*, Apr. 8, quoted in Perkins, 2:671.

2. John Janney to Alcinda "Alice" Janney, Apr. 4, transcription, box 2, Janney Papers, UVA.

3. For the fullest discussion of the hands-off strategy, see Crofts, *Reluctant Confederates*, chaps. 10–11.

4. Campbell to Davis, Apr. 3, Crist and Dix, eds., *Papers of Jefferson Davis*, 7:88.

5. Crofts, *Reluctant Confederates*, p. 290; "A Republican" to Lincoln, Apr. 3, Mearns, 2:516.

6. Confederate commissioners to Robert Toombs, Mar. 28, *OR*, ser. 1, vol. 53, p. 137 (first quotation); Campbell to Davis, Apr. 3, Crist and Dix, eds., *Papers of Jefferson Davis*, 7:89 (second quotation).

7. Russell, *My Diary*, p. 43.

8. Donald, *Lincoln*, p. 288.

9. Crofts, *Reluctant Confederates*, pp. 296–98; Donald, *Lincoln*, pp. 288–89.

10. Russell, *My Diary*, p. 47; Robert Y. Conrad to Elizabeth Whiting (Powell) Conrad, Mar. 29, Conrad Papers, VHS; dispatch from Fernando Po, Jan. 29, *New York Times*, Mar. 29; Swanberg, *First Blood*, p. 251.

11. Donald, *Lincoln*, pp. 289–90.

12. Quoted in Crofts, *Reluctant Confederates*, p. 301.

13. Quoted ibid., p. 305.

14. Ibid., pp. 301–6.

15. Ibid., pp. 308–9, quotation on p. 309.

16. Robert Y. Conrad to Elizabeth Whiting (Powell) Conrad, Apr. 6, Conrad Papers, VHS.

17. Hoogenboom, "Gustavus Fox," pp. 391–93.

18. Donald, *Lincoln*, p. 291; Beale, ed., *Diary of Gideon Welles*, 1:24.

19. David Dixon Porter to Lincoln, telegram, Apr. 6, 11:17 a.m., reel 63 (microfilm), Papers of William H. Seward, Rush Rhees Library, University of Rochester, Rochester, N.Y.

20. *New York Herald*, Apr. 7, quoted in *Richmond Dispatch*, Apr. 9.

21. Hoogenboom, "Gustavus Fox," pp. 391–93; Swanberg, *First Blood*, p. 263; Fox to wife, Apr. 8 [misdated Apr. 6] (quotation), Thompson and Wainwright, eds., *Confidential Correspondence of Gustavus Vasa Fox*, 1:26–27.

22. *Daily Chicago Times*, Apr. 9, Perkins, 2:676.

23. *Daily Nashville Patriot*, Apr. 12, Dumond, p. 493.

24. Reports from New Orleans, Montgomery, and Charleston quoted in *Richmond Dispatch*, Apr. 9.

25. *Springfield Daily Illinois State Journal*, Apr. 9, Perkins, 2:676–77.

26. *New York Times*, Apr. 8; entries for Mar. 12, 21, Apr. 5, 6, Nevins and Thomas, eds., *Strong Diary*, 3:109–17.

27. Quoted in Marvel, *Mr. Lincoln Goes to War*, p. 19.

28. Entries for Apr. 6, 7, 9, Horatio Nelson Taft diary, LC.

29. *Washington, D.C., Evening Star*, Apr. 11; Nicolay and Hay, *Abraham Lincoln*, 4:68; Lincoln to Ira P. Rankin, Apr. 5, Basler, 4:323; Lincoln to Andrew G. Curtin, Apr. 8, Basler, 4:324 (quotation).

30. Scott to Lincoln, Apr. 5, 8, 9, Mearns, 2:525 (first quotation), 2:530 (second quotation), 2:531, 534.

31. Irvin McDowell to Lorenzo Thomas, Apr. 11, *OR*, ser. 1, vol. 51, pt. i, pp. 322–23.

32. *Washington, D.C., Daily National Intelligencer*, Apr. 12 (first quotation); Levin Tilmon to Lincoln, Apr. 8, Mearns, 2:531 (second quotation).

33. Charles P. Stone to Seward, Apr. 5, Mearns, 2:526–28 (quotation); Jno. Forsyth to L. P. Walker, Apr. 10, *OR*, ser. 4, vol. 1, p. 216.

34. *Washington, D.C., National Intelligencer,* Apr. 13; Williams, *Matthew Fontaine Maury,* pp. 360–64.

6. FLASH POINT

1. Quoted in Swanberg, *First Blood,* p. 154.
2. Lowell H. Harrison, "Robert Anderson," ANB.
3. Quoted in Detzer, *Allegiance,* p. 162.
4. Walther, *Fire-Eaters,* pp. 8, 152, 297–99; Abrahamson, *Men of Secession and Civil War,* p. 47.
5. William W. Freehling, "The Divided South, Democracy's Limitations, and the Causes of the Peculiarly North American Civil War," p. 170, in Boritt, ed., *Why the Civil War Came;* Swanberg, *First Blood,* p. 25 (first quotation), p. 80 (second quotation).
6. Swanberg, *First Blood,* p. 175.
7. Klein, *Days of Defiance,* p. 142; John B. Edmunds Jr., "Francis Wilkinson Pickens," *ANB;* Detzer, *Allegiance,* p. 93 (quotation).
8. Cooper, *Jefferson Davis, American,* p. 337.
9. Holzman, *Adapt or Perish,* p. 54; Swanberg, *First Blood,* p. 218 (quotation).
10. Cooper, *Jefferson Davis, American,* p. 339.
11. Simon Cameron to Robert S. Chew, Apr. 6, Basler, 4:323–24.
12. Chew to Lincoln, Apr. 8, ibid., 4:324; Swanberg, *First Blood,* p. 280.
13. Johnson, "Fort Sumter and Confederate Diplomacy," p. 471; Washington dispatch, Apr. 10, *New York Times,* Apr. 11 (quotation).
14. Saunders, *John Archibald Campbell,* pp. 146–47.
15. Gienapp, *Abraham Lincoln,* p. 81; Marvel, *Mr. Lincoln Goes to War,* Foreword.
16. Klein, *Days of Defiance,* p. 399; Johnson, "Fort Sumter and Confederate Diplomacy," p. 473; McPherson, *Battle Cry of Freedom,* p. 272 (quotation).
17. Davis, *"A Government of Our Own,"* p. 310.
18. Johnson, "Fort Sumter and Confederate Diplomacy," p. 444; Walker to Beauregard, Apr. 10, *OR,* ser. 1, vol. 1, p. 297 (first quotation); Klein, *Days of Defiance,* p. 399; Davis, *Look Away!,* p. 112; Cooper, *Jefferson Davis, American,* p. 339 (second quotation).

19. Swanberg, *First Blood,* p. 243; Beauregard to Anderson, Apr. 7, *OR,* ser. 1, vol. 1, p. 248; Beauregard to Anderson, Apr. 8, *OR,* ser. 1, vol. 1, p. 250.

20. Charleston dispatch, Apr. 10, *New York Times,* Apr. 11.

21. Beauregard to Walker, Apr. 11, *OR,* ser. 1, vol. 1, p. 301.

22. The following summary of the fighting, relief effort, and aftermath relies on Swanberg, *First Blood,* pp. 299–322, and Klein, *Days of Defiance,* pp. 409–18.

23. Fox to Blair, Apr. 17, Thompson and Wainwright, eds., *Confidential Correspondence of Gustavus Fox,* 1:32.

24. Ibid., 1:32–33; Klein, *Days of Defiance,* pp. 413–14; Hoogenboom, "Gustavus Fox," pp. 394–95.

25. *Charleston Mercury,* Apr. 16.

26. Ibid., Apr. 15.

27. Fox to Blair, Apr. 17, Thompson and Wainwright, eds., *Confidential Correspondence of Gustavus Fox,* 1:35.

28. Hoogenboom, "Gustavus Fox," p. 395.

7. TIDINGS OF WAR

1. Entries for Mar. 14, 26 (first quotation), Feb. 18 (second quotation), Apr. 15 (third quotation), Crabtree and Patton, eds., "*Journal of a Secesh Lady,*" pp. 44, 46, 38, 49.

2. Quoted in Davis, "*A Government of Our Own,*" p. 312.

3. *Philadelphia Press,* Apr. 16, Perkins, 2:742.

4. Quoted in Davis, "*A Government of Our Own,*" p. 317.

5. Ibid., pp. 314–16.

6. Cooper, *Jefferson Davis, American,* p. 340; *New Orleans Daily Delta,* Apr. 18, Dumond, p. 499 (quotation).

7. Russell, *My Diary,* p. 92 (first and second quotations); *New Orleans Picayune,* Apr. 14 (third quotation).

8. *Philadelphia Press,* Apr. 15.

9. *Pittsburgh Post,* Apr. 15, Perkins, 2:738.

10. *Chicago Tribune,* Apr. 15.

11. *New York Times,* Apr. 15.

12. *Douglass' Monthly*, May 1.

13. Entries for Apr. 13 (quotation) and 14, Nevins and Thomas, eds., *Strong Diary*, 3:119–20.

14. *Washington, D.C., States and Union*, Apr. 15, Perkins, 2:765.

15. *Albany Atlas and Argus*, Apr. 13, ibid., 2:692.

16. Portland, Maine, *Eastern Argus*, Apr. 15, ibid., 2:767–68.

17. Newburyport, Massachusetts, *Daily Herald*, Apr. 15, ibid., 2:734.

18. *Grand Rapids Daily Enquirer*, Apr. 18, ibid., 2:744–46.

19. *Columbus Daily Capital City Fact*, Apr. 13, ibid., 2:727–28 (first and second quotations); *Douglass' Monthly*, May 1 (third quotation).

20. Mark Wahlgreen Summers, "'Freedom and Law Must Die Ere They Sever': The North and the Coming of the Civil War," p. 197, in Boritt, ed., *Why the Civil War Came*.

21. *Washington, D.C., Daily National Intelligencer*, Apr. 16, Perkins, 2:777.

22. Sitterson, *Secession Movement in North Carolina*, p. 239 (first quotation); *Louisville Courier*, Apr. 13, in *New Orleans Picayune*, Apr. 16 (second quotation).

23. *Baltimore Sun*, Apr. 15, Bailey, "Pratt Street Riots Reconsidered," p. 159 (quotation); *Baltimore American*, Apr. 15.

24. *Wheeling Daily Intelligencer*, Apr. 15.

25. Wallace Hettle, "The 'Self-Analysis' of John C. Rutherfoord," p. 103; entry for Apr. 15, John Coles Rutherfoord diary, VHS.

26. John Cochran to his mother, Apr. 14, Ayers, *In the Presence of Mine Enemies*, p. 135 (quotation); Robert Y. Conrad to Elizabeth Whiting (Powell) Conrad, Apr. 14, Conrad Papers, VHS; *Richmond Examiner*, Apr. 15.

27. F. N. Boney, "John Letcher," *ANB*; *Richmond Examiner*, Apr. 10 (first quotation), Apr. 12 (second quotation); Boney, *John Letcher*, pp. 110–12.

28. Richmond dispatch, Apr. 13, *Charleston Mercury*, Apr. 16.

29. Early, Apr. 13, Reese, 3:723.

30. *Charleston Mercury*, Apr. 17; *New York Times*, Apr. 15.

31. Nicolay and Hay, *Abraham Lincoln*, 4:70–72.

32. Quoted in Link, *Roots of Secession*, p. 336, n. 24.

33. Crofts, *Reluctant Confederates*, p. 441, n. 12.

34. Nicolay and Hay, *Abraham Lincoln*, 4:72.

35. Reply to a Committee from the Virginia Convention, Apr. 13, Basler, 4:330.

36. Ibid.

37. Nicolay and Hay, *Abraham Lincoln*, 4:76.

38. Ibid.; Alexander H. H. Stuart, Apr. 16, Reese, 4:12 (quotation).

39. H. W. Denslow to Lincoln, telegram, Apr. 13, AL-LC.

40. Davis, *"A Government of Our Own,"* p. 318.

41. *Washington, D.C., Daily National Intelligencer*, Apr. 16, Perkins, 2:774.

42. *Baltimore American*, Apr. 15.

8. CHEATED AND DECEIVED

1. Alcinda "Alice" Janney to John Janney, Apr. 14, and John Janney to Alcinda "Alice" Janney, Apr. 13, transcription, box 2, Janney Papers, UVA.

2. Entry for Apr. 16, Crabtree and Patton, eds., *"Journal of a Secesh Lady,"* p. 50.

3. *Baltimore American*, Apr. 15.

4. Proclamation, Apr. 15, AL-LC.

5. Quoted in Wells, *Stephen Douglas*, p. 282.

6. Nicolay and Hay, *Abraham Lincoln*, 4:76–77.

7. Cameron to governors, Apr. 15, *OR*, ser. 3, vol. 1, pp. 68–69.

8. Cameron to governors of Michigan, Maine, Wisconsin, Iowa, New Hampshire, and Vermont, Apr. 16, ibid., p. 75.

9. W. Dennison to Lincoln, Apr. 15, ibid., ser. 1, vol. 1, p. 73.

10. Israel Washburn Jr. to Cameron, Apr. 15, ibid., ser. 3, vol. 1, p. 71; Heather Cox Richardson, "Israel Washburn, Jr.," *ANB*.

11. O. P. Morton to Lincoln, Apr. 15, *OR*, ser. 3, vol. 1, p. 70.

12. A. G. Curtin to Cameron, Apr. 17, ibid., p. 82.

13. John W. Ellis to Cameron, Apr. 15, ibid., p. 72 (first quotation); Beriah Magoffin to Cameron, Apr. 15, ibid., p. 70 (second quotation); Isham G. Harris to Cameron, Apr. 17, ibid., p. 81 (third quotation).

14. John Letcher to Cameron, Apr. 16, ibid., p. 76.

15. Quoted in Crofts, *Reluctant Confederates*, p. 310.

16. Kruman, *Parties and Politics in North Carolina*, p. 220; Sitterson, *Secession Movement in North Carolina*, p. 241 (quotation).

17. Quoted in Crofts, *Reluctant Confederates*, p. 335.

18. Richard L. Zuber, "Jonathan Worth," *ANB*; Crofts, *Reluctant Confederates*, p. 336 (first quotation), p. 339 (second quotation).

19. Louisville dispatch, Apr. 15, in *Richmond Dispatch*, Apr. 17.

20. Quoted in Crofts, *Reluctant Confederates*, p. 337.

21. *Baltimore American*, Apr. 16 (first quotation); Ellenberger, "Whigs in the Streets?," p. 26 (second quotation).

22. Oliver Perry Temple to W. R. Hurley, Apr. 17, reel 63 (microfilm), Papers of William H. Seward, Rush Rhees Library, University of Rochester, Rochester, N.Y.

23. *Richmond Whig*, Apr. 15.

24. *New Orleans Picayune*, Apr. 16 (first quotation); *Charleston Mercury*, Apr. 17 (second quotation).

25. Davis, "*A Government of Our Own*," pp. 321–22.

26. *Richmond Dispatch*, Apr. 15.

27. Schott, *Stephens*, p. 331; Davis, "*A Government of Our Own*," p. 321 (quotation).

9. Give the Old Lady Time

1. John Janney, Apr. 17, Reese, 4:137.

2. Daniel E. Sutherland, "Roger Atkinson Pryor," *ANB*; Holzman, *Adapt or Perish*, p. 56 (quotation).

3. A. G. Smith to Letcher, Apr. 16, box 8, folder 6, Letcher Papers, LVA; *Washington, D.C., Evening Star*, Apr. 5; Greenawalt, ed., "Unionists in Rockbridge County," p. 96; Link, *Roots of Secession*, p. 240; Robert Y. Conrad to Elizabeth Whiting (Powell) Conrad, Mar. 29, Conrad Papers, VHS.

4. Reynolds, *John Brown, Abolitionist*, p. 392.

5. Entry for Apr. 10 and 11, Jones, *Rebel War Clerk's Diary*, 1:16.

6. Entry for Apr. 13, ibid., 1:18 (first quotation); Crofts, *Reluctant Confederates*, pp. 316–19; Ayers, *In the Presence of Mine Enemies*, p. 128 (second quotation).

7. Robert Y. Conrad to Elizabeth Whiting (Powell) Conrad, Apr. 14, Conrad Papers, VHS.

8. Ibid., Apr. 13.

9. Jeremiah Morton, Apr. 13, Reese, 3:716 (first quotation); *Richmond Dispatch*, Apr. 15 (second quotation).

10. Richmond dispatch, Apr. 8, *New York Times*, Apr. 10.

11. Crofts, "Virginia, the South, and the Union, 1850–1861," pp. 14–15.

12. Richmond dispatch, Apr. 15, *New York Times*, Apr. 18.

13. James Baldwin Dorman, Apr. 15, Reese, 3:756 (first quotation); Henry Wise, Apr. 15, Reese, 3:758 (second quotation).

14. Joseph Mackean Churchill to Seward, Apr. 15, reel 63 (microfilm), Papers of William H. Seward, Rush Rhees Library, University of Rochester, Rochester, N.Y.

15. John Janney to Alcinda "Alice" Janney, Apr. 16, transcription, Janney Papers, UVA.

16. George Randolph, Apr. 16, Reese, 4:5.

17. *Richmond Examiner*, Apr. 10.

18. Alexander H. H. Stuart, Apr. 16, Reese, 4:14.

19. Ibid., 4:16.

20. Robert Scott, Apr. 16, ibid., 4:40–41, 46.

21. Jubal A. Early, Apr. 16, ibid., 4:59 (first quotation); Samuel G. Staples, Apr. 16, ibid., 4:67 (second quotation).

22. John A. Campbell, Apr. 17, ibid., 4:120.

23. John S. Burdett, Apr. 17, ibid., 4:95.

24. Recollection of Waitman Willey, quoted in Hall, *Rending of Virginia*, p. 183.

25. Simpson, *A Good Southerner*, p. 250 (first quotation); Henry A. Wise, Apr. 17, Reese, 4:124 (second quotation).

26. Henry A. Wise, Apr. 17, Reese, 4:124.

27. John Baldwin, Apr. 17, ibid., 4:128 (first quotation); Simpson, *A Good Southerner*, p. 250 (second quotation).

28. Quoted from a letter from George Plater Tayloe, dated Apr. 19, in Benjamin Ogle Tayloe to Seward, Apr. 23, reel 63 (microfilm), Papers of William H. Seward, Rush Rhees Library, University of Rochester, Rochester, N.Y.

29. John Janney, Apr. 17, Reese, 4:138, 140.

30. Henry A. Wise, Apr. 17, ibid., 4:173.

31. Jubal A. Early, Apr. 18, ibid., 4:215.

32. This passage is indebted to the fuller discussion in Ayers, *In the Presence of Mine Enemies*, p. 142.

33. Crofts, "Virginia, the South, and the Union, 1850–1861," p. 15; Ayers, *In the Presence of Mine Enemies*, p. 141.

34. Entry for Apr. 17, Jones, *Rebel War Clerk's Diary*, 1:23.

10. JOHN BROWN IN GRAY

1. Alexander Stephens to Linton Stephens, Apr. 17, Davis, *"A Government of Our Own,"* p. 321.

2. *Washington, D.C., Evening Star*, Apr. 19.

3. Robert Y. Conrad to Elizabeth Whiting (Powell) Conrad, Apr. 15, Conrad Papers, VHS.

4. Crofts, *Reluctant Confederates*, p. 321; Hearn, *Six Years of Hell*, p. 50.

5. Richmond dispatch, Apr. 17, *New York Times*, Apr. 20 (quotation).

6. Letter from Staunton, Apr. 17, *Richmond Dispatch*, Apr. 19; Ayers, *In the Presence of Mine Enemies*, pp. 138–39.

7. Letcher to Gen. W. H. Harman at Staunton, Virginia, Apr. 17 (quotation); see also Letcher to Harman, Apr. 17, handwritten note on W. H. Harman to Letcher, Apr. 17, telegram; and C. A. Crump to Letcher, Apr. 17, 2 a.m., telegram, all in Letcher Papers, box 8, folder 7, LVA.

8. Entry for Apr. 17, Jones, *Rebel War Clerk's Diary*, 1:23.

9. Quoted in letter from Staunton, Apr. 17, *Richmond Dispatch*, Apr. 19.

10. Hearn, *Six Years of Hell*, pp. 4–5.

11. Quoted in Gunderson, "William C. Rives," p. 475.

12. Webster, "Last Days," p. 37.

13. Hearn, *Six Years of Hell*, p. 54 (quotation); [David Hunter Strother], "Narrative of an Eye-Witness," *Harper's Weekly*, May 11.

14. Quoted in unsigned telegram from Gordonsville, Virginia, to Wise, Apr. 17, Letcher Papers, box 8, folder 7, LVA.

15. Winfield Scott's daily report number 14, Apr. 16, Mearns, 2:562; Hearn, *Six Years of Hell*, p. 53.

16. W. Dennison to Cameron, Apr. 18, *OR*, ser. 3, vol. 1, p. 84.

17. R. Jones to assistant adjutant general, Apr. 18, 9 p.m., ibid., ser. 1, vol. 2, pp. 3–4.

18. Maj. Gen. Kenton Harper to superintendent, U.S. armory [Apr. 18], John Brown/Boyd B. Stutler Collection Database.

19. Hearn, *Six Years of Hell*, p. 55.

20. [David Hunter Strother], "Narrative of an Eye-Witness," *Harper's Weekly*, May 11.

21. *Baltimore American*, Apr. 22; Cameron to Jones, Apr. 22, *OR*, ser. 1, vol. 2, p. 5.

22. William Lucas to "Dear Dan," [c. 21–22] Apr., VHS.

23. Quoted in Burton, "*Pawnee* Sunday," p. 5 (first quotation); *Richmond Whig*, Apr. 20 (second quotation); *Richmond Dispatch*, Apr. 20 (third quotation); entry for Apr. 20, Jones, *Rebel War Clerk's Diary*, 1:25 (fourth quotation).

24. *Richmond Dispatch*, Apr. 20.

25. Riggs, "Robert Young Conrad and the Ordeal of Secession."

26. Robert Y. Conrad to Elizabeth Whiting (Powell) Conrad, Apr. 14 (first quotation), Apr. 20 (second quotation), Robert Y. Conrad to Holmes Conrad, Apr. 17, 3 p.m. (third quotation), Conrad Papers, VHS.

27. Robert Y. Conrad to Elizabeth Whiting (Powell) Conrad, Apr. 20, ibid.

11. Burning Bridges

1. Bradley, *Simon Cameron*, p. 170 (quotation); Jean Baker, "Simon Cameron," *ANB*.

2. Hicks to Lincoln, Apr. 17, Cameron to Hicks, Apr. 17, John A. Andrew to Cameron, Apr. 17, *OR*, ser. 3, vol. 1, pp. 79–80.

3. Ellenberger, "Whigs in the Streets?," pp. 24–26; Towers, *Urban South*, pp. 1, 165.

4. Compare Ellenberger, "Whigs in the Streets?," p. 26, with Towers, *Urban South*, p. 160.

5. Wigfall to Beauregard, Mar. 16, *OR*, ser. 1, vol. 1, p. 276.

6. Brown, *Baltimore and the Nineteenth of April, 1861*, p. 36.

7. Hicks to General Scott, Mar. 28, Thomas H. Hicks Papers, MHS.

8. *Baltimore American*, Apr. 19.

9. George P. Kane to William Crawford, Apr. 16, quoted in message of same date from S. M. Felton to Cameron, Apr. 16, *OR*, ser. 1, vol. 2, p. 577 (quotation); Cameron to Hicks, Apr. 18, ibid.

10. *Baltimore American*, Apr. 19; Quarles, *The Negro in the Civil War*, pp. 24–25; Worthington G. Snethen to Seward, Apr. 18 (quotation), reel 63 (microfilm), Papers of William H. Seward, Rush Rhees Library, University of Rochester, Rochester, N.Y.

11. Bohner, *John Pendleton Kennedy*, p. 227 (first quotation); entries for Apr. 14 (second and third quotations) and Apr. 18 (fourth quotation), John P. Kennedy diary, John Pendleton Kennedy Papers (microfilm), Enoch Pratt Free Library, Baltimore.

12. *Boston Daily Advertiser*, Apr. 18.

13. Entry for Apr. 18, Nevins and Thomas, eds.; *Strong Diary*, 3:124.

14. *Philadelphia Press*, Apr. 19.

15. Report of Col. Edward F. Jones, Apr. 22, *OR*, ser. 1, vol. 2, p. 7.

16. Extracts from the message of the mayor of Baltimore, July 11, ibid., p. 16.

17. Report of Col. Edward F. Jones, Apr. 22, ibid., p. 7; Henry Stump to his sister-in-law, Mrs. Mary Alicia Stump, Apr. 20 (quotation), Clark, "Baltimore," p. 47.

18. Extracts from the message of the mayor of Baltimore, July 11, *OR*, ser. 1, vol. 2, pp. 16–17.

19. Report of Col. Edward F. Jones, Apr. 22, ibid., p. 9.

20. Statement of George M. Gill, July 12, ibid., pp. 20–21.

21. Frederick Bernal to Richard Lyons, Apr. 20, Barnes and Barnes, eds., *The American Civil War Through British Eyes*, 1:63.

22. Quoted in Ellenberger, "Whigs in the Streets?," p. 27.

23. Entry for Apr. 19, Marks and Schatz, eds., *Between North and South*, p. 30 (first quotation); Ellenberger, "Whigs in the Streets?," p. 28 (second quotation).

24. Brown to Lincoln, Apr. 19 (misdated Apr. 18), AL-LC.

25. Report of Col. Edward F. Jones, Apr. 22, and extracts from report of the president of Baltimore police commissioners, May 3, *OR*, ser. 1, vol. 2, pp. 7–11.

26. Brown's speech, *Baltimore American*, Apr. 20.

27. Hicks to Scott, Mar. 18, and Hicks to Cameron, Apr. 17, *OR*, ser. 1, vol. 51, pt. 1, pp. 317, 326–27; Hicks to Governor Burton of Delaware, Jan. 2, Thomas H. Hicks Papers, MHS; Baker, *Politics of Continuity*, pp. 49–50.

28. *Baltimore American*, Apr. 20.

29. Quoted in Towers, *Urban South*, p. 167.

30. Report of Hon. George William Brown, May 9 [?], *OR*, ser. 1, vol. 2, p. 12.

31. Mitchell, "'The Whirlwind Now Gathering,'" pp. 220–21.

32. Bailey, "The Pratt Street Riots Reconsidered," p. 158.

33. *Richmond Whig*, Apr. 20.

34. *Philadelphia Press*, Apr. 20 (first quotation); *New York Times*, Apr. 19 (second quotation).

35. *New Orleans Picayune*, Apr. 21.

36. "A letter from Baltimore," Apr. 19, quoted in *Washington, D.C., Evening Star*, Apr. 22.

37. Ibid.

12. ALONE

1. Entry for Apr. 18, Hay diary, Dennett, ed., *Lincoln and the Civil War*, p. 1.

2. Elizabeth B. Pryor, "Clara Barton," *ANB* (quotation); Oates, *A Woman of Valor*, pp. 3–6; *Washington, D.C., Evening Star*, Apr. 20.

3. Russell, *My Diary*, p. 75.

4. *Washington, D.C., Evening Star*, Apr. 15.

5. Entry for Apr. 14, Nevins and Thomas, eds., *Strong Diary*, 3:120.

6. Quoted in Peskin, *Winfield Scott*, p. 243.

7. Scott to Lincoln, Apr. 18, Mearns, 2:567.

8. Scott to Lincoln, Apr. 12, 13, ibid., 2:544, 550; *Washington, D.C., Evening Star*, Apr. 15, 16.

9. Scott to Lincoln, Apr. 16, Mearns, 2:562.

10. The best modern account of Stone's contribution, and his later unfair treatment by the army, is in Marvel, *Mr. Lincoln Goes to War*.

11. Cooling, "Defending Washington," p. 318; Leech, *Reveille in Washington*, p. 58; Stone, "A Dinner with General Scott in 1861," pp. 528–32.

12. Entry for Apr. 17, Horatio Nelson Taft diary, LC (first quotation); Scott, general order number 4, Apr. 26, *OR*, ser. 1, vol. 2, p. 602 (second quotation).

13. *Washington, D.C., Evening Star*, Apr. 18 (quotation); *Washington, D.C., Daily National Intelligencer*, Apr. 22.

14. Entry for Apr. 12, Horatio Nelson Taft diary, LC (first quotation); *Washington, D.C., National Intelligencer* (triweekly), Apr. 20 (second quotation).

15. Furgurson, *Freedom Rising*, p. 66.

16. Quoted in Leech, *Reveille in Washington*, p. 59.

17. Jacob Dodson to Cameron, Apr. 23, *OR*, ser. 3, vol. 1, p. 107; *Washington, D.C., Evening Star*, Apr. 23.

18. Frank Morn, "Allan Pinkerton," *ANB*; Pinkerton to Lincoln, Apr. 21, Mearns, 2:576–77.

19. Neal Dow to Lincoln, Apr. 22, AL-LC.

20. Kielbowicz, "The Telegraph, Censorship, and Politics," pp. 95–98.

21. *Washington, D.C., Evening Star*, Apr. 19; dispatch, Apr. 20, *New York Times*, Apr. 24.

22. Dispatch, Apr. 20, *New York Times*, Apr. 24; Lyman Furber to mother, Apr. 20 [?], Lyman Van Buren Furber Collection, MHS (quotation).

23. Quoted in Allen, *History of the United States Capitol*, p. 313.

24. Dispatch, Apr. 20, *New York Times*, Apr. 24.

25. *Washington, D.C., Daily National Intelligencer*, Apr. 23; *Washington, D.C., Evening Star*, Apr. 22.

26. *Washington, D.C., Evening Star*, Apr. 23.

27. Beale, ed., *Diary of Gideon Welles*, p. 19 (first quotation); *New York Times*, Apr. 24 (second quotation); Morrison, "*The Best School in the World*," p. 134; MacDonnell, "The Confederate Spin," note 1.

28. Lunsford Lindsay Lomax to Billy [George Dashiell Bayard], Apr. 21, VHS; Furgurson, *Freedom Rising*, p. 82 (quotation).

29. *Washington, D.C., National Intelligencer* (triweekly), Apr. 25.

30. Quoted in Swartz, "Franklin Buchanan," pp. 65, 66.

31. McCaslin, *Lee in the Shadow of Washington*, pp. 67–75.

32. Entry for Apr. 21, Hay diary, Dennett, ed., *Lincoln and the Civil War*, p. 6.

33. Leech, *Reveille in Washington*, p. 63; Nicolay and Hay, *Abraham Lincoln*, 4:140–41; Furgurson, *Freedom Rising*, p. 81 (quotation).

34. *Washington, D.C., Evening Star*, Apr. 24.

35. Ibid.

36. Ibid.

13. BROAD STRIPES AND BRIGHT STARS

1. Entry for Apr. 18, Nevins and Thomas, eds., *Strong Diary*, 3:123.

2. St. Clairsville, Ohio, *Gazette and Citizen*, Apr. 18, Perkins, 2:784 (first quotation); Tucker, *Cincinnati During the Civil War*, p. 11 (second quotation).

3. O. P. Morton to Cameron, Apr. 24, *OR*, ser. 3, vol. 1, p. 108.

4. J. Edgar Thomson to Cameron, Apr. 23, ibid., ser. 1, vol. 2, p. 597.

5. *New York Times*, Apr. 21.

6. Quoted in Furgurson, *Freedom Rising*, p. 85.

7. *Chicago Tribune*, Apr. 17.

8. Ibid., Apr. 19.

9. *The Liberator*, Apr. 26 (quotation); *Boston Daily Advertiser*, Apr. 17, 18.

10. *Philadelphia Press*, Apr. 15–17, 24 (quotation on Apr. 16).

11. Entries for Apr. 17, 18, Wister, ed., "Sarah Butler Wister's Civil War Diary," p. 277.

12. Atkins, *The Life of Sir William Howard Russell*, 2:23 (first quotation); McPherson, *For Cause and Comrades*, p. 16 (second quotation); *New York Times*, Apr. 19 (third quotation).

13. *New York Times*, Apr. 21.

14. Entry for Apr. 20, Nevins and Thomas, eds., *Strong Diary*, 3:127.

15. *New York Times*, Apr. 18; Edward G. Longacre, "Elmer Ephraim Ellsworth," *ANB*.

16. *New York Times*, Apr. 20, quoted in Stampp, *And the War Came*, p. 291.

17. New York dispatch, Apr. 15, *Charleston Mercury*, Apr. 20 (first quotation); New York dispatch, Apr. 18, *Richmond Dispatch*, Apr. 22 (second quotation).

18. J. M. Thayer to Cameron, Apr. 17, and Samuel W. Black to Cameron, Apr. 27, *OR*, ser. 3, vol. 1, pp. 83, 123 (quotation on p. 83).

19. *Charleston Mercury*, Apr. 20.

20. *Richmond Examiner*, Apr. 20.

21. *Charleston Mercury*, Apr. 25.

22. *Chicago Tribune*, Apr. 16, 19 (first and second quotations); *Richmond Examiner*, Apr. 20 (third quotation).

23. James McPherson, "Ulysses S. Grant," *ANB*; U. S. Grant to Frederick Dent, Apr. 19 (first quotation), and U. S. Grant to Jesse Root Grant, Apr. 21 (second quotation), Simon, ed., *Papers of Ulysses S. Grant*, 2:3, 7.

14. SUNDAY REST

1. Abstract log of USS *Pawnee*, Apr. 21, *ORN*, ser. 1, vol. 4, p. 292.

2. Entry for Apr. 21, Giles Buckner Cooke diary, VHS.

3. Operator, City Point, to Letcher, Apr. 21, 7 p.m. (quotation), Letcher Papers, box 9, folder 3, LVA; Burton, "*Pawnee* Sunday," pp. 4–9.

4. John Janney to Alcinda "Alice" Janney, Apr. 21, 5 p.m., transcription, Janney Papers, UVA.

5. Russell, *My Diary*, p. 81 (first quotation); Robertson, "War Comes to Norfolk Harbor, 1861," p. 64 (second quotation).

6. Long, "The Gosport Affair, 1861," p. 156.

7. John Niven, "Gideon Welles," *ANB*.

8. Welles to Capt. C. S. McCauley, Apr. 10, *ORN*, ser. 1, vol. 4, p. 274; Welles to Comdr. James Alden, Apr. 11, ibid., p. 275; Samuel L. Breese to Welles, Apr. 15, ibid., p. 276.

9. Tazewell Taylor to Letcher, Apr. 17, box 8, folder 7, and J. J. Cropper to Letcher, Apr. 18, box 8, folder 8, both in Letcher Papers, LVA.

10. John Rodney to Secretary of the Navy, Apr. 18, 9 p.m., and report of Charles F. McIntosh, Apr. 19, *ORN*, ser. 1, vol. 4, p. 271.

11. Elizabeth Noble Shor, "Benjamin Franklin Isherwood," *ANB*; report of B. F. Isherwood, Apr. 18, *ORN*, ser. 1, vol. 4, pp. 280–81.

12. Beale, ed., *Diary of Gideon Welles*, 1:43.
13. Welles to Paulding, Apr. 18, and M. N. Falls to W. W. Hunter, Apr. 19, enclosure in W. W. Hunter to Welles, Apr. 20, *ORN*, ser. 1, vol. 4, pp. 282, 286–87.
14. John A. Dahlgren to Welles, Apr. 20, ibid., pp. 287–88.
15. Old Point Comfort dispatch, Apr. 20, *New York Times*, Apr. 25.
16. J. J. Cropper to Letcher, Apr. 20, 11:50 a.m., Letcher Papers, box 9, folder 2, LVA.
17. Report of Capt. Charles Wilkes, USS *Pawnee*, to Flag Officer Hiram Paulding, Apr. 22, *ORN*, ser. 1, vol. 4, pp. 293–96.
18. Ibid.
19. Abstract log of USS *Pawnee*, Apr. 20–23, ibid., pp. 292–93.
20. Report of Major General Taliaferro, Apr. 23, ibid., pp. 306–9; J. J. Cropper to Letcher, Apr. 18, telegram, box 8, folder 8, Letcher Papers, LVA.
21. G. T. Sinclair to S. R. Mallory, Apr. 22 (quotation), *ORN*, ser. 1, vol. 4, p. 306; report of Capt. H. G. Wright, Apr. 26, ibid., pp. 296–98; Robertson, "War Comes to Norfolk Harbor, 1861," pp. 73–74.
22. John Janney to Alcinda "Alice" Janney, Apr. 28, transcription, box 2, Janney Papers, UVA.
23. Report of Capt. H. G. Wright, Apr. 26, *ORN*, ser. 1, vol. 4, p. 297; John Rodgers to Letcher, Apr. 21 (quotation), Letcher Papers, folder 385, VHS.
24. Report of Capt. Charles Wilkes, Apr. 22, *ORN*, ser. 1, vol. 4, p. 295.

15. WILD EXCITEMENT

1. Brown to Lincoln, Apr. 19, AL-LC.
2. Towers, *Urban South*, pp. 66–67; Reynolds, *John Brown, Abolitionist*, p. 317.
3. Hungerford, *Baltimore & Ohio*, 1:359, 369 (quotation).
4. Ibid., 1:370–72.
5. Brown to Lincoln, Apr. 19, AL-LC (first quotation); L. Thomas, Adjutant General, to S. M. Felton, Apr. 19, *OR*, ser. 1, vol. 2, p. 578 (second quotation).

6. Brown, *Baltimore and the Nineteenth of April, 1861*, p. 36; *Baltimore American*, Apr. 22.

7. Worthington G. Snethen to Seward, Apr. 23, reel 63 (microfilm), Papers of William H. Seward, Rush Rhees Library, University of Rochester, Rochester, N.Y. (first quotation); letter from Baltimore signed "X. Y. L.," Apr. 20, *Philadelphia Press*, Apr. 25 (second quotation).

8. *Baltimore Sun*, Apr. 22, quoted in Mitchell, "'The Whirlwind Now Gathering,'" p. 206 (first quotation); Brown, *Baltimore and the Nineteenth of April, 1861*, p. 60 (second quotation); Mitchell, "'The Whirlwind Now Gathering,'" pp. 207–8 (third quotation); entry for Apr. 20, John P. Kennedy diary, John Pendleton Kennedy Papers (microfilm), Enoch Pratt Free Library, Baltimore (fourth quotation).

9. Hicks to Cameron, Apr. 20, *OR*, ser. 1, vol. 2, p. 581.

10. Lincoln to Hicks and Brown, Apr. 20, Basler, 4:340.

11. Brown to Lincoln, Apr. 20, Mearns, 2:574.

12. Lincoln to Hicks and Brown, Apr. 20, Basler, 4:341.

13. *Baltimore Sun*, Apr. 22, in Mitchell, "'The Whirlwind Now Gathering,'" p. 206.

14. *Baltimore American*, Apr. 22; Capt. John C. Robinson to Col. L. Thomas, Apr. 20, *OR*, ser. 1, vol. 2, p. 582.

15. *Baltimore American*, Apr. 22 (first and second quotations). The newspaper printed the verse correctly but attributed it incorrectly to Psalms 3 rather than Joel 3:10 (King James Version).

16. Quoted in Mitchell, "The Whirlwind Now Gathering," p. 212.

17. *Baltimore American*, Apr. 22.

18. Brown to Lincoln, Apr. 21, AL-LC (original in all capitals).

19. Garrett to Brown, Apr. 21, quoted in *Baltimore American*, Apr. 22.

20. F. J. Porter to Col. Lorenzo Thomas, May 1, *OR*, ser. 1, vol. 51, pt. 1, pp. 345–51.

21. Wilmot to Scott, Apr. 20, *OR*, ser. 1, vol. 2, p. 582.

22. *Baltimore American*, Apr. 24; letter of Apr. 21, *Washington, D.C., Evening Star*, Apr. 23 (quotation).

23. *Baltimore American*, Apr. 23 (quotation), Apr. 24.

24. J. Edgar Thomson to Cameron, Apr. 23, *OR*, ser. 1, vol. 2, p. 597 (first quotation); Cameron to J. Edgar Thomson, Apr. 27, ibid., p. 604 (second quotation).
25. G. H. Steuart to John Letcher, Apr. 25, ibid., ser. 1, vol. 51, pt. 2, pp. 34–35.
26. Jabez D. Pratt to John C. Pratt, Apr. 20, transcription, Pratt Papers, MHS.
27. *Baltimore American*, Apr. 22.
28. John C. Pratt to Jabez D. Pratt, Apr. 27, "Brother Against Brother," p. 6.
29. Jabez D. Pratt to John C. Pratt, Apr. 27, ibid., p. 7.
30. Jabez D. Pratt to John C. Pratt, May 3, transcription, Pratt Papers, MHS; *The Liberator*, May 3.

16. COUNTLESS RUMORS

1. *Athens, Ohio, Messenger*, quoted in *Washington, D.C., National Intelligencer* (triweekly), Apr. 23.
2. Nicolay and Hay, *Abraham Lincoln*, 4:148; *Washington, D.C., Daily National Intelligencer*, Apr. 22 (quotation).
3. Entry for Apr. 22, Hay diary (first quotation), Dennett, ed., *Lincoln and the Civil War*, p. 7; reply to Baltimore Committee, Apr. 22 (second quotation), Basler, 4:341–42.
4. Basler, 4:342.
5. James M. McPherson, "Edward Bates," *ANB*; Bates's memorandum to cabinet, Apr. 23, Beale, ed., *Diary of Edward Bates*, p. 185 (quotation).
6. *New Orleans Picayune*, Apr. 21.
7. L. Q. Washington to L. E. Harvie, Apr. 18, Letcher Papers, box 8, folder 8, LVA; Campbell to Davis, Apr. 23 (quotation), Crist and Dix, eds., *Papers of Jefferson Davis*, 7:117–18.
8. *Charleston Mercury*, Apr. 23 (quotation); Pickens to Davis, Apr. 16, Crist and Dix, eds., *Papers of Jefferson Davis*, 7:104–6.
9. H. D. Bird to L. P. Walker, Apr. 20, *OR*, ser. 1, vol. 2, p. 772 (first quotation); Davis to Letcher, Apr. 22, ibid., p. 773 (second quota-

tion); *Richmond Dispatch*, Apr. 23 (third quotation); extracts from the proceedings of the Advisory Council of the State of Virginia, Apr. 22, *OR*, ser. 1, vol. 2, p. 773.

10. Hans L. Trefousse, "Benjamin Franklin Butler," *ANB*.

11. *Boston Daily Advertiser*, Apr. 19.

12. J. Edgar Thomson and S. M. Felton to Cameron, Apr. 19, *OR*, ser. 1, vol. 2, p. 578.

13. Roehrenbeck, *The Regiment That Saved the Capital*, pp. 72–77; Butler, *Butler's Book*, p. 188.

14. Abstract log of USS *Constitution*, Apr. 21, *ORN*, ser. 1, vol. 4, p. 398.

15. G. S. Blake to Welles, Apr. 15, ibid., p. 269 (first quotation); Welles to George S. Blake, Apr. 20, ibid., p. 272 (second quotation).

16. Hicks to "Commander of the Volunteer Troops on board the steamer," Apr. 21, *OR*, ser. 1, vol. 2, pp. 586–87.

17. Butler to Hicks, Apr. 22, ibid., p. 590 (quotation); abstract log of the USS *Constitution*, Apr. 21–22, *ORN*, ser. 1, vol. 4, pp. 398–99; Butler, *Butler's Book*, pp. 194–95; Butler to Governor of Maryland, Apr. 21, [Butler], *Private and Official Correspondence of Gen. Benjamin F. Butler*, 1:22.

18. Butler, *Butler's Book*, p. 195.

19. Hicks to Lincoln, Apr. 22, *OR*, ser. 1, vol. 2, pp. 588–89.

20. *Baltimore American*, Apr. 25.

21. Butler to Hicks, Apr. 23, [Butler], *Private and Official Correspondence of Gen. Benjamin F. Butler*, 1:28–29.

22. *Annapolis Gazette*, Apr. 25; R. J. to "my dear Cousin, [Hester]," May 2, MHS.

23. Butler, *Butler's Book*, p. 200.

24. Butler to Hicks, Apr. 23, *OR*, ser. 1, vol. 2, p. 593.

25. Andrew to Butler, Apr. 25, and Butler to Andrew, May 9, [Butler], *Private and Official Correspondence of Gen. Benjamin F. Butler*, 1:37–40.

26. Swinton, *History of the Seventh Regiment*, p. 95.

27. *Baltimore American*, Apr. 24.

28. Ibid., Apr. 23.

29. Mitchell, "'The Whirlwind Now Gathering,'" p. 228.
30. *Washington, D.C., Daily National Intelligencer,* Apr. 26.
31. Swinton, *History of the Seventh Regiment,* p. 21.
32. *Washington, D.C., Evening Star,* Apr. 25.
33. Entry for Apr. 25 (quotation), Horatio Nelson Taft diary, LC; R. C. Wood to Cameron, Apr. 25, *OR,* ser. 3, vol. 1, p. 115.
34. *Washington, D.C., Daily National Intelligencer,* Apr. 24.
35. Wall, *Andrew Carnegie,* pp. 157–60; Joseph Frazier Wall, "Andrew Carnegie," *ANB;* Carnegie, *Autobiography of Andrew Carnegie,* pp. 95–96.

17. DISMEMBERING THE NATION

1. *Joliet Signal,* Apr. 23, Perkins, 2:788.
2. Fox to Blair, Apr. 17, Thompson and Wainwright, eds., *Confidential Correspondence of Gustavus Vasa Fox,* 1:31–35.
3. Blair to Fox, Apr. 26, ibid., 1:37.
4. Crofts, *Reluctant Confederates,* p. 324 (quotation); W. R. Hurley to Letcher, Apr. 21, Letcher Papers, folder 385, VHS.
5. Entry for Apr. 25, John P. Kennedy diary, John Pendleton Kennedy Papers (microfilm), Enoch Pratt Free Library, Baltimore.
6. W. H. Winder to John Letcher, Apr. 19, Letcher Papers, folder 385, VHS.
7. *Kenosha Democrat,* Apr. 19, Perkins, 2:788.
8. *Joliet Signal,* Apr. 23, ibid., 2:789.
9. McPherson, *Battle Cry of Freedom,* pp. 306–7.
10. *New Orleans Picayune,* Apr. 19 (first quotation); *Richmond Dispatch,* Apr. 23 (second quotation).
11. Alcinda "Alice" Janney to John Janney, Apr. 21, transcription, box 2, Janney Papers, UVA.
12. Ibid., Apr. 30.
13. *Wheeling Daily Intelligencer,* Apr. 20, Perkins, 2:904 (first quotation); letter to editor, Apr. 25, *Washington, D.C., Daily National Intelligencer,* Apr. 26 (second quotation); Bates to Botts, May 5, Botts, *The Great Rebellion,* p. 273 (third quotation).

14. *Wellsburg Herald,* May 3 (first quotation); Curry, "A Reappraisal," p. 403 (second quotation).

15. Ayers, *In the Presence of Mine Enemies,* p. 142; Crofts, *Reluctant Confederates,* p. 329; *Baltimore American,* Apr. 25 (quotation).

16. *Daily Nashville Patriot,* Apr. 24, Dumond, p. 511.

17. Harris, *North Carolina and the Coming of the Civil War,* p. 43 (first quotation), p. 54 (second quotation); Sitterson, *Secession Movement in North Carolina,* p. 242 (third quotation); Crofts, *Reluctant Confederates,* p. 333 (fourth quotation).

18. Gilmer to Seward, Apr. 21, quoted in Crofts, *Reluctant Confederates,* p. 340.

19. Abrahamson, *Men of Secession and Civil War,* p. 157; H. M. Rector to Cameron, Apr. 22, *OR,* ser. 1, vol. 1, p. 687 (quotation).

20. *St. Louis Daily Missouri Republican,* Apr. 19, Dumond, p. 500.

21. *Chicago Tribune,* May 2 (first quotation); *Washington, D.C., Daily National Intelligencer,* Apr. 29 (second quotation).

22. *Baltimore American,* Apr. 27.

23. Lincoln to Scott, Apr. 25, AL-LC; Scott to Butler, Apr. 26, *OR,* ser. 1, vol. 2, pp. 601–2. The federal government thus avoided provoking moderate Marylanders and waited until autumn to arrest the most pro-Confederate legislators.

24. McPherson, *Battle Cry of Freedom,* p. 289 (first quotation); Gienapp, *Abraham Lincoln,* p. 84 (second quotation).

25. Evitts, *A Matter of Allegiances,* p. 189; Ellenberger, "Whigs in the Streets?," p. 30.

26. *Richmond Examiner,* Apr. 20.

27. James S. Murrow to Letcher, Apr. 22, Letcher Papers, box 9, folder 4, VHS.

28. Robert Y. Conrad to Elizabeth Whiting (Powell) Conrad, Apr. 20, Conrad Papers, VHS.

29. Davis, *Look Away!,* p. 117 (first quotation); Botts, *The Great Rebellion,* p. 279 (second quotation).

30. Ayers, *In the Presence of Mine Enemies,* p. 233.

31. *Chicago Tribune,* Apr. 18 (first quotation); *Richmond Examiner,* Apr. 22 (second quotation).

32. *Peoria Daily Transcript*, Apr. 24, Perkins, 2:875 (first quotation); *Boston Journal*, cited in *Baltimore American*, Apr. 27; *Richmond Dispatch*, Apr. 20 (second quotation).

33. A. W. Spies [?] to Letcher, Apr. 28, Letcher Papers, folder 385, VHS (first quotation); John S. Burton to Letcher, Apr. 21, ibid. (second quotation); Edmund James McGarn and William Fairchild to Lincoln, Apr. 20, AL-LC (third quotation).

34. *Richmond Examiner*, Apr. 24.

35. Charles Royster, "Fort Sumter: At Last the War," p. 204, Boritt, ed., *Why the Civil War Came* (quotation); McPherson, *Battle Cry of Freedom*, p. 238.

36. Quoted in Crofts, *Reluctant Confederates*, p. 345.

37. *Brooklyn Eagle*, Apr. 17.

38. Thomas E. Stephens, "John Jordan Crittenden," *ANB*.

39. Cooper, *Jefferson Davis, American*, p. 343; Lincoln to Ephraim and Phoebe Ellsworth, May 25, AL-LC (quotation).

40. Victor, *The History, Civil, Political, and Military, of the Southern Rebellion*, 2:172–73.

Epilogue

1. Speech at Great Central Sanitary Fair, Philadelphia, June 16, 1864, Collected Works of Abraham Lincoln (www.hti.umich.edu/l/lincoln).

2. Potter, *The Impending Crisis*, p. 583.

3. Swanberg, *First Blood*, pp. 333–39.

4. Simpson, *A Good Southerner*, pp. 280–82; Michael B. Chesson, "Henry Alexander Wise," *ANB*.

5. Simpson, *A Good Southerner*, p. 292.

6. Ibid., pp. 288, 292; Peterson, *John Brown*, p. 38; Siviter, *Recollections of War and Peace*, p. 218.

BIBLIOGRAPHY

The multiplicity of sources for studying the American Civil War intimidates the most experienced researchers; those for the period leading up to the war seem hardly less daunting in number. Even though this book focuses on a few weeks, not four years, and concentrates mainly on events in Virginia, Maryland, and Washington, D.C., not the whole country, a wealth of evidence abounds. Because I wanted to view the story through the eyes of Americans as they experienced it at the time and not in hindsight, I tended not to favor the vast array of memoirs and other accounts written after spring 1861, in many cases long after. This was not an absolute rule. Some accounts written in retrospect offer insight, just as many contemporaneously written letters and diaries entirely misrepresent the events they purport to describe. Even so, my tendency was to give greater weight to writings of eyewitnesses who did not know the outcomes of the events they observed.

I found the most rewarding sources for *Cry Havoc!* in the unpublished treasures of seven archives in particular: in Richmond, the Virginia Historical Society, the Library of Virginia, and the Eleanor S. Brockenbrough

Library of the Museum of the Confederacy; in Charlottesville, the Albert and Shirley Small Special Collections Library of the University of Virginia; in Baltimore, the H. Furlong Baldwin Library of the Maryland Historical Society; and in Washington, D.C., the manuscripts reading rooms of the Library of Congress and the National Archives. I am most grateful to the staffs of each of these institutions for their generous help.

The published primary sources listed in the bibliography that follows illustrate the wealth of documentation readily available through interlibrary loan and, more and more every year, through myriad online sites that are revolutionizing historical research. A decade ago, few if any of these electronic resources were available. A historian writing on the same topic a decade hence will have vastly more primary documents readily to hand through the Internet.

Published Primary Sources

[Baldwin, John B., comp.]. *Interview Between President Lincoln and Col. John B. Baldwin, April 4th, 1861: Statement & Evidence.* Staunton, Va.: D. E. Strasburg, 1866.

Barnes, James J., and Patience P. Barnes, eds. *The American Civil War Through British Eyes: Dispatches from British Diplomats.* Volume 1, *November 1860–April 1862.* Kent, Ohio: Kent State University Press, 2003.

Basler, Roy P., et al., eds. *The Collected Works of Abraham Lincoln.* New Brunswick, N.J.: Rutgers University Press, 1953–55.

Beale, Howard K., ed. *The Diary of Edward Bates, 1859–1866.* Washington, D.C.: U.S. Government Printing Office, 1933.

Beale, Howard K., assisted by Alan W. Brownsword. *Diary of Gideon Welles: Secretary of the Navy Under Lincoln and Johnson.* 3 volumes. New York: Norton, 1960.

Berlin, Ira, et al., eds. *Freedom: A Documentary History of Emancipation, 1861–1867.* Series 1, volume 1. *The Destruction of Slavery.* Cambridge: Cambridge University Press, 1985.

Botts, John Minor. *The Great Rebellion: Its Secret History, Rise, Progress, and Disastrous Failure.* New York: Harper & Brothers, 1866.

Brown, George William. *Baltimore and the Nineteenth of April, 1861: A Study of the War*. Baltimore: N. Murray, 1887.

Butler, Benjamin F. *Autobiography and Personal Reminiscences of Major-General Benj. F. Butler: Butler's Book. . . .* Boston: A. M. Thayer, 1892.

[————]. *Private and Official Correspondence of Gen. Benjamin F. Butler During the Period of the Civil War*. N.p.: Privately printed, 1917.

[Carnegie, Andrew]. *Autobiography of Andrew Carnegie*. Garden City, N.Y.: Doubleday, Doran, 1933.

Catton, Bruce, ed. "Brother Against Brother." *American Heritage* 12 (1961): 4–7, 89.

Cole, Donald B., and John J. McDonough, eds. *Witness to the Young Republic: A Yankee's Journal, 1828–1870* [Benjamin Brown French]. Hanover, N.H.: University Press of New England, 1989.

Crabtree, Beth G., and James W. Patton, eds. *"Journal of a Secesh Lady": The Diary of Catherine Ann Devereux Edmondston, 1860–1866*. Raleigh: Division of Archives and History, 1995.

Crist, Lynda Lasswell, and Mary Seaton Dix, eds. *The Papers of Jefferson Davis*. Volume 7. Baton Rouge: Louisiana State University Press, 1992.

Dahlgren, Madeleine Vinton, ed. *Memoir of John A. Dahlgren, Rear-Admiral United States Navy*. Boston: James R. Osgood, 1882.

Dennett, Tyler, ed. *Lincoln and the Civil War in the Diaries and Letters of John Hay*. New York: Dodd, Mead & Company, 1939.

Douglass, Frederick. *The Life and Times of Frederick Douglass . . .* Electronic edition. Frederick Douglass Papers, American Memory, LC. (Originally published in Hartford, Conn., 1881.)

Dumond, Dwight Lowell, ed. *Southern Editorials on Secession*. Gloucester, Mass.: Peter Smith, 1964.

Greenawalt, Bruce S., ed. "Unionists in Rockbridge County: The Correspondence of James Dorman Davidson Concerning the Virginia Secession Convention of 1861." *VMHB* 73 (1965): 76–102.

Jones, J. B. *A Rebel War Clerk's Diary at the Confederate States Capital*. 2 volumes. Edited by Howard Swiggett. New York: Old Hickory Bookshop, 1935.

Marks, Bayly Ellen, and Mark Norton Schatz, eds. *Between North and South: A Maryland Journalist Views the Civil War: The Narrative of William Wilkins Glenn, 1861–1869.* Rutherford, N.J.: Fairleigh Dickinson University Press, 1976.

Mearns, David C., ed. *The Lincoln Papers: The Story of the Collection with Selections to July 4, 1861.* Volume 2. Garden City, N.Y.: Doubleday, 1948.

Morgan, William James, et al., eds. *Autobiography of Rear Admiral Charles Wilkes, U.S. Navy, 1798–1877.* Washington, D.C.: Department of the Navy, 1978.

Nevins, Allan, and Milton Halsey Thomas, eds. *The Diary of George Templeton Strong.* 4 volumes. New York: Octagon Books, 1974.

Perkins, Howard Cecil, ed. *Northern Editorials on Secession.* 2 volumes. Gloucester, Mass.: Peter Smith, 1964.

Rachal, William M. E., ed. "'Secession Is Nothing but Revolution': A Letter of R. E. Lee to His Son 'Rooney.'" *VMHB* 69 (1961): 4–6.

Reese, George H., ed. *Journals and Papers of the Virginia State Convention of 1861.* 3 volumes. Richmond: Virginia State Library, 1966.

———. *Proceedings of the Virginia State Convention of 1861.* 4 volumes. Richmond: Virginia State Library, 1965.

Russell, William Howard. *My Diary: North and South.* Boston: T. O. H. P. Burnham, 1863.

Scarborough, William Kauffman, ed. *The Diary of Edmund Ruffin.* 3 volumes. Baton Rouge: Louisiana State University Press, 1972–79.

Simon, John Y., ed. *The Papers of Ulysses S. Grant.* Volume 2, *April–September 1861.* Carbondale, Ill.: Southern Illinois University Press, 1969.

Stone, Charles P. "A Dinner with General Scott in 1861." *Magazine of American History* 11 (1884): 528–32.

———. "Washington in March and April, 1861." *Magazine of American History* 14 (1885): 1–24.

Thompson, Robert Means, and Richard Wainwright. *Confidential Correspondence of Gustavus Vasa Fox, Assistant Secretary of the Navy, 1861–1865.* 2 volumes. New York: Printed for the Naval History Society by the De Vinne Press, 1918.

United States Naval War Records Office. *Official Records of the Union and Confederate Navies in the War of the Rebellion.* 27 volumes. Washington, D.C.: Government Printing Office, 1894–1922.

United States War Department. *The War of the Rebellion: A Compilation of the Official Records of the Union and Confederate Armies.* 128 volumes. Washington, D.C.: Government Printing Office, 1880–1901.

Victor, Orville J. *The History, Civil, Political, and Military, of the Southern Rebellion . . .* 4 volumes. New York: J. D. Torrey, 1861–68.

Wister, Fanny Kemble, ed. "Sarah Butler Wister's Civil War Diary." *Pennsylvania Magazine of History and Biography* 102 (1978): 271–327.

SELECTED ONLINE PRIMARY SOURCES

Abraham Lincoln Papers at the Library of Congress. American Memory. A Collaborative Project of the Library of Congress Manuscript Division and the Lincoln Study Center, Knox College.
memory.loc.gov/ammem/alhtml/malhome.html

American Memory: Historical Collections from the National Digital Library. Library of Congress.
memory.loc.gov/ammem/ammemhome.html

Brooklyn Daily Eagle, 1841–1902 Online. Brooklyn Public Library.
www.brooklynpubliclibrary.org/eagle

John Brown/Boyd B. Stutler Collection Database. West Virginia Archives and History.
wvmemory.wvculture.org/imlsintro.html

Collected Works of Abraham Lincoln. Sponsored by the Abraham Lincoln Association.
www.hti.umich.edu/l/lincoln

Horatio Nelson Taft Diary, 1861–1865. American Memory. Library of Congress.
memory.loc.gov/ammem/tafthtml/tafthome.html

The Valley of the Shadow: Two Communities in the American Civil War. Edward L. Ayers.
valley.vcdh.virginia.edu

The War of the Rebellion: A Compilation of the Official Records of the Union and Confederate Armies and *Official Records of the Union and Confederate Navies in the War of the Rebellion.* Making of America. Cornell University.
cdl.library.cornell.edu/moa/moa_browse.html

SECONDARY SOURCES

Abrahamson, James L. *The Men of Secession and Civil War, 1859–1861.* Wilmington, Del.: Scholarly Resources Inc., 2000.

Allen, William C. *History of the United States Capitol: A Chronicle of Design, Construction, and Politics.* Washington, D.C.: Government Printing Office, 2001.

Ambler, Charles Henry. *Francis H. Pierpont: Union War Governor of Virginia and Father of West Virginia.* Chapel Hill: University of North Carolina Press, 1937.

———. *Sectionalism in Virginia from 1776 to 1861.* Chicago: University of Chicago Press, 1910.

Andrews, J. Cutler. *The North Reports the Civil War.* Pittsburgh: University of Pittsburgh Press, 1955.

Atkins, John Black. *The Life of Sir William Howard Russell, C.V.O., LL.D.: The First Special Correspondent.* London: John Murray, 1911.

Ayers, Edward L. *In the Presence of Mine Enemies: War in the Heart of America, 1859–1863.* New York: W. W. Norton, 2003.

Ayers, Edward L., and John C. Willis, eds. *The Edge of the South: Life in Nineteenth-Century Virginia.* Charlottesville: University Press of Virginia, 1991.

Bailey, Robert F., III. "The Pratt Street Riots Reconsidered: A Case of Overstated Significance?" *MHM* 98 (2003): 153–71.

Baker, Jean H. *The Politics of Continuity: Maryland Political Parties from 1858 to 1870.* Baltimore: Johns Hopkins University Press, 1973.

Bancroft, Frederic. *The Life of William H. Seward.* 2 volumes. Gloucester, Mass.: Peter Smith, 1967.

Barton, William E. *The Life of Clara Barton: Founder of the American Red Cross.* New York: AMS Press, 1969.

Billings, Elden E. "Social and Economic Conditions in Washington During the Civil War." In Francis Coleman Rosenberger, ed., *Records of the Columbia Historical Society of Washington, D.C., 1963–1965.* Washington, D.C.: The Society, 1966.

——. "Military Activities in Washington in 1861." *Records of the Columbia Historical Society of Washington, D.C.* 52 (1989): 123–33.

Blondheim, Menahem. *News over the Wires: The Telegraph and the Flow of Public Information in America, 1844–1897.* Cambridge, Mass.: Harvard University Press, 1994.

Blue, Frederick J. *No Taint of Compromise: Crusaders in Antislavery Politics.* Baton Rouge: Louisiana State University Press, 2005.

Bohner, Charles H. *John Pendleton Kennedy: Gentleman from Baltimore.* Baltimore: Johns Hopkins University Press, 1961.

Boney, F. N. *John Letcher of Virginia: The Story of Virginia's Civil War Governor.* University: University of Alabama Press, 1966.

Boritt, Gabor S., ed. *The Historian's Lincoln: Pseudohistory, Psychohistory, and History.* Urbana: University of Illinois Press, 1998.

——. *Why the Civil War Came.* New York: Oxford University Press, 1996.

Bowman, Shearer Davis. "Conditional Unionism and Slavery in Virginia, 1860–1861: The Case of Dr. Richard Eppes." *VMHB* 96 (1988): 31–54.

Bradley, Erwin Stanley. *Simon Cameron, Lincoln's Secretary of War: A Political Biography.* Philadelphia: University of Pennsylvania Press, 1966.

Bridges, Peter. *Pen of Fire: John Moncure Daniel.* Kent, Ohio: Kent State University Press, 2002.

Burton, David L. "*Pawnee* Sunday." *VC* 32 (1982): 4–9.

Carmichael, Peter S. *The Last Generation: Young Virginians in Peace, War, and Reunion.* Chapel Hill: University of North Carolina Press, 2005.

Carp, Benjamin L. "Nations of American Rebels: Understanding Nationalism in Revolutionary North America and the Civil War South." *CWH* 48 (2002): 5–33.

Clark, Charles B. "Baltimore and the Attack on the Sixth Massachusetts Regiment, April 19, 1861." *MHM* 56 (1961): 39–71.

Connor, Henry G. *John Archibald Campbell: Associate Justice of the United States Supreme Court, 1853–1861.* Boston: Houghton Mifflin, 1920.

Cooling, Benjamin Franklin. "Defending Washington During the Civil War." In Francis Coleman Rosenberger, ed., *Records of the Columbia Historical Society of Washington, D.C., 1971–72.* Washington, D.C.: The Society, 1973.

Cooper, William J., Jr. *Jefferson Davis, American.* New York: Alfred A. Knopf, 2000.

Crofts, Daniel W. "Late Antebellum Virginia Reconsidered." *VMHB* 107 (1999): 253–86.

———. *Reluctant Confederates: Upper South Unionists in the Secession Crisis.* Chapel Hill: University of North Carolina Press, 1989.

———. "A Reluctant Unionist: John A. Gilmer and Lincoln's Cabinet." *CWH* 24 (1978): 225–49.

———. "Virginia, the South, and the Union, 1850–1861." Paper presented at Southern Historical Association, Nov. 7, 1997.

Crozier, Emmet. *Yankee Reporters, 1861–65.* Westport, Conn.: Greenwood Press, 1956.

Curry, Richard O. "A Reappraisal of Statehood Politics in West Virginia." *JSH* 28 (1962): 403–21.

Davis, William C. *The Deep Waters of the Proud.* Garden City, N.Y.: Doubleday, 1982.

———. *"A Government of Our Own": The Making of the Confederacy.* New York: Free Press, 1994.

———. *Look Away!: A History of the Confederate States of America.* New York: Free Press, 2002.

Davis, William C., and James I. Robertson Jr. *Virginia at War, 1861.* Lexington: University Press of Kentucky, 2005.

d'Entremont, John. *Southern Emancipator: Moncure Conway, the American Years, 1832–1865.* New York: Oxford University Press, 1987.

Detzer, David. *Allegiance: Fort Sumter, Charleston, and the Beginning of the Civil War.* New York: Harcourt, 2001.

————. *Dissonance: The Turbulent Days Between Fort Sumter and Bull Run*. New York: Harcourt, 2006.

Dew, Charles B. *Apostles of Disunion: Southern Secession Commissioners and the Causes of the Civil War*. Charlottesville: University Press of Virginia, 2001.

Donald, David Herbert. *Lincoln*. New York: Simon & Schuster, 1995.

Dozier, Graham T., comp. *Virginia's Civil War: A Guide to Manuscripts at the Virginia Historical Society*. Richmond: Virginia Historical Society, 1998.

Egnal, Marc. "Rethinking the Secession of the Lower South: The Clash of Two Groups." *CWH* 50 (2004): 261–90.

Eisenhower, John S. D. *Agent of Destiny: The Life and Times of General Winfield Scott*. New York: Free Press, 1997.

Ellenberger, Matthew. "Whigs in the Streets?: Baltimore Republicanism in the Spring of 1861." *MHM* 86 (1991): 23–38.

Elliott, Charles Winslow. *Winfield Scott: The Soldier and the Man*. New York: Macmillan, 1937.

Evitts, William J. *A Matter of Allegiances: Maryland from 1850 to 1861*. Baltimore: Johns Hopkins University Press, 1974.

Finkelman, Paul, ed. *His Soul Goes Marching On: Responses to John Brown and the Harpers Ferry Raid*. Charlottesville: University Press of Virginia, 1995.

Foote, Shelby. *The Civil War: A Narrative*. Volume 1, *Fort Sumter to Perryville*. New York: Random House, 1958.

Foster, Gaines M. "Guilt over Slavery: A Historiographical Analysis." *JSH* 56 (1990): 665–94.

Freehling, William W. "The Editorial Revolution, Virginia, and the Coming of the Civil War: A Review Essay." *CWH* 16 (1970): 64–72.

————. *The South vs. the South: How Anti-Confederate Southerners Shaped the Course of the Civil War*. New York: Oxford University Press, 2001.

Freeman, Douglas Southall. *R. E. Lee: A Biography*. New York: Charles Scribner's Sons, 1935.

Furgurson, Ernest B. *Ashes of Glory: Richmond at War*. New York: Alfred A. Knopf, 1996.

———. *Freedom Rising: Washington in the Civil War.* New York: Alfred A. Knopf, 2004.

Gaines, William H., Jr. *Biographical Register of Members, Virginia State Convention of 1861.* Richmond: Virginia State Library, 1969.

Gallagher, Gary W. *The Confederate War.* Cambridge, Mass.: Harvard University Press, 1997.

Gienapp, William E. *Abraham Lincoln and Civil War America: A Biography.* New York: Oxford University Press, 2002.

Golden, Alan Lawrence. "The Secession Crisis in Virginia: A Critical Study of Argument." PhD dissertation, Ohio State University, 1990.

Green, Constance McLaughlin. *Washington: Village and Capital, 1800–1878.* 2 volumes. Princeton: Princeton University Press, 1962.

Greenawalt, Bruce Stephan, ed. "Unionists in Rockbridge County: The Correspondence of James Dorman Davidson Concerning the Virginia Secession Convention of 1861." *VMHB* 73 (1965): 76–102.

Gunderson, Robert G. "William C. Rives and the 'Old Gentlemen's Convention.'" *JSH* 22 (1956): 459–76.

Hall, Granville Davisson. *The Rending of Virginia: A History.* Chicago: Mayer & Miller, 1902.

Harris, William C. *North Carolina and the Coming of the Civil War.* Raleigh: Division of Archives and History, North Carolina Department of Cultural Resources, 1988.

Harrison, Lowell H., and James C. Klotter. *A New History of Kentucky.* Lexington: University Press of Kentucky, 1997.

Hearn, Chester G. *Six Years of Hell: Harpers Ferry During the Civil War.* Baton Rouge: Louisiana State University Press, 1996.

Heck, Frank H. "John C. Breckinridge in the Crisis of 1860–1861." *JSH* 21 (1955): 316–46.

Hettle, Wallace. "The 'Self-Analysis' of John C. Rutherfoord: Democracy and the Manhood of a Virginia Secessionist." *Southern Studies* 5, nos. 1 and 2 (1994): 81–116.

Hitchcock, William S. "The Limits of Southern Unionism: Virginia Conservatives and the Gubernatorial Election of 1859." *JSH* 47 (1981): 57–72.

———. "Southern Moderates and Secession: Senator Robert M. T. Hunter's Call for Union." *JAH* 59 (1972–73): 871–84.

Holzman, Robert S. *Adapt or Perish: The Life of General Roger A. Pryor,* *C.S.A.* Hampden, Conn.: Archon Books, 1976.

Hoogenboom, Ari. "Gustavus Fox and the Relief of Fort Sumter." *CWH* 9 (1963): 383–99.

Howard, Charles McHenry, ed. "Baltimore and the Crisis of 1861." *MHM* 41 (1946): 257–81.

Hungerford, Edward. *The Story of the Baltimore & Ohio Railroad,* *1827–1927.* 2 volumes. New York: G. P. Putnam's Sons, 1928.

Inscoe, John C., and Robert C. Kenzer. *Enemies of the Country: New* *Perspectives on Unionists in the Civil War South.* Athens: University of Georgia Press, 2001.

Jaffa, Harry V. *A New Birth of Freedom: Abraham Lincoln and the* *Coming of the Civil War.* Lanham, Md.: Rowman & Littlefield, 2000.

Johnson, Clint. *Bull's-Eyes and Misfires: 50 People Whose Obscure* *Efforts Shaped the American Civil War.* Nashville: Rutledge Hill Press, 2002.

Johnson, Ludwell H. "Fort Sumter and Confederate Diplomacy." *JSH* 26 (1960): 441–77.

Johnson, Timothy D. *Winfield Scott: The Quest for Military Glory.* Lawrence: University of Kansas Press, 1998.

Kammen, Michael. *Mystic Chords of Memory: The Transformation of* *Tradition in American Culture.* New York: Alfred A. Knopf, 1991.

Kielbowicz, Richard B. "The Telegraph, Censorship, and Politics at the Outset of the Civil War." *CWH* 40 (1994): 95–118.

Kimball, Gregg D. *American City, Southern Place: A Cultural History* *of Antebellum Richmond.* Athens: University of Georgia Press, 2000.

King, Alvy L. *Louis T. Wigfall: Southern Fire-Eater.* Baton Rouge: Louisiana State University Press, 1970.

Klein, Maury. *Days of Defiance: Sumter, Secession, and the Coming of* *the Civil War.* New York: Vintage Books, 1999.

Kornblith, Gary J. "Rethinking the Coming of the Civil War: A Counterfactual Exercise." *JAH* 90 (2003): 76–105.

Kruman, Marc W. *Parties and Politics in North Carolina, 1836–1865.* Baton Rouge: Louisiana State University Press, 1983.

Lankford, Nelson. *Richmond Burning: The Last Days of the Confederate Capital.* New York: Viking, 2002.

Leech, Margaret. *Reveille in Washington, 1860–1865.* New York: Harper & Brothers, 1941.

Link, William A. *Roots of Secession: Slavery and Politics in Antebellum Virginia.* Chapel Hill: University of North Carolina Press, 2003.

Long, E. B., with Barbara Long. *The Civil War Day by Day: An Almanac, 1861–1865.* Garden City, N.Y.: Doubleday, 1971.

Long, John Sherman. "The Gosport Affair, 1861." *JSH* 23 (1957): 155–72.

Lull, Edward P. *History of the United States Navy-Yard at Gosport, Virginia (Near Norfolk).* Washington, D.C.: Government Printing Office, 1874.

McCaslin, Richard B. *Lee in the Shadow of Washington.* Baton Rouge: Louisiana State University Press, 2001.

MacDonnell, Francis. "The Confederate Spin on Winfield Scott and George Thomas, Southern Unionists." *CWH* 44 (1998): 255–66.

McDowell, Robert Emmett. *City of Conflict: Louisville in the Civil War, 1861–1865.* Louisville: Louisville Civil War Round Table, 1962.

McGregor, James C. *The Disruption of Virginia.* New York: Macmillan, 1922.

McPherson, James M. *Battle Cry of Freedom: The Civil War Era.* New York: Ballantine Books, 1988.

———. *For Cause and Comrades: Why Men Fought in the Civil War.* New York: Oxford, 1997.

McPherson, James M., and William J. Cooper Jr. *Writing the Civil War: The Quest to Understand.* Columbia: University of South Carolina Press, 1998.

Marvel, William. *Mr. Lincoln Goes to War.* Boston: Houghton Mifflin, 2006.

Mitchell, Charles W. "'The Whirlwind Now Gathering': Baltimore's Pratt Street Riot and the End of Maryland Secession." *MHM* 97 (2002): 203–32.

Morrison, James L., Jr. *"The Best School in the World": West Point, the Pre–Civil War Years, 1833–1866.* Kent, Ohio: Kent State University Press, 1986.

Nicolay, John H., and John Hay. *Abraham Lincoln: A History*. Volume 4. New York: Century Company, 1890.

Oates, Stephen B. *To Purge This Land with Blood: A Biography of John Brown*. New York: Harper & Row, 1970.

———. *A Woman of Valor: Clara Barton and the Civil War*. New York: Free Press, 1994.

Osborne, Charles C. *Jubal: The Life and Times of General Jubal A. Early, CSA, Defender of the Lost Cause*. Chapel Hill, N.C.: Algonquin Books, 1992.

Perret, Geoffrey. *Lincoln's War: The Untold Story of America's Greatest President as Commander in Chief*. New York: Random House, 2004.

Perry, James M. *A Bohemian Brigade: The Civil War Correspondents—Mostly Rough, Sometimes Ready*. New York: John Wiley & Sons, 2000.

Peskin, Allan. *Winfield Scott and the Profession of Arms*. Kent, Ohio: Kent State University Press, 2003.

Peterson, Merrill D. *John Brown: The Legend Revisited*. Charlottesville: University of Virginia Press, 2002.

Plum, William R. *The Military Telegraph During the Civil War in the United States . . .* Chicago: Jansen, McClurg, 1882.

Potter, David M. *The Impending Crisis, 1848–1861*. Completed and edited by Don E. Fehrenbacher. New York: Harper & Row, 1976.

———. *The South and the Sectional Conflict*. Baton Rouge: Louisiana State University Press, 1968.

Quarles, Benjamin. *The Negro in the Civil War*. Boston: Little, Brown, 1953.

Rable, George C. *The Confederate Republic: A Revolution against Politics*. Chapel Hill: University of North Carolina Press, 1994.

Radcliffe, George L. P. *Governor Thomas H. Hicks of Maryland and the Civil War*. Baltimore: Johns Hopkins Press, 1901.

Reynolds, David S. *John Brown, Abolitionist: The Man Who Killed Slavery, Sparked the Civil War, and Seeded Civil Rights*. New York: Alfred A. Knopf, 2005.

Riggs, David F. "Robert Young Conrad and the Ordeal of Secession." *VMHB* 86 (1978): 259–74.

Robertson, Alexander F. *Alexander Hugh Holmes Stuart, 1807–1891: A Biography*. Richmond: William Byrd Press, 1925.

Robertson, J. H. "War Comes to Norfolk Harbor, 1861." *VC* 50 (2001): 64–75.

Robinson, Armstead L. *Bitter Fruits of Bondage: The Demise of Slavery and the Collapse of the Confederacy, 1861–1865*. Charlottesville: University of Virginia Press, 2005.

Roehrenbeck, William J. *The Regiment That Saved the Capital*. New York: Thomas Yoseloff, 1961.

Rubin, Anne Sarah. *A Shattered Nation: The Rise and Fall of the Confederacy, 1861–1868*. Chapel Hill: University of North Carolina Press, 2005.

Saunders, Robert, Jr. *John Archibald Campbell, Southern Moderate, 1811–1889*. Tuscaloosa: University of Alabama Press, 1997.

Schott, Thomas E. *Alexander H. Stephens of Georgia*. Baton Rouge: Louisiana State University Press, 1988.

Shanks, Henry T. *The Secession Movement in Virginia, 1847–1861*. Richmond: Garrett & Massie, 1934.

Simpson, Craig M. *A Good Southerner: The Life of Henry A. Wise of Virginia*. Chapel Hill: University of North Carolina Press, 1985.

Sitterson, Joseph Carlyle. *The Secession Movement in North Carolina*. Chapel Hill: University of North Carolina Press, 1939.

Siviter, Anna Pierpont. *Recollections of War and Peace, 1861–1868*. New York: G. P. Putnam's Sons, 1938.

Snay, Mitchell. *Gospel of Disunion: Religion and Separatism in the Antebellum South*. New York: Cambridge University Press, 1993.

Snyder, Timothy R. "Border Strife on the Upper Potomac: Confederate Incursions from Harpers Ferry, April–June 1861." *MHM* 97 (2002): 79–108.

Sowle, Patrick. "The Trials of a Virginia Unionist: William Cabell Rives and the Secession Crisis, 1860–1861." *VMHB* 80 (1972): 3–20.

Stampp, Kenneth M. *And the War Came: The North and the Secession Crisis, 1860–1861*. Chicago: University of Chicago Press, 1964.

———. *The Imperiled Union: Essays on the Background of the Civil War*. New York: Oxford University Press, 1980.

Standage, Tom. *The Victorian Internet: The Remarkable Story of the*

Telegraph and the Nineteenth Century's On-Line Pioneers. New York: Walker, 1998.

Sutton, Robert P. *Revolution to Secession: Constitution Making in the Old Dominion.* Charlottesville: University Press of Virginia, 1989.

Swanberg, W. A. *First Blood: The Story of Fort Sumter.* New York: Charles Scribner's Sons, 1957.

Swartz, Oretha D. "Franklin Buchanan: A Study in Divided Loyalties." *United States Naval Institute Proceedings* 88: no. 12 (1962): 60–69.

Swinton, William. *History of the Seventh Regiment, National Guard, State of New York, During the War of the Rebellion . . .* New York: Fields, Osgood, 1870.

Thomas, William G., III, and Edward L. Ayers. "An Overview: The Differences Slavery Made: A Close Analysis of Two American Communities." *American Historical Review* 108 (2003): 1298–1307 and www.vcdh.virginia.edu/AHR.

Thompson, Robert Luther. *Wiring a Continent: The History of the Telegraph Industry in the United States, 1832–1866.* New York: Arno Press, 1972.

Towers, Frank. *The Urban South and the Coming of the Civil War.* Charlottesville: University of Virginia Press, 2005.

Tucker, Louis Leonard. *Cincinnati During the Civil War.* Columbus: Ohio State University Press for the Ohio Historical Society, 1962.

Tyler-McGraw, Marie. *At the Falls: Richmond, Virginia, and Its People.* Chapel Hill: University of North Carolina Press, 1994.

Wall, Joseph Frazier. *Andrew Carnegie.* New York: Oxford University Press, 1970.

Wallenstein, Peter, and Bertram Wyatt-Brown, eds. *Virginia's Civil War.* Charlottesville: University of Virginia Press, 2005.

Walther, Eric H. *The Fire-Eaters.* Baton Rouge: Louisiana State University Press, 1992.

———. *The Shattering of the Union: America in the 1850s.* Wilmington, Del.: Scholarly Resources, 2004.

Webster, Donald B., Jr. "The Last Days of Harpers Ferry Armory." *CWH* 5 (1959): 30–44.

Wells, Damon. *Stephen Douglas: The Last Years, 1857–1861.* Austin: University of Texas Press, 1971.

White, Ronald C., Jr. *The Eloquent President: A Portrait of Lincoln Through His Words*. New York: Random House, 2005.

———. *Lincoln's Greatest Speech: The Second Inaugural*. New York: Simon & Schuster, 2002.

Williams, Frances Leigh. *Matthew Fontaine Maury: Scientist of the Sea*. New Brunswick, N.J.: Rutgers University Press, 1963.

Wright, William C. *The Secession Movement in the Middle Atlantic States*. Rutherford, N.J.: Fairleigh Dickinson University Press, 1973.

Wyatt-Brown, Bertram. *The Shaping of Southern Culture: Honor, Grace, and War, 1760s–1890s*. Chapel Hill: University of North Carolina Press, 2001.

INDEX